Mission-Critical Security Planner
When Hackers Won't Take No for an Answer

Eric Greenberg

WILEY

Wiley Publishing, Inc.

Publisher: Robert Ipsen
Executive Editor: Carol A. Long
Editorial Manager: Kathryn A. Malm
Developmental Editor: Janice Borzendowski
Managing Editor: Angela Smith
Text Design & Composition: Wiley Composition Services

This book is printed on acid-free paper. ∞

Published by Wiley Publishing, Inc., Indianapolis, Indiana

Published simultaneously in Canada

For general information on our other products and services please contact our Customer Care Department within the United States at (800) 762-2974, outside the United States at (317) 572-3993 or fax (317) 572-4002.

Wiley also publishes its books in a variety of electronic formats. Some content that appears in print may not be available in electronic books.

Library of Congress Cataloging-in-Publication Data:

ISBN: 0-471-21165-6

Printed in the United States of America

10 9 8 7 6 5 4 3 2 1

Acknowledgments

I cannot sufficiently acknowledge, in the few words here, the contributions of so many people who helped with the completion of this book. This book was a very long, challenging, but ultimately very satisfying endeavor, and many people played one role or another, directly and indirectly, in its completion.

I'd like to thank Carol Long, the Wiley executive editor I worked very closely with in conceiving this book and during the long writing process. Carol has years of experience in the technical book industry and has served as executive editor on some of the most successful modern technical books written. In my opinion, she is the finest in the business. Carol did not simply negotiate a contract with me and wait for the book, a common practice in the technical publishing industry. She very heavily collaborated with me on it and shaped the book considerably, going through endless phone and email exchanges even before the book began to take any recognizable form. She demonstrated enormous confidence in the importance of security planning. Books like this one have a very long development lead time. There are few editors who would "stay the course" as Carol did. It was a tremendous opportunity to work with her.

Tom McKnight, my business partner in the NetFrameworks consulting practice, also happens to be my closest friend of more than 20 years. It would have been impossible to write this book without Tom's help. By taking on my business responsibilities for extended periods of time while I wrote this book, Tom cleared the path for it to be written.

Janice Borzendowski, the Wiley developmental editor assigned to this book, is enormously talented and dedicated. After going through many reviews and revisions, this book still required enormous amounts of work. I recall how anxious I was once Janice was given the manuscript to work on. I wondered how she would react, fearing she'd run for the hills after seeing so much work to do. Instead, she displayed infinite patience and continuously went "above and beyond" as she performed very heavy lifting in the manuscript. We worked collaboratively and efficiently. Very importantly, she's just a plain nice person; it was a pleasure to work with her.

The overall developmental editing process was managed by Kathryn Malm. Kathryn is one of those folks inside the publishing company who presides over the management and completion of hundreds of books. You'd think she would become hardened to the process after a while and become cynical about books in general. This was not at all the case. During critical periods of the manuscript's development, she jumped in with every bit of talent, enthusiasm, and energy you could imagine. I'd also like to thank the entire Wiley production and copyediting team, including Angela Smith. The production team did an excellent job handling the unique layout requirements of this book and its many worksheets.

I'd like to thank Stephanie Lokmer, a neighbor, friend, and business consultant. She played a critical role in motivating me during the early days of this book's development. Showing endless interest in security, she regularly spurred me on to complete this book.

The book was reviewed by the NetFrameworks security consulting team and others working in the security industry. I'd like to recognize those who made an extra special effort during the review process.

First, Steve Orgill, a top security architect and great writer, went above and beyond during his review of this book. Steve regularly emailed me at 3 or 4 A.M. with his comments, clearly indicating that he chose to not sleep in order to help out with this book and still fulfill his busy schedule. Steve reviewed with great skill and completeness. He also went further: Instead of simply critiquing something he read, he made comments *and* frequently offered a rewritten version of how he thought it should be. I can't tell you what a help this is when, as an author, you are adrift in an endless sea of pages, words, edits, figures, and so forth.

Pam Arya, an industry consultant and friend, performed a very close review of the manuscript, regularly visiting me with large numbers of marked-up pages she sweated over the days and evenings before. Pam's father also wrote technical books, and so she was able to provide a deeper level of understanding about what I was going through in trying to complete this one. Pam put serious time into helping with this book, providing support and much needed close review.

Greg Gallant, Dale Gustafson, Carmin McLaughlin, Jim Miller, and Jeff Treuhaft rounded out the group of dedicated reviewers providing invaluable help. They provided interesting "war stories" and perspectives on security planning, and important comments on manuscript organization.

Contents

Introduction

Security—of our systems, our organizations, our personal identities—is more important than ever, and we, as an industry, need to advance the art and technology of security to make it less elusive, more readily achievable. I'm well aware that being responsible for security in an organization is not an easy job, and my objective for *Mission-Critical Security Planner* is to make that job easier and the results more effective. Few if any comprehensive security planning guides are available today that present a consistently workable methodology and perspective derived from an author's first-hand experience. This book seeks to fill that gap. Whereas most books provide tutorials and implementation tips relating to specific security technologies or an overview of security technologies, this book introduces a system of worksheets that enables you, the reader, to immediately have a hands-on experience in security planning.

As you go through the security planning process in this book, keep in mind the adage that actions speak louder than words; that is, in the end, we will have to evaluate our ultimate commitment to security planning by what we do, not by what we say we *should* do. Otherwise, we end up with what I call the "soft spots" in most security implementations. To name just a few I commonly see: Too many organizations do not adequately and effectively address the physical security elements of our corporate offices, incorrectly assuming that physical security relates in only a small way to electronic security. Too many people routinely email confidential information "in the clear" over public networks. Too many deploy systems without proper security review and implementation. Simply put, too many build what can only be described as playgrounds for hackers.

The other side of the coin, equally detrimental, is to try to incorporate too much into the security planning process. This causes lack of focus. Security planning, as I define it here, is concerned with the protection of information and infrastructure against risks introduced through the acts of one or more human beings, either intentional or accidental.

Who Should Read This Book

This book is intended for the working IS/IT manager and administrator, security officer, security consultant, operational executive concerned about security, and the CTO who spends most of his or her workday putting out fires. If you fill one of these roles at your company, I'm betting you need an approach to security planning that relates to the technology you see every day. You need answers—a road map, really—and advice about how to sort through the morass of security technologies, directions, and options that proliferate today. This book is intended for that purpose, again to make your job easier. In it you will find a plan and template to follow, one that will help you find your way through the tangle of security technology and challenges.

Let me assure you that you will not need to take out the equivalent of a slide rule to perform solid security risk analysis. Nor will you need to become a technical expert—though, ideally, you should be familiar with a range of technologies. (For those not familiar with common industry terms such as *filter* or *proxy server*, a comprehensive glossary is provided at the end of the book.) In this book I do not ask you to understand something fundamentally if you can get the job done by understanding just enough to manage the problem. I attempt to provide answers; I do not expect you to learn to derive them on your own from first principles.

I have deliberately kept the book's style conversational and friendly. It shares my philosophies, perspectives, and viewpoints on the topic of security planning. And though it does not provide specific command-line tips and techniques for configuring Cisco routers, an Entrust PKI, or a Checkpoint firewall, it does present the issues associated with these classes of products and related technology for the purpose of planning security.

And to address a fundamental challenge of security planning faced by all IS/IT managers today—that of justifying cost—I provide a quantitative risk analysis methodology, which I call *impact analysis,* as a means to do just that: justify security expenditures. Using this method will help you to understand the risks, how to estimate the costs, if any, and to lower them, and how to assess the resultant impact risk reduction.

With that said, it's important to point out that security planning is not all about spending more money to reduce risk. In fact, spending money often does not solve the problem or reduce the risk (though it's probably safe to say that a well-funded security group will perform, on average, better than a poorly funded one). Security is as much about sound policies, procedures, implementation, and operations as it is about investment. So, of course, this book addresses those issues as well as part of the security planning process.

Finally, I want to elaborate on what can be considered the heart of the book: the worksheets. For the busy IT professional, few things are more helpful than a template showing how to complete a new and complex task. These worksheets provide such a guide. They are tools you can use directly in your work. You can integrate them into your planning documents, use them as the basis for important security policies and procedures, and include completed worksheets in memos that you distribute within your company. You can even customize worksheets for the various implementation groups, who can use them to verify that they have completed all of the steps delineated in the worksheets.

NOTE To save you time the worksheets are included in two forms: fill-in-the-blank versions to view as you read and Microsoft Word-formatted electronic versions. Feel free to customize these worksheets to include more questions and pointers related to your particular needs. Electronic copies of the worksheets included in this book are available from the Web site maintained by the author at www.criticalsecurity.com or from the publisher's Web site at www.wiley.com/compbooks/greenberg.

How the Book Is Organized

I think you'll find that *Mission-Critical Security Planner* is logically organized to ensure that you get the most from the material. The chapters break down as follows:

Chapter 1: Setting the Stage for Successful Security Planning. This chapter introduces you to a security planning approach that works. In it I identify challenges, problems, and pitfalls associated with less-than-optimal approaches so that you'll know how to avoid them. The chapter also introduces a method for guiding and justifying your security budget, and it addresses the important topic of successfully "selling" security inside your organization. The chapter closes with a summary of security business process improvement. All of these topics are expanded on throughout the remainder of the book.

Chapter 2: A Security Plan That Works. This chapter describes how to form the security planning team, whose members will be responsible for carrying out the security plan for your organization. This chapter also introduces the security planning template that we will use throughout the remainder of this book and that, subsequently, you will be able to use to develop an effective security plan for your own organization.

Chapter 3: Using the Security Plan Worksheets: The Fundamentals. In this chapter you will begin to learn how to fill out the worksheets that will serve as your guide throughout the security planning process. The worksheets contain an important starter set of questions and pointers. When you address these conscientiously and plan accordingly, the result will be a comprehensive security plan.

Chapter 4: Using the Security Plan Worksheets: The Remaining Core and Wrap-up Elements. In this chapter you continue to learn how to fill out the worksheets that will serve as your guide throughout the security planning process.

Chapter 5: Strategic Security Planning with PKI. This chapter offers a primer on the business, technical, and planning issues associated with a poorly understood but very important strategic security planning technology, public key infrastructure (PKI) technology.

Chapter 6: Ahead of the Hacker: Best Practices and a View of the Future. In this concluding chapter I review the best practices for security planning presented throughout the book. I also invite you to look with me into the future at what we might expect from hackers and how our approach to security planning can be continually applied to protect our information and infrastructure as we face those oncoming challenges.

For Further Reading.

Glossary.

The security planning process detailed in Chapters 1 to 4 is summarized in Figure I.1.

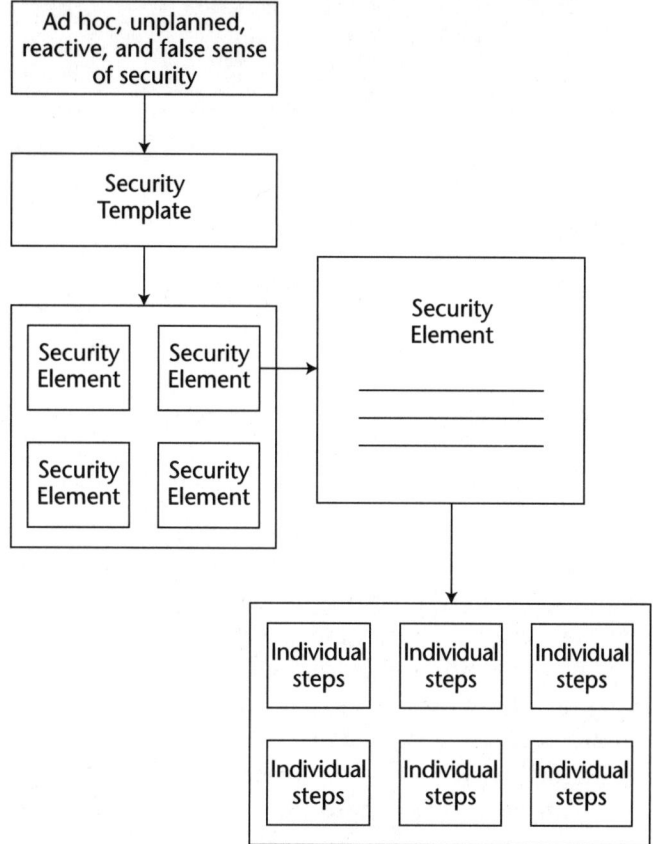

Figure I.1   Security planning process.

Now let's get started on securing our systems.

About the Author

Eric Greenberg is CTO and cofounder of NetFrameworks, Inc. (http://www.NetFrameworks.com), where he leads the security consulting practice. Eric Greenberg is well-known in the security, networking, and commerce areas. He led Netscape's security group, managing the deployment of a range of groundbreaking technologies including the one used for nearly all security on the Internet today, the Secure Sockets Layer (SSL) protocol. As Director of Engineering of Global SprintLink, he led the deployment of one of the world's largest international networks of its time. He has served on the staff of Bell Communications Research and holds a bachelor's and master's degree in electrical engineering from the University of Maryland and Cornell University. Mr. Greenberg is also author of the book *Network Application Frameworks* (Addison Wesley Longman, 1999), writes for leading industry magazines, serves on corporate advisory boards, and is frequently quoted in leading media outlets.

Setting the Stage for Successful Security Planning

Security isn't a product, a feature, or anything that we can simply acquire and then implement, confident that it will work now and forever after. It is a highly complex, organic process, one we must manage heuristically and optimize in an ongoing process. Security is also a way of thinking; it is neither an absolute science nor a purely technical subject. Security planning demands an understanding of the psychology of the hacker, of the key variables influencing information and infrastructure vulnerability, and of the organization's business. Security also requires a framework for weighing these variables, for the purpose of driving security implementation decisions and associated budgets.

This chapter sets the stage for a security planning approach that works. Along the way, we'll identify the challenges, problems, and pitfalls associated with less-than-optimal approaches so that we know how to avoid them. We will address the important topics of security risk (impact) analysis, to give our security plan focus and justification. To that end, the chapter introduces a method for guiding and justifying your security budget and addresses the important topic of successfully "selling" security inside your organization. The chapter closes with a summary of security business process improvement. All of the topics introduced are then expanded on throughout the remainder of the book.

TIP Refer to the comprehensive glossary of this book whenever you see a term or an acronym you don't understand.

Not an Absolute Science

Protecting information or defending a computing infrastructure is not an absolute science. Effective security planning requires that we understand the relative value of what we're protecting, the cost of protecting it, and the probability that what we're protecting will be violated in spite of the security measures we put into place. Security planning is also about learning to manage the trade-off between these things—think of the process as balancing a "security diet."

A balanced security diet incorporates the realization that security is about managing risk in an environment with limitations, *not* about finding a way to prevent loss at any cost and level of inconvenience. As with any diet, attempts to impose overly rigid security measures will paralyze an organization, causing it to adopt, as a knee-jerk reaction, too few security measures. This is tantamount to saying there's no value to locking doors and windows in a house because someone can just break them; therefore, we might as well leave the windows and doors unlocked and instead arm ourselves with a submachine gun. Such an attitude will result in an unbalanced security environment.

As we'll see throughout this book, security is not a single thing. Optimal configuration of a firewall, for example, is not security. Nor is a powerful virus scanner or an intrusion detection system (IDS). Security touches every aspect of an organization, from physical security starting at the front door of its buildings to detailed and tedious details about the way we configure our networks to how we run our infrastructure to the information we provide when we answer our phones. It's far broader even than these examples. In Chapter 2, we'll start the process of defining security in terms of a well-structured security technology model, business model, and a view of the life cycle management of security. In doing so, we'll have the beginnings of a security planning approach that will work for your organization. But before we do that, we need to establish an effective mind-set for security planning.

A Way of Thinking

Security is a way of thinking, and we need to think it through better than our adversaries. Effective security planning is the way we accomplish that. But though most of us instinctively believe planning is a good idea, when it comes to complex and difficult-to-manage problems like security, we sometimes resist. This is understandable for two basic reasons. First, because we are on tight budgets and under difficult time constraints, we look for steps we can skip. Second, security is a difficult problem to solve, and we feel we don't have the time it takes to address it adequately. But, as most of us are learning, time and again, we'll be hacked repeatedly unless we take the time to do security right. Ultimately, we come to accept that security planning is a *requirement*, not an optional exercise.

Avoiding the Pitfalls

Once we accept the value of planning, however, we often open the door to some of the problems associated with it. In general, planning, whether for security purposes or anything else, is frequently practiced ineffectively in large organizations. In addition to those who use planning (whether intentionally or not) to escape real work (and so impede, rather than aid, progress), most of us have seen the planning process taken to extremes by the types of planners characterized here as the *ultra-planner*, the *nonplanner*, and the *shock-advisor*.

The Ultra-Planner

For the ultra-planner, planning is its own end, not the means to a more important end. As you might guess, there are many ultra-planners in the security arena. You know the scenario: While you and your colleagues are focusing on securing your organization's information and data infrastructure against hacker threats, the ultra-planner is talking to you about protecting against the business equivalent of sandstorms and locusts. To the ultra-planner, focus is for small thinkers; your insistence that the scope be narrowed only reinforces what a small thinker you must be.

In fact, a lack of focus is the enemy of security. Security administrators routinely admit that one of the biggest challenges they face is deciding which of the hundreds of known security flaws they should protect against at any given time because they do not have the resources to address all of them. Solving the problem requires knowing what to focus on. But to do that, you need to genuinely understand, starting at least from a technology standpoint, which classifications of problems truly apply to you. To do that, you need to understand the underlying technologies; for example, you need to understand that one way to deal with the 100 risks relating to a particular protocol is simply to disable that protocol altogether, or at least isolate it onto its own Ethernet segment where it can be more carefully controlled and monitored. In this example, not only is there a technology issue (understanding what the protocol is and what it means to disable it), but there's a business issue as well: understanding why anyone might need it within your organization in the first place.

The issue of focus is prevalent throughout the book, as you'll see in examples such as this one; learning from these examples will help you develop your own security plan.

> **AN EFFECTIVE SECURITY PLANNER**
>
> **An effective security planner combines a good understanding of technology, the planning process, and business implications. These things are necessary to go beyond believing we're safer to truly being safer.**

The Nonplanner

The nonplanner is the cowboy in all of us. We think we can "just do it": shoot from the hip and move on. When we're in this mode (and most of us fall into it at one time or another), we become very busy. We put lots of effort and energy into our work, but we know, in the end, that we weren't nearly as efficient as we could have or should have been.

We are then reminded of the value of planning the right way. That's when we sit back down and consider more carefully how to proceed. This and future chapters will direct you where to go, and you'll discover a planning path that works for you, one that is practical, comprehensible, and implementable.

The Shock-Advisor

In many organizations today, the state-of-the-art security planner plays the role of the shock-advisor. This resident security expert typically finds himself or herself in a temporary position of power, generally as a result of a recent security breach. As a result of the breach, staff, many—or most—of whom were only peripherally concerned with security issues, have received a wake-up call, so they are alarmed and ready to listen.

Going from meeting to meeting, the shock-advisor warns everyone that if they don't pay attention, another breach is bound to happen—and with potentially worse results. "You fools," the advisor's words imply, "do as I say or lose it all." Unfortunately, over time, people simply do not respond to these dire warnings; they tune out, turn off. In short, the shock approach doesn't work more than once or twice. And without a change in tactics, things return to the way they were with little or no difference. The point is, we need to *sell* security, not *force-feed* it.

In conclusion, the hard lesson we must learn about security is that we can't go from one extreme or another. What we need—what we *know* we need—is a balanced approach to security planning. Without balanced planning, we are not nearly as secure as we could and should be.

Identifying Risk

If security is a way of thinking, one aspect of this way of thinking is to operate, to a certain degree, in a state of suspicion, so that you can identify the risks your business faces and distinguish between the real and the imagined. For example, you should understand that hackers are becoming more professional. They are more than young adults who are very good with computers and who satisfy themselves by showing you how vulnerable you are. Increasingly, hackers are paid professionals who intend either to extort money from you or to sell your secrets to the highest bidder. Even if yours is a small, relatively unknown company, your systems may be hijacked and used by hackers attacking others.

For example, one company I know of had spread workstations around its customer conference rooms for the purpose of demonstrating its products. These workstations gave unbridled access to all internal corporate and development systems. Such a setup is not unusual: I find this same scenario in four out of five companies (I recommend that you check yours).

Hackers and others engaged in corporate espionage visited this customer conference center disguised as potential customers; they slipped right past front-door security—that is, they didn't even need to be known by anyone to gain access to the customer conference area. Information and infrastructure security starts with strong building security, yet this is one of the weakest areas of security for most organizations.

BAD HACKER, GOOD HACKER

It's important to note that using the term *hacker* in a negative connotation is a misnomer because initially the term referred not to a "bad guy," but rather to someone who was engrossed in computer technology—a computerphile, if you will. The term is now commonly used to refer to someone attacking your information or infrastructure. Twenty years ago, many people referred to me as a hacker simply because I was proficient with computers. To confuse matters further, some now use *hacker* to refer to a "good security person"; they use *cracker* or other terminology to refer to an unwanted attacker. The meaning of the term *hacker* is, therefore, not standardized. What's somewhat new is the commonplace interpretation of the word to refer to an attacker. In this book, I keep it simple: When I talk about a hacker, unless otherwise stated, I'm talking about an attacker of one kind or another.

The point here is this: Security is much more than identifying the risks presented by your network connections. In addition to attacking you via the Internet, hackers disguised as customers, repair technicians, and contractors look for open cubicles, offices, and, especially, empty conference rooms having LAN connections to the corporate network. They call on the phone and extract private information. Lazy hackers or those not so adept at conning the receptionist often simply sit out in the parking lot with a wireless 802.11b-enabled notebook computer and access many corporate networks behind the firewall, an invasion made possible because corporations are increasingly using wireless networks, many of which offer no security.

These types of intrusion are so prevalent now that if someone doesn't believe it's as easy as I say it is and challenges me to prove it, I can "break in" almost on demand. While unknowing victims feel secure with their firewall investment, these hackers just walk right into the building or use the telephone and get what they're after. As this book will demonstrate over and over, security is not about any one feature. Security is not a firewall.

Profiling Hackers

To be a successful security planner, you will help your organization understand and appreciate what and where the real risks are. As part of this undertaking, you need to familiarize yourself with the various types of hackers and their range of motivations. Those who attack your information or infrastructure fall into the following primary categories: the attention seeker, the malicious, the curious, the thief, and the unintentional hacker. All present considerable danger. Let's profile them one by one.

The Attention Seeker

Attention seekers are the most common variant of attacker. They attack systems for the pleasure of showing off their hacking skills. They enjoy being noticed and particularly relish the press exposure associated with revealing a flaw in a major organization's system.

Often the best way to deal with such attackers is to give them the attention they seek; that is, give them your full attention, as opposed to giving an attacker the opportunity to make the attack widely known—in short, a PR nightmare. If possible, keep the attack quiet, at least until you can notify the affected parties in an effective way and get people working to remove the security vulnerability. In parallel with all of this, you should turn your attention to the attacker: Make him or her feel important. Learn everything you can from the attacker about your vulnerabilities. Often these people just want to be heard—and well they should be, for they have valuable information to share.

Though not everyone would agree with me, I also consider it reasonable to compensate these individuals with gifts or payment. Those who consider this "extortion" fail to factor in the motivations of this type of hacker. They aren't directly asking you for money or gifts; it's your attention that motivates them. Typically, they are not trying to hurt you. Furthermore, taking an openly provocative posture with a hacker is not in anyone's best interest.

The Malicious

Those who do not like your organization or someone working there, for whatever reason, fall into this category. Also, competing organizations may indirectly sponsor malicious activities using third parties. Thus, the malicious may be someone paranoid, a former employee, a competitor, a terrorist, or, often, simply an angry person. The malicious category also may include the truly delusional, someone, for example, who proclaims the evils of the organization they are attacking in an exaggerated fashion. Needless to say, it is very difficult to reason with such people, who typically enjoy toying with you and amplifying your fear about what they have done or will do.

As when dealing with the attention seeker, you do not want to be openly provocative with malicious attackers, nor do you want them to see you panic. This is the reaction they're hoping for. The best tactic is to distract them so that they believe you are taking a direction that leaves them safe and undetected while, in fact, you are working to get closer to them.

You may never have the opportunity to confront a hacker directly, though the opportunity presents itself far more frequently than you might expect. Most communication will be in the form of anonymous email, an Internet relay chat (IRC), or a phone call. And note that the way you change your system configurations in response to an attack or the manner in which you electronically track an attacker can also be considered forms of communication on your part.

The Curious

Not necessarily seeking attention or intending to cause damage, the curious like to poke around in others' systems and often leave a "trail"; their presence highlights various security holes. The danger presented by the curious type, as with all those who attack your system, is that you're never quite sure what they have seen or done. Their intent isn't clear at first (if ever) because they do not seek attention nor do their exploits reflect any particular objective; often they do not like to talk. And when you study their behavior, you cannot tell whether they have malicious intent or theft in mind; and you are, therefore, left in the frustrating state of not knowing exactly what they are up to.

When dealing with the curious, I attempt to find out what made them curious in the first place and then develop a plan of action accordingly. If you get the opportunity to communicate with them directly, be casual about it. Do not approach them in an aggressive and threatening manner as, chances are, you will not accomplish anything constructive.

The Thief

The motivations of the thief are pretty clear, and for that reason thieves are easier to profile from a behavioral standpoint. Unfortunately, they are, in general, also significantly more skilled at going unnoticed, getting what they are after, and covering their tracks. They are adept at various methods of breaking system security and often possess greater levels of interpersonal skills than the other categories of hackers. And they are better than most at so-called social hacking (for example, calling on the phone to gain information useful in their hacking endeavor).

If thieves are caught, they may try to con you by masquerading as one of the other forms of hackers (the curious or the attention seeker). More often than not, they leave only faint traces that they've been present with nothing to lead you to them. Thieves are often professionals, and most organizations are in over their heads when trying to deal with them. Many organizations also put themselves at a disadvantage by failing to acknowledge that paid "hired guns" are going after their information and infrastructure. This is a mistake.

The Unintentional Hacker

Security holes are often introduced accidentally by someone working within or on behalf of your company. Often their accidents resemble the footprints of one of the other types of hackers. Unrealistic and difficult-to-manage security policies can render an organization accident-prone because individuals naturally skip steps and work to bypass overly complex security policies and procedures. Security measures must not introduce so many details as to cause them to be ignored or otherwise implemented improperly by someone whose job is not security, but the organization's mainline business. This is why the security planning process must consider the business process needs of the organization. Security measures developed in absence of an understanding of an organization's business processes are inherently problematic.

Negotiating with Hackers

As I touched on in the preceding descriptions of the types of hackers, you cannot afford to take the perspective that all hackers are bad people and, if and when you communicate with one of them, that your objective should be to try to intimidate them and prosecute them maximally. This mind-set runs counter to the nature of the problem. There will always be hackers; you cannot stop them. Yes, you must deal with them, but to do so successfully, you need to understand them and learn to handle them with finesse, which doesn't mean immediately poking out your chest and starting a fight. Generally, you have more of an opportunity to communicate civilly with hackers than you realize. The best way to promote communication with a hacker is to provide an easily identifiable email address such as security@yourorganization.com on your Web site for anyone to email security concerns. For example, you can put a link to this address on your Contact Us or similar Web page. You need to make someone responsible for conscientiously sifting through these emails for real security issues and for answering them. In my experience, for every one email having something to do with security, you'll receive 500 that do not. For those that do, the information you learn will be invaluable. Also, if your company provides products and maintains a customer support interface (phone, Web form, or email), the customer support staff should be told to forward concerns from customers about security to a designated point of contact. Make sure the people handling these security inquiries take the task seriously and are trained well enough to know when to escalate a security concern. There's no better way to anger hackers than to ignore their efforts at trying to help you. Typically, they respond by redoubling their effort to embarrass you.

Again, not all hackers are bad; they don't all have malicious intent. And even if you are dealing with one that does, do you really want to anger him or her before you have the situation under control? Remember, these are people who thrive on the feeling of power they get from hacking. Your rage only motivates them further.

A company I was once associated with made the headlines sometime after I left by taking an aggressive tack against a hacker who was attempting to extort money from it. The company poked their chest out and became very confrontational with the hacker. In fairness, some hackers simply cannot be dealt with in a rational manner. But it's always best to try to do so initially. For example, it may seem that the hacker wants money, but, in fact, it's often attention and notoriety. The point is, you need to be sure you know what it is they want. Consider all of your options *calmly*, balanced against the risks. The presumption here is that you are vulnerable in some way and that they have some level of expertise in that area. If you look at it that way, the picture may change from one of a stand-off to a process of learning and negotiation.

The truth is that against the best hackers, especially the hired guns with criminal intent, the best offense is a good defense, in form of a solid security implementation, as described in this book.

STEALING YOUR CREDIT

According to *The Washington Post* (May 17, 2002), credit reports of 13,000 wealthy people were stolen from the credit-reporting company Experian's database by intruders posing as Ford Motor Credit employees. These private credit reports could allow the intruders to run up large balances on existing credit card accounts or to open up new ones in the victims' names. Federal Trade Commission officials and computer database experts said they'd never heard of anyone stealing so many key identities from a credit-report provider, the sort of company generally believed to have very tight security.

Selling Security

Remember I said earlier that we need to *sell* security, not force-feed it to an organization? To sell security successfully—that is, to achieve *buy-in*—you first must have a clear understanding of how people typically solve problems in general. Consider these basic observations as they relate to an organization's executive staff, middle management, and staff members:

Executive management.   Executive managers spend money to gain something (as in revenue), to save money (as in cost reduction), or increasingly, to reduce corporate exposure to potentially devastating losses from a security breach. Executive managers today are learning the hard way that a security breach of great-enough magnitude can destroy their company's business (you'll see examples of such breaches throughout this book). Executive managers, by charter, *must* manage the exposure of the organization to these risks. In fact, most managers are quite willing to learn to do so if security planners would communicate their options in terms they understand. Communicating security options effectively is one of the objectives of this book.

Middle management.   Middle managers understand processes and procedures that do not impede their main business objectives. Their focus is more on the particular systematic objectives of their department and associated tight schedules. Within the classical corporate organizational structure, middle managers typically do not own the same bottom-line dollar and asset responsibility that executive management does. At the same time, they are typically one step removed from the day-to-day tasks of staff members.

Staff members.   The staff understands the task of implementing their day-to-day functions and appreciates changes that help them do their jobs better, but only when these changes are carefully communicated in terms of their day-to-day job description. Conversely, they rebel against corporate overhead of any kind that they don't understand to be a benefit.

Rarely will these groups effectively support anything they cannot relate to on these terms. Herein lies the reason why, historically, organizations have resisted large-scale investment in security systems, processes, and procedures, or if they do invest, why adoption is so poor. If security experts do not fully understand the business, organizational roles, and people in general, they will not make the security sale. Security experts must be educators, which means they must understand human beings outside of their world, because all parties influenced and affected by security (and that's everybody) need to understand, in a balanced fashion and in terms they understand, what security means to them.

We'll consider a simple example of this in a moment, but first let's quickly review authentication, tokens, smart cards, and biometrics to ensure we're all on the same page here.

Authentication, Tokens, Smart Cards, and Biometrics: An Overview

Authentication is the process of validating a user, ensuring that you are who you say you are. Solutions range from traditional username/password regimens to the use of complex devices such as *tokens, smart cards*, and *biometric scanners*. A smart card is a specific example of a token.

A system can authenticate you by examining three things: *what you know, what you have,* and *what you are*. Not all solutions use all three, though. Tokens (what you have) must be paired with passwords (what you know) or biometric technology (what you are) to produce a stronger solution. This helps prevent the use of stolen tokens.

One popular token design, used in the RSA SecurID card, displays a constantly changing numeric identifier on a tiny LCD screen; the number is synchronized with server software. A user logs on by entering a username, a password, and the identifier currently displayed on the token. The server-side software computes the correct identifier for that token at that moment. Although such tokens improve security, they can be expensive and have a finite battery life. The entire token must be discarded when its batteries expire because its tamper-proof design does not allow for batteries to be replaced. Another type of token called a smart card contains an embedded chip that can be programmed to send and receive data and perform computations. The underlying electronics are small and can be shaped into a wide range of physical packages. Most smart cards are driver's-license- or credit-card-shaped. There are three categories of smart cards:

Memory-only.   This kind of smart card is capable of storing and returning information, but no more. Such devices have limited use in network security and are generally relegated to applications such as phone cards, gift cards, and the like.

CPU-based.   This device is capable of processing information.

CPU- and crypto-coprocessor-based.   This type of smart card is typically tied to a public-key infrastructure (PKI) and sometimes called PKI-enabled smart cards. PKI is a combination of software, services, and encryption technologies that facilitate secure communications and transactions. The only way to get a smart card to perform cryptographic operations is to provide a password or biometric information.

Smart cards offer many benefits but require smart card readers or some other way to interface with your computer. As interfaces like Universal Serial Bus (USB) continue to proliferate, the challenges of deployment will decrease; manufacturers are already integrating the smart cards and USB interfaces into single units and providing simple USB-compatible smart-card readers. Biometric authentication systems capture and store physiological traits, such as those of the finger, hand, face, iris, or retina, or behavioral characteristics, such as voice patterns, signature style, or keystroke dynamics. To gain access to a system, a user provides a new sample, which is then compared with the stored biometric sample. Biometric systems offer great promise in user validation but can, for some environments, be expensive and complicated to administer; this deters many companies from deploying them. If these deterrents can be addressed, the technology offers benefits.

Making the Security Sale: An Example

For our example, we'll suppose that an organization is considering the deployment of tokens to strengthen authentication.

- The executive will be concerned with the dollar cost of the deployment (cost addresses tokens, integration, software, servers, staff time, and any other impact on existing business objectives), so he or she will want to know if any cost-savings benefit or revenue enhancement can be had from the deployment. The executive will also expect a clear explanation of the reduction in exposure (risk of loss) if the deployment is carried out versus if things are left as they are.

- Managers, who are concerned with schedules, processes, and procedures, will be concerned with how to manage the deployment of the tokens and how this effort will affect their existing commitments.

- Employees, who tend to take a nuts-and-bolts view of proposals like this, will want to understand the impact that using this token will have on their performance of their daily tasks. Will it get in the way of doing their jobs? What, if anything, will it add to their daily experience: Will it give them any additional flexibility? Or will it impose greater restrictions?

Now let's evaluate how the three types of "extremist" security planners described earlier might try to sell this proposal:

- The shock-advisors typically will try to sell something like tokens by telling staff that if they don't implement such measures, they will forever be victims of hacking, which potentially could cause the demise of the company. People quickly numb to this argument because their experience dictates that this all-or-nothing view is not the only option.

- The nonplanners will often be cynical about such a proposal because it will require an intensity of focus that they are not accustomed to or not capable of investing.

- The ultra-planners will gridlock the organization by excessively broadening the scope of the "security sell." They will instigate unbounded debates on topics such as token standards and product selection. For example, the ultra-planner may embark on an endless study hyperfocused on the merits of one token design over another and the lack of associated industry standards

Clearly, none of these ways of pitching the smart card token deployment will be successful. A better way, one that considers the audience and their points of view, is delineated in Table 1.1.

Table 1.1   Selling a Smart Card Deployment

INDIVIDUAL	POINT OF VIEW	SECURITY SELL
Executive	Revenue, savings, quantitative exposure	Tokens, particularly smart cards, will enable us to sign documents digitally, rather than sign them by hand. We will also be able to streamline workflow in quantifiable ways. Here are specific processes we will bring to an entirely electronic form: [insert specific implementations].
		As we move forward, a combined building entry and computer access token can be deployed, allowing us to save $X [insert number] per year per employee, money that would otherwise be spent on building access technology. By strengthening authentication we will reduce our exposure to authentication, and impersonation-based security breaches by X percent (later in this chapter, and throughout the remainder of the book, we will learn how to estimate reduction in exposure to security breaches). By administering a single token identity rather than the typical seven passwords that employees must remember, it is estimated that administrative overhead will be reduced by X percent, reducing workload by x number of work hours per month.
Manager	Commitments, processes, schedules, budgets	Tokens will streamline workflow processes by reducing the number of required passwords that must be administered, from seven on average to just a single identity. This will reduce the time required to grant new employees access to network-based applications to approximately four days on average. Worker efficiency will increase by reducing, on average, three manual steps out of the top five processes carried out by employees. Instead, those steps will be automated through an electronic digital signing process. By reducing exposure to security hacks by X percent, risk to schedules caused by the need to respond to such hacks will also be reduced by X percent.

INDIVIDUAL	POINT OF VIEW	SECURITY SELL
Staff	Impact on daily tasks	Employees will no longer need to remember and manage an average of seven passwords. Each employee will manage a single identity, the token assigned to him or her. Over time, the same token used for building access and access to employee benefits online will also be used to gain access to other electronic resources. The ability to sign documents digitally and send them electronically, rather than sign them manually and send physical paper, will save time, make everyone's job easier, and make key processes more reliable.

Doing the Math

Once we decide to plan security effectively, it becomes clear that we need a business equation to help us decipher the morass of security problems, challenges, and technology we face in the process. The equation should help us prioritize our (usually scarce) security dollars and resources so that we focus them on the infrastructure that, if hacked, presents the greatest negative impact to our organization. The objective then becomes to implement security solutions that reduce the risk of such a hack occurring.

And because security is not an absolute science, such a business equation will be an approximation, not the result of a formal scientific derivation . Most of us have a very difficult time predicting and estimating things we cannot analytically dissect to the most discrete level of logic. Security risk management, therefore, is somewhat of a challenge. But in the face of as-yet-unknown threats and scarce preventive resources, we must do just that: approximate and predict. Furthermore, we need a risk management business equation tailored specifically to the problem set of security. That's what I introduce here and what we'll use throughout the book: a form of risk analysis tailored to the needs of the security planner and the business needs of the organization. I call it *security impact analysis.*

Understanding Impact Analysis

The first step in developing a security plan is to perform a security impact analysis. This analysis attempts to evaluate the effects of a security breach on your business, so that you can identify the areas of greatest vulnerability. The next step involves developing a sound security implementation, which is driven by your impact analysis, thereby giving you the most bang for the buck.

These two steps are not as straightforward as they might seem, however, because a security breach has several dimensions when it comes to assessing its impact on your business. That is, it's not simply a matter of determining the raw value of information and then predicting how much money you will lose when it's rendered inaccessible, stolen, or destroyed by a hack attack. Consider, for example, that systems offering an opportunity for bad press in a public forum are also very attractive to hackers. Therefore, when evaluating the technical and business impact of a security compromise, you need to consider four important exposure parameters:

Relative value of the information or infrastructure component (V).   For example, product plans, accounting systems, customer databases, and so forth typically have a high value, while a company newsletter has a lower value.

Degree of public exposure (P).   A defaced Web site, for example, means, at a minimum, embarrassment to a company. This can translate to loss of consumer confidence in an organization's products and services.

Denial-of-business (DoB) potential.   Will an attack affect your ability to do business? It's one thing to be inconvenienced, quite another if your ability to operate your business is entirely halted.

Ease of attack (E).   The easier a component is to attack, the more often it will be. Components closest to the public Internet are clearly more accessible and, thus, the best first targets. These systems also act as excellent "jumping-off points" for further attacks. Hackers compromise such systems, install their tools on them, and then launch attacks from those systems, perhaps leveraging any preconfigured trusts these systems possess, relative to other components in your infrastructure.

These are the factors to consider when performing a security impact analysis. In a large company, a security team drawn from business and technical areas would likely do the analysis. In a large company, the analysis might be very complex, requiring the team to assess the relative value and vulnerability of dozens of components. (See Chapter 2 for a discussion of the formation and dynamics of a security planning team.)

Performing Security Impact Analysis: An Example

In this section we'll look at these factors within the context of an imaginary company with five key systems. Table 1.2 describes these five systems, and Table 1.3 assigns values (0 through 25) to each of the impact analysis parameters for these systems. A value of 0 means the parameter represents no risk of impact on the organization (no security worries), whereas a value of 25 translates to a maximum impact for that parameter (serious problems may be in store for the company unless changes are made to better protect the environment). Each of the exposure parameters is assigned values based on the current security mechanisms in place within the company. (In this chapter and in Chapter 2, I'll explain how you can organize and conduct meetings to assign impact parameters and perform impact analysis.)

We'll call the sum of these four parameters the *security impact value.* This value is used to help drive our security plan priorities. The maximum impact value is the maximum of the sum of each parameter and is, therefore, 100. An impact value of 100 indicates that the security item needs to be addressed immediately by your security plan; a value of 0 means there is no impact for the security item. A higher impact value, therefore, equates to greater impact on the company should the system be compromised, and thus that security item demands priority positioning in the security planning process. Assigning values in this way enables a company to distribute scarce resources where they are needed most.

WHAT'S IN A NUMBER?

In performing security impact analysis for clients, I have concluded that it helps to keep numbers simple; that is, that they add up to a round, easy-to-understand and -remember number, such as 100. I've seen people become distracted by something as simple as averaging four numbers. In contrast, by taking four variables that add up to 100 in the maximum case, it eliminates the need to compute a simple average. You may be surprised to learn that, over time, people's "gut" takes over, and these impact numbers become surprisingly accurate, as opposed to a number in the range of 1-4 or word values such as "poor," "good," or "excellent." In summary, people are capable of estimating to a better level of granularity using simple numbers—at the same time, they don't want to take out their calculators. Adding four numbers that total to 100 (in the worst case) tends to work best when factoring in the realities of the process and the people involved in that process.

Table 1.2   Five Systems

RISK ELEMENT	DESCRIPTION
Public Web site	Not critical to day-to-day operations. Used for customer support, product information, and investor information.
Mail servers	Used in day-to-day operations by managers and employees. If a mail server is down, business does not stop, but it is hampered.
Accounting systems	Holds all key company financial information, hence is required for the company to do business.
Desktop virus	All employee operations, including manufacturing, can be brought to a standstill if a destructive virus is spread to desktop computer systems in the organization.
Corporate network uptime	This mission-critical internal network connects corporate systems and desktop systems.

As you can see from Table 1.3, the overall impact for our imaginary company is highest (95) for the accounting systems because of high scores on the parameters. The accounting system should, therefore, be the first focus, meaning that the security plan should be developed to reduce accounting system vulnerability.

Table 1.3   Example Impact Analysis

RISK ELEMENT	VALUE OF INFORMATION (V)	PUBLIC EXPOSURE (P)	DENIAL OF BUSINESS (D)	EASE (E) OF ATTACK	OVERALL IMPACT
Public Web site	13	25	5	23	66
Mail servers	23	15	20	18	76
Accounting systems	25	25	25	20	95
Desktop virus	25	15	25	23	88
Corporate network uptime	25	18	25	20	88

Counting the Cost of Security

The security planning process can be realistic only if cost is considered. Not recognizing this is the number-one reason well-intentioned security planning efforts fail. Organizations have finite resources—their budgets, staff, and ability to accommodate security overhead are all limited. Therefore, the objective is to intelligently reduce vulnerability to the lowest acceptable level, minimizing the cost required to do so.

The objective is to avoid throwing all the money you have at the first challenge. Rather, you want to spend money to reduce vulnerability for each of your high-impact systems. After applying your security measures, you revise values for the four exposure parameters for your systems and compute a new impact value, one that is acceptably lower.

For the sake of providing a simplified framework for analyzing cost scenarios for reducing impact based on improved security, we can group the costs of security plan preventive measures into three categories: *low, moderate,* and *high.* Each group implies a particular level of security and a corresponding reduction in predicted impact on the company should the component in question be compromised.

Returning to our example, we'll assume the security team met and, using the planning tools provided in this book, developed three potential security solutions intended to reduce vulnerability in the accounting systems:

Low cost.   Maximum use of freeware and implementation of good practices. Estimated impact reduction is 35 percent.

Medium cost.   Enhanced use of commercial software products with additional security measures and improved vendor support. Predicted impact reduction is 50 percent.

High cost.   Enhanced solution with greater diversity, redundancy, and stronger authentication. Impact reduction is 60 percent.

Figure 1.1 illustrates how the analysis might proceed. The vertical axis shows cost; the horizontal axis is the impact value for that given cost solution. The lines dividing the graph into four sections represent maximum allowable impact and cost (these maximum values were selected by the security impact analysis team, a process we'll talk about in a moment). This produces four categories of solutions, as drawn in the figure. Here, the team placed its low-, medium-, and high-cost solutions on the graph. The medium-cost solution was considered the best solution (low vulnerability + acceptable cost).

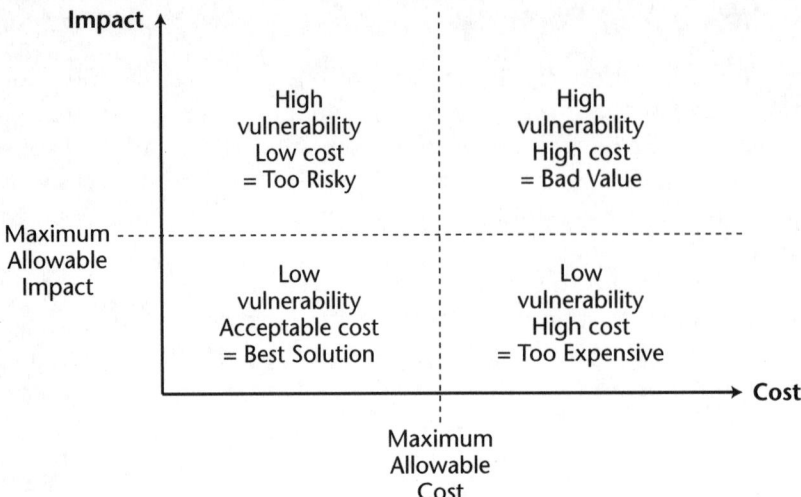

Figure 1.1   Impact analysis graph.

Establishing Maximum Impact, Cost, and the Security Budget

As the security team becomes more comfortable with its ability to perform impact analysis consistently and see positive results, its members will gain a better feel for what represents excessive impact to the organization. Eventually, the team will reach a consensus view on what is meant by, for example, an impact value of 75 versus 40. Over time, the team will become comfortable producing guidelines that say, for example, that given the current available security budget, anything with an impact value greater than 75 is not acceptable.

The maximum cost parameter represents the team's consensus view on how much of its budget can be allocated to this particular security item. The cost of security is both relative and absolute. Clearly, the costs of the solutions in our analysis (low, medium, and high) are relative to each other, in that, for example, one may cost $500 while another may cost $50,000 to implement. They are also relative in that if the value of the protected information or infrastructure is very high, arguably more costly security measures are in order. For example, if we allow for a 5 percent protection cost (a total cost for staffing, software, hardware, training, organizational awareness programs, and so forth), then we might accept that information or infrastructure valued at $1 million could easily justify a relative security investment of $50,000. The concept of allocating security dollars based on the value of an asset is directly analogous to the way we buy insurance today. When we insure our home or car, for example, our insurance premiums increase right along with the value of the home or car.

Returning to our example, the cost is absolute in the sense that we must have $50,000 in the bank if we go this route. This whole discussion of relative and absolute costs at first may seem academic; however, when we try to communicate and sell security within our organization, it becomes clear that people, at least subconsciously, think along these lines and that such a thought process can be used to drive their decisions more effectively.

None of this discussion about relative costs, insurance premiums, and so forth is meant to imply that simply throwing dollars at the problem improves security. Intelligence, experience, common sense, and savvy are also important factors in successfully securing systems. But, on average, a well-managed security group that is better funded will do better work and offer improved security. It will have the budget to hire sufficient staff and invest in important security infrastructure software and systems, and it will have the time and money to enforce security policies and procedures and to provide training within the organization.

Estimating the Value of Security

When you do an impact analysis, you are required to make some tough decisions about the value of security. To make those decisions, you must first determine the answers to relevant questions. How valuable are your product plans? How about your company phone directory? (Relative to phone numbers, for example, some companies publish these on the Web, while others view them as highly confidential and would never consider that level of exposure, given that the phone is an excellent tool for social attacks—to gather confidential information from individuals—not to mention that competitors can use your phone directory to attempt to hire your employees away from you.) How might your customers react if your company's Web site was defaced by hackers? If yours is a publicly held company, how might this form of attack affect confidence in your service and products, or in your stock value?

Depending on your company and the type of product or service it offers, everything might be mission-critical, with no shades of gray—the company phone list is as sensitive as your product plans. That said, remember that security planning calls for making tough decisions to control costs and maintain workplace efficiency, which means, in part, avoiding overly cumbersome security processes and procedures. Consequently, someone in your company might need to stand up and say that company phone numbers are important and should be kept confidential, but they're not as security-critical as product plans. Asked to assign a weighting of 0 to 25 (again, where 0 is unimportant and 25 is most sensitive), this individual might assign a 20 to product plans and a 15 to company phone numbers; the company's financial system, crucial to its daily operation, might be assigned a 25.

Laying the Security Foundation

Security policies and procedures define the organization's security-related processes, guidelines, and standards. A procedure might define the process by which an individual in the organization is authenticated and granted access to key applications. A policy might define a standard that requires firewalls from at least two vendors be implemented to protect against a vulnerability in any one vendor's product or that backup filters be resident in all the organization's routers. You will learn more on policies and procedures in the remainder of the book, but for now understand that you must define and maintain them as living documents. In turn, of course, employees also must read and adhere to them. That, then, requires education and an effective security sell. (There's that important verb "sell" again.)

Policies and procedures will be driven by your impact analysis; that is, when you know you might have a lot to lose, it becomes evident that defining policies and procedures to prevent such a loss is essential. Keep these important points in mind as we proceed:

- Publish procedures and policies to all affected people.

- Give appropriate staff members "ownership" responsibility for implementation and oversight of policies and procedures.

- Policies and procedures grow with the organization. They must be kept up to date by accountable staff members to reflect that growth.

- Establish clear accountability and define metrics, to ensure that policies and procedures are followed (you will be given a framework for these metrics later).

- Gather, on a regular basis, input from staff members, always with an eye to improving policies and procedures.

A real-life example is in order here. Consider a grocery store in the United States just beginning the process of installing an auto-checkout capability. With it, customers will be able to check themselves out after selecting their food items, without the help of a clerk behind a cash register. A friend of mine, interested in this installation, noted that the grocery store had wisely implemented a thumbprint biometric scan as part of the registration process. Customers would use their thumbprint cards at the checkouts, where computers would check the cards and thumbprints before automatically authorizing payment from a credit card. This gave my friend a "warm fuzzy feeling" about the process, and he decided to sign up. Part of the sign-up process involved revealing highly personal information, the kind an attacker could use to steal your identity (Social Security number, driver's license number, name, address, and historical information). My friend entered his personal information directly into a workstation set up at the store, provided his thumbprint, and went home.

At home, he realized he had left his driver's license at the store. Upon returning to the store, as he walked over to the enrollment workstation, he noticed that a store clerk had printed his application for manual processing, complete with all his private information, and the clerk had *left it on a desk in the middle of the store*. Needless to say, my friend wasn't very happy. The clerk attending the workstation either hadn't been trained in the *policies and procedures* associated with the process or had none to guide him in the first place.

The result? The security of this customer registration process for auto-checkout, complete with a thumbprint scan, was greatly diminished by the absence of or lack of adherence to security policies and procedures. Clearly, if we're going to spend time, money, and effort to implement security technologies, we need to be sure to implement the policies and procedures that will make them effective in practice.

Improving Security as Part of the Business Process

Throughout the remainder of this book, we will employ an approach to security planning that is as much about business process improvement as it is about technology. We will work to understand our organization, our policies, and our procedures; and we will measure the cost and effectiveness of our security planning effort by defining appropriate measures (metrics) and a means of tracking and analyzing them.

Like business process improvement, security demands that we address the relationship of people to our processes and procedures. When we define a security process, we define a *process owner*. We present a method for streamlining our security and for continuously improving it. Very importantly, our security plan addresses education, training, and the selling of security to people and their organizations. The entire approach is summarized in Figure 1.2.

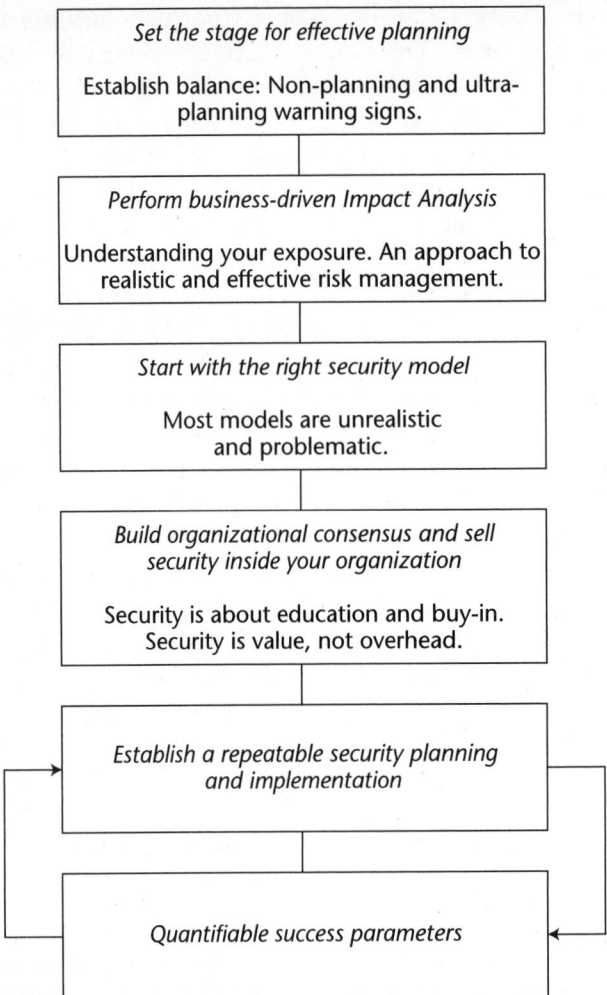

Figure 1.2   Security is business process improvement.

Conclusions

This chapter laid the groundwork for our planning approach, essentially defining the fundamental staples of security planning. We now have at our disposal a way to prioritize and focus our goals: We have gained a perspective on balanced security planning; we have the beginnings of an approach to selling security; and, finally, we have the framework for a security business improvement model. We will put all of this to work in future chapters, starting in Chapter 2, where we address forming a security planning team and developing a detailed security planning template.

A Security Plan That Works

The purpose of this chapter is twofold: First, it describes how to form the security planning team, whose members will have the responsibility for carrying out the security plan for your organization. Without them in place, each fully understanding his or her role in the process, the security plan cannot be implemented successfully. Second, this chapter introduces the security planning template that we will use throughout the remainder of this book and that, subsequently, you will be able to use to develop an effective security plan for your own organization. This template focuses on 28 core elements of security. Beginning in Chapter 3, we'll put this template to work, incorporating it step by step into a sequence of straightforward worksheets that will effectively prepare you to complete your own plan. With those worksheets in hand, we'll delve deeper into security, building a security plan that works, and one that you can tailor specifically to your needs and those of your organization.

Forming a Security Planning Team

Security demands buy-in; it's a collaborative effort that involves human beings, not just technology, doors, locks, buildings, badges, and the like. It's about business as much as anything else. Before we embark on our security planning effort, we need to form a team of people who can work together effectively in the effort. What characteristics and capabilities should those people have?

To begin with, it doesn't hurt if they're a little (just a little) paranoid because, as described in Chapter 1, individuals working in organizational security have to recognize that hackers come in myriad shapes, sizes, and motivations (ranging from self-satisfaction to extortion to espionage and sabotage on behalf of a competitor or a nationalistic, political, or terrorist cause), all of whom may seek to undermine the security of their organization.

Clearly, then, we need a formal cross-functional team, whose members will come from business, technical, and operational arenas:

- Business members will be especially useful in assisting with the impact analysis, as well as a myriad of other business workflow-related issues, security selling, and people-focused responsibilities, all of which we will address in the remainder of this book. Team members are chosen based on their ability to understand mission-critical business processes, customer service, and owner/investor sensitivities and objectives. These members must also understand, or seek to understand, the crucial relationship between the company's business and its use of technology.

- Technical staff will work, first, to communicate the challenges and risks and then offer solutions. Team members having in-depth expertise in the organization's physical, network, application, and operating systems from a systems-level perspective, as well as comprehensive experience with security-focused tools and technologies, should be selected. Also, technical staff will be responsible for setting up a testing laboratory and for certifying new technology.

- Operational staff members will contribute on issues associated with maintaining, on a daily basis, security technologies, policies, and procedures. Senior operations staff on the team should be involved in IT administration, customer support, and help desk staffing.

- Training/human resources staff members will offer insight into security-related education and organizational awareness, as well as on issues relating to managing terminated employees. Training and human resource functions may be consolidated or distributed within any company. Those who will be concerned with training employees and those responsible for staff management and personnel-related issues should be represented on the team.

These four groups will work closely together and must demonstrate a common commitment to security. Once the team is formed, it's a good idea to have a first meeting to establish a security planning agenda. Acting as a lead security planner in your organization, one person needs to be assigned the responsibility of managing the logistics and performance of this team. In many organizations, this will be the security officer, chief security officer, or some similar individual. I refer to the person heading this team as the *chief security planner.*

In preparation for the first meeting, all team members should read this book to ensure that they are all focused on relevant, high-impact items and concerns relating to security. Doing so will ensure that they will start the meeting with a more holistic view on security.

At the First Meeting

For the purpose of this discussion, we'll assume that the team members have familiarized themselves with the 28 elements that make up the security planning template (introduced later in this chapter) and the worksheets (introduced in Chapter 3) and that each is prepared to offer initial concerns as a starting point for the meeting.

Also during this first meeting, each group in the security team will elect a "security champion," the person who will be responsible for driving his or her group toward accomplishing its part of the overall security plan. The security champions, along with all individual team members and the chief security planner, should be held accountable for their progress in building a dynamic security plan that meets quality management objectives (as described in Chapter 3). Next, the team should also put on the agenda the need to select members for a security incident response team. (Incident response team member requirements are discussed later in this chapter.) Note that there may be considerable overlap between security planning team members and the incident response team. Some members of the incident response team, though, such as those working in public relations, would not likely also be members of your security planning team.

The security team, led by the security group champions and the chief security planner, should report to an *executive security review board,* a group charged with and capable of making executive-level decisions relative to security budgets, business processes, and anything else that may broadly affect the organization. The executive review board is important not only for its authority and ability to approve, or not approve, broad solutions; the establishment of such a board is a clear indicator that top management understands and appreciates the importance of security.

OWNING SECURITY

In my experience, purely matrix-managed teams, wherein everyone contributes to but nobody truly "owns" security, fail. By "ownership" I mean that an individual's job performance is measured by the success of his or her contributions to the security team's work overall progress.

A senior management mandate and sponsorship are critical; without them, this team will die on the vine. Supportive senior management can "grease the wheels," meaning that the security team's recommendations will stand a much better chance of actually being implemented and supported throughout the company. An example of such a mandate would be this: "Our company is committed to maintaining shareholder value and protecting the interests and privacy of our customers and employees. Actively maintaining the security of our technology infrastructure is crucial to this commitment." The mandate could be followed up with specific performance goals, the meeting of which are tied to the performance evaluations (and to the compensation) of company executives.

After working to identify immediate high-impact concerns, the team should begin the impact analysis process. The process, when first performed in an organization, will be confusing and difficult simply because most people will, on their first attempt, not have an intuitive feel for what it means to assign numbers to variables like "denial of business." After working through four or five analyses, looking at the numeric results for overall impact, then weighing those results against their intuitive feel for what the real relative impact might be, and revising accordingly any of their previously assigned values to reflect that, the team will begin to feel comfortable assigning values to impact parameters. It's a somewhat self-correcting process the first few times. The results become more consistent as the team adapts to the process.

In the beginning, the team should meet at least once a week. Between meetings, team members should collaborate as they work on their individual assignments. Soon the team will know how frequently to meet—whether once a week or once a month—based on the organization's needs.

The team should increasingly alternate between impact analysis and worksheet development. Security worksheets are the backbone of the security planning process presented in this book. When an aspect of the security plan is implemented and the impact is reduced, this fact is recorded in the security worksheets. In this way, the organization has an ongoing record and methodology for understanding its exposure.

As the plan is further developed and implementation proceeds, the team will evolve into one fully capable of managing the security model introduced in the next chapter, one focused on managing security technology, its life cycle, and its relationship to business in a fluid and repeatable manner.

Anatomy of an Effective Security Plan

An effective security plan incorporates three main components (see Figure 2.1):

- A security-centric model of your business
- An approach to security life-cycle management
- A full and complete view of all security-related technology, which I refer to as the *security stack,* a layered ordering of the security-focused technologies we put in place

The Importance of a Security-Centric Business Model

At the heart of all this is the business of our organization. Developing security in the absence of business awareness rarely works. In terms of what we protect for our business, the entire range of things can be categorized as *information, infrastructure*, and *people* (see Figure 2.2).

Information

Information is a database, a transaction, a data file, an email message, some combination of these things while in transport, and so forth. When you focus on securing information, you need to understand the entire life span of that information, from when and where it was created to when it was last used, backed up, archived, and, at some point, retired.

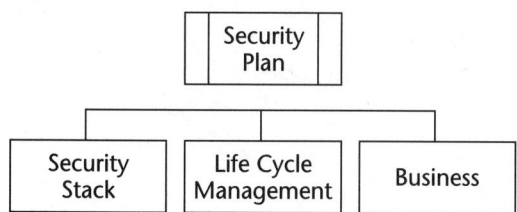

Figure 2.1   Essential components of a successful security plan.

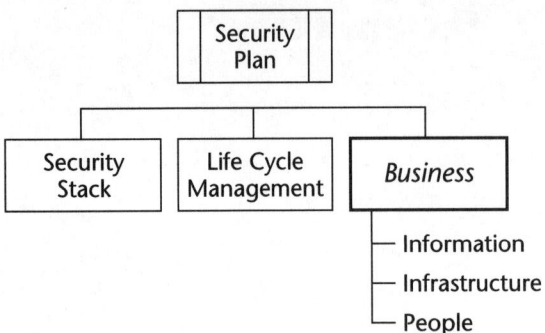

Figure 2.2   Security business modeling.

Infrastructure

Infrastructure is a support service for information; as such, it may be a network connection, a router, a switch, a desktop computer, a file server, an application server, or a firewall. Infrastructure also includes your office space and data center—that is, your physical environment.

The impact analysis introduced in Chapter 1 applies equally to information and infrastructure. That means you can perform the same analysis to determine how to protect your accounting system data as well as the routers in your network. There is, of course, overlap in that when we protect infrastructure, we also protect information. When it comes to, for example, protecting infrastructure from a denial-of-service (DoS) attack, we are protecting the infrastructure from becoming inoperable; we are preventing a hacker from stopping service by, for example, flooding our infrastructure with unwanted malicious data packets. At the same time, we are protecting access to information. When we encrypt, say, important accounting information, we are protecting only that information; we are not protecting infrastructure.

People

To protect people, we have to understand their roles within the organization, and we have to consider their views on information and infrastructure accordingly. In trying to identify the high-impact information assets on which your security plan should focus, it's important to determine how the individuals in your organization view that information. You need to ask, for example, if it is particularly valuable or important to them personally or to their job.

Table 2.1 The Human Factor in Information

ENTITY	INFORMATION EXAMPLES
Employees	Social Security numbers and health records. Access to confidential company planning documents.
Customers	Contact information, payment details, and buying patterns. Access to company information shared under nondisclosure.
Owner(s) and Investors	Sales projections, profit/loss statements, and press releases.
Suppliers	Access to company information, such as product plans and buying patterns, that might reveal confidential company plans, such as preparing to launch a new product/service and stocking up on items needed to accomplish that.
Partners	Access to considerable amounts of sensitive and confidential company information, including product plans, employee contact lists, organizational structures, and so forth.

To better understand this, take a look at the groups of people categorized in Table 2.1: For each there is sensitive and/or confidential information that falls under company control; conversely, each controls or influences some level of information that is sensitive and/or confidential to the company. Let's look at the different types of information each of these groups might consider sensitive.

Let's get more specific and consider a range of information and infrastructure examples typical in many organizations. As you review the two lists that follow, keep in mind the questions raised in Chapter 1 relative to assessing the value and impact of components such as these. That is, we need to ask ourselves what the relative value is of the component (V), degree of public exposure (P), denial-of-business opportunity (DoB), and ease of attack (E). Examples of information elements include the following:

- Accounts payable and accounts receivable
- Authentication data
- Building access systems
- Business process documentation

- Competitive plans
- Customer information of all types
- Email
- Employee accounts/authorization to resources
- Employee badge information
- Employee Social Security numbers
- Financial projections
- Internal application/server design documentation
- Internal network design documentation
- IS/IT configuration-management information
- Manufacturing data
- Marketing plans
- Partner-related information
- Payroll
- Press releases
- Product/service design plans
- Product/service performance metrics
- Product/service strategy documentation
- Product/service source code (computer programs)
- Public Web site content of all kinds
- Sales records
- Security polices and procedures documentation
- Staffing plans
- System logs of all kinds

Examples of infrastructure elements include the following:

- Application servers
- Authentication servers
- Authorization servers
- Backup/recovery systems
- Building access systems
- Conference rooms
- Configuration-management servers
- Database servers

- Dial-up systems/services
- Directory servers
- File servers
- Firewalls
- Frame relay network
- Gateways
- Intrusion detection systems
- Intranet Web servers
- Leased lines
- Logging servers
- Mail servers
- Manufacturing systems
- Network-based appliances
- PKI components
- Public Web servers
- Reception areas
- Remote employee access
- Routers
- Switches
- Terminal servers
- Testing and staging area
- Token infrastructure (SecurID, smart cards, etc.)
- Vulnerability analysis systems

As we begin this process of focusing on specific information and infrastructure assets, it's a good time to reiterate the importance of making the connection between these assets and security. Unless we make this connection, our security efforts will have no specific direction—other than to make it safer, whatever safer means. One mind-set that flies in the face of the directed focus necessary to a successful planning effort is the idea that, "Why bother focusing on anything in particular because there's probably some tool—some *thing*—that I can implement and that will, by default, secure *everything*?"

A security engineer once said to me, "Why put those additional safeguards behind the firewall (within the corporate network)? It's like wearing a belt with suspenders: The firewall already protects against those things." This engineer clearly had no concept of the range of opportunities available to hackers should they make it past one line of defense to find no others behind it. Achieving "theoretical security" with the firewall was the end of the story for him, the end of the thought process with regard to a certain set of threats; he did not concern himself with details, prioritization, information, or additional infrastructure. Another engineer similarly argued that his organization had no need for a method to encrypt passwords and other traffic (SSH, which we'll talk about later) because of its firewall. It didn't occur to the engineer that, if the first line of defense were broken, then most administrative passwords, including superuser passwords, would be available to a hacker by compromising just one machine. That is, compromising just one weak machine would mean the compromise of all of them because passwords in the clear or those weakly encrypted can be sniffed right off the LAN from a compromised machine placed into promiscuous (that is, sniffing) mode.

Keep in mind as we proceed to the next section on the security life cycle that the goal is to employ solid security mechanisms *deep inside* the organization and to focus our security measures on our most valuable assets.

Security Life Cycle

This section breaks down and details the basic elements of security life-cycle management. These elements are diagrammed in Figure 2.3. The first stage in this cycle is to choose the technology we will need to implement the security plan.

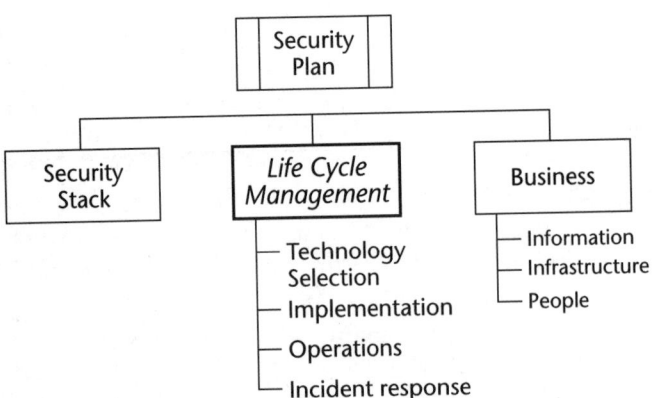

Figure 2.3 Security life-cycle management.

Choosing Technology

Proper technology selection requires that we first understand distributed computing technology in general, not just security tools. But what technology do we really need to understand? My experience indicates that the answer isn't as simple as it would seem, and many organizations today are making the wrong assumptions about what technology their security staff needs to understand. As we'll see when we discuss the *security stack* later in this chapter, security planners must work to fully comprehend the complete range of physical security, networking, application, and operating system technologies in their organization. The security planner can't be effective when seeking to understand only security tools such as firewalls, filters, and intrusion detection systems. Yet many companies hire security planners based on their experience in only those tools. As we'll see throughout this book, effective planners must fully understand the very technologies they are protecting, not just the tools used to protect them. Unfortunately, many security planners are today evolving as experts in security tools alone; instead, as effective security planners, we need to work to broaden our knowledge base considerably.

Next we add parameters that include quality, support, ease of implementation/operation, reliability, and—dare I mention them—features. The reason for my caveat on features is that we've become much too feature-focused when it comes to technology, a fact that becomes apparent when we address security. Flaws in security-related hardware and software are typically much more significant than the absence of a feature or two. Unfortunately, vendors have learned that having more feature checkmarks next to their products means they "look better," and that translates to more sales. What you, the security planner, need to be concerned with, however, is not the number of checkmarks next to a product or service; you need to understand its *quality*.

To understand quality, you must take the time to learn about and from the experiences of others, via newsgroups, vendor and technology user groups, and so forth. Study security advisories and security discussions on sites such as Slashdot (www.slashdot.org) and CERT (www.cert.org). Subscribe to newsgroups focused on the security of your high-impact infrastructure. Regularly visit the security pages of the vendors on whom you rely, and subscribe to their vendor-specific security newsgroups; for example, subscribe to Microsoft security (www.microsoft.com/security), the security advisory pages for your Linux operating system provider, Sun Microsystems security (www.sun.com/security), and newsgroups such as those sponsored by Checkpoint (www.checkpoint.com). And don't be too influenced by product reviews because many of those, too, focus on features. True, assessing quality requires more work, but that's what you need to do.

Typically, during the technology selection phase, cost concerns emerge. A tight budget doesn't necessarily mean sacrificing quality, for sometimes the best technology is inexpensive or even free. Using the methodology described in Chapter 1, work to get the budget required to secure the technology you need to properly implement your security plan, taking care not to overestimate your requirements. Too many engineers design much more expensive systems than what's needed for the job because they don't research the market adequately. This is not the way to get buy-in from the executive staff. Remember, executives are charged with controlling costs, so rest assured that if you've gone off the deep end with your recommendations, they may shut you down entirely. The point is, be reasonable and search for value in this process. Your goal is effective security, not security at any cost. In Chapters 3 and 4, specific guidance will be provided on technology selection in the security planning process.

Generally speaking, in terms of cost drivers, a popular debate right now (one likely to continue for years) involves the trade-off between the use of open source software, which is essentially free, and software that is sold by vendors and supported by them. In between all of this is open-source software that includes vendor support, as in some versions of the hugely popular Linux operating system. In large organizations, vendor accountability and support are important; as such, they often make less use of open-source software with no vendor support than smaller organizations. At the same time, open-source software offers, arguably, the ultimate support flexibility by making the source code freely available to you. That's a double-edged sword for some organizations because working with source code control implies that you have people available who can modify and recompile source code. For high-impact infrastructures, some contend that keeping track of the security of open-source software is difficult because there are many contributors to the software and too little scrutiny. The concern is that, for example, a malicious intruder could plant a backdoor security hole into an open software product you rely on. Others argue that open-source software, because the source code is freely available, receives exceptional scrutiny—the scrutiny of a world of software developers.

All that said, concern about backdoors in any software, including open-source software and commercial software, is a valid point that supports the notion that we should keep people around who can read source code to evaluate the security of open-source software before we use it and to test all software. A further argument is that many vendors today blindly incorporate open-source software straight into their products, which means they could fall prey to the very same backdoor security holes if they are not careful.

In sum, when it comes to technology selection there is no simple solution. Your organization has to apply the resources it can afford to develop an adequate comfort level with the technologies you select based on your impact analysis and available budget. One important way to do this is to test the systems you plan to deploy. A common recurring theme throughout this book is the importance of security testing your systems as part of the technology selection and implementation processes.

Hitting the On Switch: Implementation

After we select technology, we are ready to implement. Implementation is obviously fraught with risks, which we'll address as they arise throughout the book. You need to run a tight ship during implementation and operations to get things right. Your team must be properly trained, and they will need a dedicated implementation lab environment in which to work. Too often, engineers connect devices to the network and then begin to "harden them" against attacks. The problem with this approach is that, while they are hardening the system, someone is breaking into them and planting backdoors. You need to secure things *offline,* so ensure that this implementation laboratory is not connected to the network at large.

Another important aspect of implementation is testing—that is, verifying that the plan works as expected and that the technology doesn't crash your systems. Some overly aggressive vulnerability analysis and intrusion detection systems (IDS), for example, have been known to crash the very devices they have been implemented to protect.

Understand performance impacts, if any, keeping in mind that giving up some amount of performance should be something you are willing and able to do in the name of security.

Testing should be done as part of the technology selection process; experience has proven that implementation teams prefer to "kick the tires" as they proceed because exposure to the live network tends to reveal problems rarely encountered in up-front focused testing (which is not to downplay the value of such up-front testing). The best approach is to test up-front during technology selection, simulating as much as you can of your live environment. Next, during implementation, you should test again to assess the validity of any assumptions you made during your earlier technology selection testing.

Keeping a Lookout: Operations

If the implementation is poor, the operations folks won't have a fighting chance. Successful operations is highly dependent on a quality plan, technology, and implementation, and especially on solid policies and procedures. Policies and procedures relating to software updates, patches, monitoring and response, trends, configuration rules, and so forth will ultimately determine the strength of your security implementation.

Only after you've put all these elements in place is it time to operate your security implementation. A day-to-day operations group will monitor systems, respond to issues, and perform updates and patches. An operations group ranges from those who answer phones to support employees needing assistance with their computers or network connections to those who interface with customers (that is, customer service representatives).

Dealing with Threats, Hacks, and Mistakes: Incident Response

If you do not have an incident response plan, complete with staffing, roles, and procedures, you do not have a security plan. It's a requirement. I'm going to go into some detail here on incident response simply because it *is* so important, and then I'll revisit it as part of the discussions on security planning worksheets.

Each aspect of the incident response process must be defined in terms of policies and procedures. Policies should define the criteria for determining whether an incident should be escalated to the incident response team and exactly how subsequent escalations will be handled through your company's chain of command. They also define roles, responsibilities, accountability, and performance metrics related to carrying out an incident response. Procedures delineate the steps members of the incident response team will take in the event of a hack attack.

Unfortunately, for many organizations, the idea of an incident response process is the IT administrator running around installing security patches and restoring systems from tape. That type of reactive solution typically leaves the organization's exposure at an unacceptably high level. A solid, proactive incident response plan takes into account the following five areas:

- Activities
- Team members and coordination
- Notifying authorities
- Incident reports
- Testing incident handling

The following sections define each of these areas in more detail.

Activities

Incident response activities include gathering evidence, classifying the attack, defining the mechanism of the attack, and responding.

Gathering Evidence

The incidence response team collects evidence to drive its actions and decision-making process.

Logs. The question of what you log and how often you do it will be addressed throughout the book. The incident response team must institute a formal log collection and analysis procedure.

Vulnerability scanner. Collect the most recent output from vulnerability scanners. Be prepared to go back into your vulnerability scanner archive to determine when in the past a particular vulnerability has existed, one that may have been leveraged by a patient hacker as part of the current incident.

Intrusion detection. Collect recent output from intrusion detection systems (IDSs). As with vulnerability scanner output, be prepared to review archives as-needed.

Reliability assessment. Any evidence collected may have been tampered with or otherwise destroyed by the attacker. Therefore, the chief security planner should assign a reliability value of between 0 and 1 to all evidence: 0 means the evidence is believed to have no reliability; 1 indicates that the chief security planner believes the evidence can be relied on without question.

Correlation with past incidents and observations (incident reports). Correlate all evidence with past incident reports.

Comparison to known vulnerabilities/attacks. Compare all evidence collected to a top-10 list of most common attacks at the time of the incident. Such a list can be assembled by the security lead and officer by visiting Web sites that compile such information, of which there are many on the Internet today (e.g., www.sans.org). The security officer and lead should then investigate other known attacks to determine if the evidence points to a known attack. Most attacks your organization will encounter will already be known. It's rare to be the first victim of a particular attack variant, though, of course, it can happen. Odds are, though, that you are not the first, and information will be available on Web sites or on newsgroups (but be careful when polling the latter for information, as this can make your organization vulnerable in many ways; do so anonymously). By playing the odds, generally you will be able to respond faster and with better accuracy.

Internal and external organization coordination. Coordinate evidence across internal and external organizations. While doing this, ensure that the company's name is kept confidential because any information reported about an attack, if reported at all, must be cleared through the organization's public relations/communications department.

> **KNOWING WHEN TO GO PUBLIC**
>
> Here's a good example of a security plan lacking the proper incident response policies and procedures and resulting in the type of publicity no organization can afford. After a public utility company was hacked, and during the incident response process (before the incident was resolved), an intern assisting the system administrator sent out a corporate email letting the entire company know what happened. To try to help the situation, the intern also sent email messages to several public mailing lists to see if "anyone knew who could be breaking into the system." As a result of these email messages, the press published a story on the hack, all of this before the utility could formulate its complete response and resolve potential vulnerabilities relating to the hack.

Classifying the Attack

It's essential to determine the type of attack you have experienced. You may likely have encountered more than one type of attack because many hacks involve a sequence of actions to achieve an end or ends. To do this you will need to establish a standard terminology that all incident response team members understand and use in the same way. Here are examples of a basic terminology. We will discuss these and other forms of attacks in future chapters; these terms are also defined in the Glossary.

- Denial of Service (DoS)
- Distributed DoS (DdoS)
- Unauthorized data access
- Data tampering
- Data destruction
- Communications infrastructure attack
- Host attack
- Desktop attack
- Firewall attack
- Virus (identify component(s))
- Trojan horse
- Worm
- Physical attack (as in media or computer theft)
- Unauthorized execution of code
- Impersonation

Defining the Attack Mechanism

The team should determine as much as they can about the mechanism of the attack. The mechanism is defined by the following parameters:

Person.   Identify the individual behind the attack if this is determined to be advantageous (for example, if the attacker is malicious and you plan to seek prosecution). Profile the attacker as previously described.

Path(s).   Define the path used to implement the mechanism. This would include physical intrusion, such as access to an employee laptop, the actual path of packets through the network, and the levels of obfuscation, spoofing, and impersonation that might have been employed. Determine which programmatic, resource, and protocol mechanisms were employed.

Resources targeted.   Define the resources attacked, to include network components, hosts, desktops, firewalls, specific data elements, specific services, applications, and so forth. Try to determine if there is a pattern in what the hacker is going after—this pattern may become more evident to you as you consider the hacker's profile.

Purpose.   As part of the process of profiling the hacker, work to understand what his or her motivation was for the attack.

Formulating a Response

Obviously, the team must formulate a technical response quickly, and in doing so must address the following issues:

Exposure.   Determine roughly what your current exposure probability (EP) is and what the revised EP (REP) will be as the team takes actions.

Rebuilds.   If a system has been hacked, you can rarely be sure of exactly what has been done to it because, even if you deploy an IDS system, it can't track, in a guaranteed manner, every data element on the server for tampering. You need to rebuild your system *offline* so that the system is not attacked again while you are rebuilding. When restoring from tape, do so carefully so as to not reintroduce the vulnerability that was leveraged in the attack. Of course, apply the appropriate changes needed to prevent the hacker from relaunching the attack.

Configuration management.   Carefully track revisions of all system components (software versions, hardware versions) prior to and after the attack. Record this information in the incident report.

Backup and recovery.   Carefully back up any hacked systems in their exact states. This information is needed for future analysis and may be needed if your company intends to prosecute a hacker.

Potentially hacked data.   The hacker may have tampered with data (including customer data) on the server. You need a process to somehow "scrub" and analyze data for unusual activities. You will be tempted to restore data on the server—customer data, for example—to your new system from the old system at the time it was taken offline in response to the attack. If you must restore data in this way, institute a checkpointing procedure to validate data. This validation may include establishing a certain level of acceptable corporate exposure.

Readdressing, repartitioning, isolating, observing.   Place vulnerable systems on separate network segments (such as switched Ethernet segments) wherever possible. This is particularly crucial for systems that have been attacked, for by isolating them you can observe protocols and packets much more easily and closely; this also lets your IDS do its job (more on this in later chapters). If you can, assign a new IP address to the attacked system to throw off the hacker and to allow you to easily determine if attacks are still being launched against the old IP address. Such information may be helpful in collecting path evidence and in profiling the hacker.

Disablement, disconnection.   As soon as you discover the hack, determine if any systems should be immediately disconnected from the network. Assess the business impact of taking the component offline. Remember, as a security expert you are also a disablement engineer. Quickly assess if there's anything else you can afford to disable to further protect you from an attack in the future. In short, disable maximally, meaning, for example, that if you choose to filter out a protocol, do so at multiple levels in your infrastructure, such as in all firewalls, in all routers, and, of course, in hosts themselves. In this way, if one line of defense is compromised, such as the firewall, you will still have backup filters that may protect you.

Testing and staging redeployment.   Don't just, for example, rebuild your system, choose what to disable, and then deploy it. In your test lab, quickly test any systems before you connect them to the live network. Once the system is connected to the live network, establish a quick test plan to validate correct operation; and be prepared to back the new system out rapidly if there are problems.

Notification of affected parties (customers, employees, etc.)   Do this only as required and in accordance with guidance from the public relations/corporate communications group and member of the executive team.

Public relations (PR) response plan.   After you have the situation under control internally and know what you're dealing with, determine whether it is necessary to inform the public about the security incident or how to respond to reports already in the press about it. The goal is to achieve balanced coverage: Don't cover up the incident, but don't blow it out of proportion (as the press will sometimes do). Work to keep the incident in perspective, and calm fears wherever possible. At the same time, take responsibility where you need to, clearly communicate what you intend to do about the breach, and reassure the public that you are now more secure than you were before as a result of addressing it. Your PR group should be prepared to manage the press successfully. (Keep in mind that anything you say that is reported in the press will ultimately be seen or heard by the hackers. Depending on the hacker profile, you may be playing into his or her hands or further enrage or motivate the hacker, thereby spurring him or her to cause you further harm. Keep all this in mind as you craft your PR responses.)

Internal and external organization coordination.   Your incident response team should be capable of quickly coordinating internal and external organizations to collect evidence and act on it. Maintain confidentiality in accordance with guidance from public relations/corporate communications departments. Such confidentiality should not impede your ability to share technical information, but it may influence how you share it (anonymously, under nondisclosure with regard to the company name in particular).

Vendor and service provider escalation process and service-level agreement.   Vendors and service providers must respond to an attack on you according to your service-level agreement (SLA) with them. (Note: You should put an attack SLA in place where possible for key vendors and service providers.) For example, in the event that you come under a DoS attack, your Internet service provider (ISP) should have a rapid escalation procedure to deal with it. Also, establish a solid point of contact within the ISP, someone who can rapidly coordinate upstream packet filters within the network and ISP peers (other ISPs to which they connect) to protect your network from a bombardment of unwanted traffic.

Manage communication with hacker according to his or her profile.   Be sure effective communications mechanisms are in place to communicate with the hacker if such an opportunity presents itself.

Craft your response.   Consider the hacker profile where applicable.

Coordinating Team Members

For an organization to take security seriously, the members of its incident response team must be accessible 24 hours a day, 7 days a week for the most critical attacks. To that end, maintain up-to-date contact information for each member of the team, to include office, home, and cell phone numbers, email addresses, and pagers. Establish an escalation procedure based on estimated impact to the company and the company's allowable thresholds. For example, after you've completed your first impact analysis for major information and infrastructure, you can develop value ranges on which you'd escalate—for example, that for any system with a security incident with an impact value of 90 or greater you would immediately notify executives. Those in the 50-60 range, with an unresolved incident lasting more than 4 hours might be escalated to the director level in your organization. Your escalation needs will be specific to your organization. However they are defined, it should be evident that very sensitive security incidents might benefit from greater levels of awareness and support within your organization.

The incident response team should include members from the following departments within the organization:

- Chief security planner and security planning team members
- Affected business unit representatives
- Representatives from public relations/corporate communications
- Legal counsel
- Human resources (in the event an employee or contractor is involved)
- Executives, in escalation path from CIO to COO, then CEO and CFO, then board of directors

Notifying Authorities

Based on guidance from your public relations/corporate communications department, the chief security planner may find it necessary to contact and coordinate with law enforcement organizations and security advisory groups such as CERT. Within the United States, the Federal Bureau of Investigation (FBI) has a special group focused on electronic security called the National Infrastructure Protection Center (NIPC).

NOTE As of this writing, a government proposal has been put forth to absorb the NIPC and several related government agencies into the new Department of Homeland Security.

Filing an Incident Report

The incident report, prepared under the leadership of the chief security planner and presented to the executive security review board, should include the following items:

- A summary of the security incident (the attack)
- A qualitative summary of the incident's impact on the organization
- A summary of the low-, medium-, and high-cost measures, and the one chosen, including details of your associated impact analysis
- Documentation of all key activities
- Suggestions for improvements in the incident-handling process, to set the stage for establishment of any new security policies believed to be necessary to avoid similar attacks in the future

In addition to the report, a tape of the hacked system(s) should be securely archived offline.

NOTE Quality management worksheets, presented in Chapter 3, define specific reporting mechanisms that will help you to better trend incident response activity and incident process improvement objectives.

Testing Incident Handling

Don't wait to have an incident to test your incident response process. Implement the entire process using a well-known attack, such as a buffer exploit performed on your Web servers or a newly discovered desktop vulnerability, as an example. Simulate the impact it might have on your organization and the decision processes you might follow.

Creating Order from Chaos: The Security Stack

In the networking world, technology is organized into a seven-layer model called the Open Systems Interconnect (OSI) model, developed by the International Standards Organization (ISO). We will use a similar model to develop our security plan, one composed of four layers, delineated as follows (see Figure 2.4):

Physical.   Anything you can touch, listen to, or see. Cables, physical media (floppy disks, CDs, tapes, hard drives, flash cards), buildings, doors, ports, building passes, smart cards, tokens, biometrics, wireless signals, locks, cameras, and so forth all fall under the physical layer of the security stack.

Network.   The network, by our definition, is the collection of protocols, transmission standards, and physical components that come together to produce a path for voice, video, or data. The network is the Internet, intranet, extranet, virtual private network (VPN), public switched telephone network (PSTN), private branch exchange (PBX) network, frame relay network, wireless LAN, switched network, and so forth.

Application.   The line between applications and operating systems has blurred because operating systems increasingly come bundled with so much application software. For that reason, the distinction has become somewhat arbitrary. In this book, applications refer primarily to those used to accomplish a business objective.

Operating system.   This is the core environment used to execute applications and manage local and network resources, wherein resources are objects, files, printers, and so forth.

These categories are not strict delineations; they overlap. Directory services in general, for example, overlap the network, application layer, and operating system layer to some extent. So directory services may be discussed multiple times within the model.

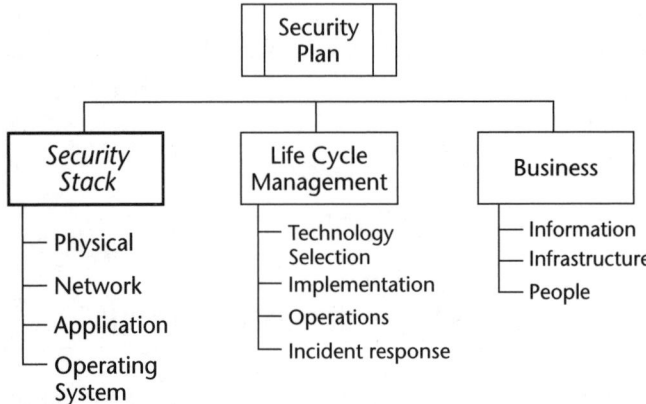

Figure 2.4   Security stack.

Mapping the Template: The Keys to the Kingdom

We have thus far defined the three components of our security plan: the security stack, life-cycle management, and business model. Keep them in mind, for we will revisit them over and over again in our worksheets. *They make up the template for our security planning process.*

Our security plan template is mapped to 28 *security elements,* carefully selected core topics of security that, when combined and used with our template, result in an organic security planning process that works. The template is applied repeatedly to each of the security elements. The relationship between our security template and the security elements is illustrated in Figure 2.5.

Preparing to Work with the Security Elements

In preparation for working with the security elements, which is crucial to the security planning effort, I want to take a moment to alert you to a few of the things to avoid when security planning. As we explore our security elements in detail, the importance of this list will become increasingly clear. Here, in my opinion, are the top-10 most serious mistakes people make when planning security:

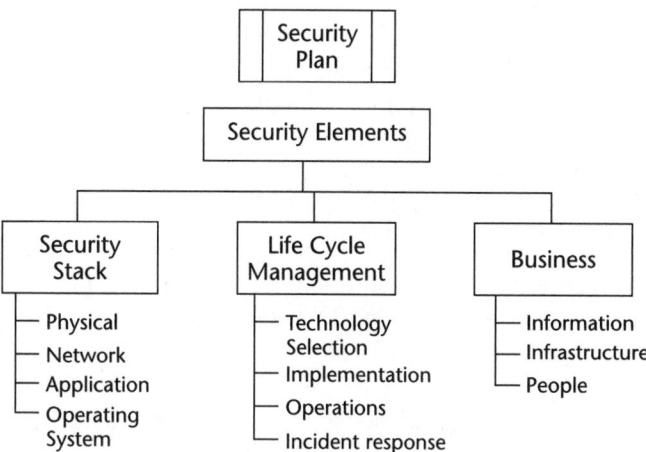

Figure 2.5   Relationship between security template and security elements.

1. **Presuming that one line of defense is adequate.** This is the "belt-and-suspenders-are-redundant" mind-set. People with this mind-set design only single points of failure into their entire security architecture. Thus, if a single component is compromised, all bets are off, and the hacker wins. How can this be effective security?

2. **Insufficiently understanding the technology and its nuances, including the many approaches a hacker can take to attack you.** For example, many security engineers do not understand the range of applications that send passwords "in the clear" or are so poorly encrypted that they can be easily deciphered by a hacker. These applications offer little more than one or two lines of defense.

3. **Thinking enablement, as opposed to disablement.** If there's only one piece of advice you take away from reading this book, it should be this one: Disable capabilities you do not absolutely need. Disable them everywhere—in your desktop computers, servers, communication devices, and every other bit of technology we discuss. (I'll have much more to say on this topic and why it's such a problem in today's technology.)

4. **Forgetting that security is part of a life cycle.** I've said it before, but it bears repeating: Security is an evolving process. You can't just finish it, put it on the shelf, and move on to some other problem. Security is a dynamic part of your organization, and your security plan should grow and adapt with your organization's changing security needs.

5. **Overlooking the physical aspects of security—buildings, rooms, data centers, physical computer access, and so forth.** The list of opportunities for making this mistake, thereby opening the door to hackers, is endless; we will address many of them throughout the book. For now, realize that you are kidding yourself if you believe a hacker will not enter your building to launch an attack. Depending on the attacker's profile, it may be the very first thing he or she does. And, sadly, it does not take a rocket scientist or James Bond to gain unauthorized entry into the buildings of most organizations.

6. **Relying excessively on weak trust mechanisms.** A good example of this mistake is relying only on source IP address filtering, something we'll talk more about later. True, source IP address filtering is a very worthwhile thing to do, but, again, it cannot be your primary line of defense because IP addresses are easily spoofed. We must raise the bar higher than that to protect our organization adequately.

7. **Failing to understand exposure to attacks on information and infrastructure.** I've discussed this previously in this chapter. This is the

mistake of not prioritizing or focusing security, instead assuming that there is one thing (such as a firewall) that will solve all security risks.

8. **Failing to understand and address the relationships between network, application, and operating system security.** We need to understand the technology we are protecting, not just security tools. I touch on this throughout the book.

9. **Architecting a system that issues far too many "false alarms."** This mistake will cause the incident response team to become numb to real threats.

10. **Inadequately addressing the risk of security breaches from those within your organization.** Though it's no longer true that most hackers can be found within an organization, these "insiders" do still exist, so you must be aware of the possibility. In short, you need to protect your organization both from within and from outside.

With an eye toward not making those same mistakes, let's look more closely at our security elements.

Introducing the Security Elements

I define the 28 security elements in two categories: *core* and *wrap-up*. The first 15 are the core security elements; they represent the heart of our security plan, addressing all key security planning challenges in a distributed computing environment. The 13 wrap-up elements are summary elements that relate heavily to others: They will come to represent something of a final checklist as we complete our security plan—a catchall for anything we've missed.

In completing your security plan for high-impact information and infrastructure components, you may be tempted to choose, up front, those elements from the 28 that most directly relate to your component. After all, this list of elements, presented numerically, does resemble a card catalogue of sorts, tempting you to simply thumb through it casually, selecting only those items you're most interested in. In most cases, though, every single one of these elements is directly or indirectly related to the high-impact component you are focusing on in your security plan. These elements strike at the heart of distributed computing, and a distributed computing environment is what we're trying to secure.

In general, rather than trying to assume which elements apply to a particular high-impact component, I advise you to keep an open mind and to walk through each and every element. In this way you can be assured that you haven't missed something very important in the planning process.

The Core Elements

Core security elements reflect the organizational and technology needs that are most applicable to a modern distributed computing environment. Of the 15 core elements defined, 6 of them are what I call *fundamental*. These fundamental elements represent the main ingredients of security—they address the challenges of knowing who you are dealing with (authentication), what is authorized and what isn't (authorization and access control), the importance of hiding secret information (encryption), the need to maintain incorruptible information (integrity), the importance of accountability (nonrepudiation), and the mission of maintaining privacy.

After addressing the fundamentals, we focus on the central role of routing, addressing, and communication and application protocols in general (core element number 7). In this element, we focus our security plan on the way our applications and networking systems communicate in a distributed computing environment. In the next security elements, we delve deeper into the realities of designing and operating information and infrastructure, addressing a range of problem sets that include the challenge of managing the configuration of our systems (configuration management), securing software development, and subtle but very important aspects of security such as managing the security of timekeeping among our systems, a problem set grossly overlooked in the area of security to date, yet providing an opportunity for a great many attacks.

The Fundamentals

There are six fundamental security elements, and they are all policy- and procedure-intensive. For example, while your security plan may ultimately call for the temporary disablement of a user account after 10 incorrect password attempts, a *policy* should exist that states that such disablement will occur; furthermore, a *procedure* should be defined to detail how the disablement will be performed and how it will be reversed in the event the problem was caused by a forgetful or careless employee. Before we dive into the fundamentals and the core elements in detail, let's jump ahead and see how these policies, procedures, and security elements are interrelated. You might skim through these policies and procedures (without feeling compelled to understand everything now), then return and reread them after you have reviewed all 28 security elements. In this way you'll have all of the background you need to understand the interrelationship of the core elements as they relate to these policies and procedures:

- Define policies identifying which individuals and roles within the organization are responsible for authenticating an individual and granting him or her access rights and accounts for specific applications. Define related procedures to describe how these accounts, and access to them, are created and removed. Clearly define new employee authentication and access control initiation.

- Relating to staff management policies and procedures (discussed later), define policies regarding disablement of terminated employee accounts in all systems, within a prestated minimum timeframe after termination notification. Record metrics for how quickly this disablement will be achieved in practice. Write procedures for performing a complete terminated employee disablement. These procedure should call for clear traceabilty/validation/checkpointing to prove that a terminated employee was removed from all systems, and they should include a record of the time each task was completed.

- Relating to intrusion detection policies and procedures, define full auditing of failed authentication attempts over a certain preconfigured threshold or according to a certain pattern.

- Maintain policies for archiving authentication logs. Define procedures for archiving these records.

- Define policies and procedures surrounding key management for systems performing encryption.

- Define the corporate privacy policy and document any associated procedures. The corporate privacy policy should be clearly understood by all employees.

I will address these and other policies and procedures in future chapters as they will become an increasingly important part of our security plan vocabulary. But now let's move on to the fundamental security elements.

1. Authorization and Access Control: Opening and Closing the Gates

Once the user identity is known, generally the next question a server must answer is, which resources is this client allowed to access or what activities is this user allowed to perform. This is called authorization or, simply, access control. Once you have authenticated a user, the user may be authorized for different levels of access or activity.

Authorization information is typically stored on a server inside of something called an *access control list* (ACL). ACLs are defined for resources that are controlled by the server and that require protection, such as files. Increasingly, directory server technology is used to streamline the management of access control simultaneously across network, application, and operating system resources. ACLs may be used to limit resource access to individual users or to users who have been configured to be part of a group. For example, the human resources group may get access to employee salary history, whereas the group representing the sales department may not.

Not only do users authenticate themselves to servers, but servers will, depending on the application, need to authenticate themselves to each other and to the clients. In addition, communication devices such as network routers may need to authenticate themselves to each other when they, for example, exchange routing information or establish a virtual private network (VPN) connection. Network management workstations must authenticate themselves to network devices such as routers. The security plan must address all of these scenarios.

Unfortunately, too many security professionals lose sight of the fact that authentication without a well-managed authorization infrastructure typically won't get them far. The ability to manage access control lists (the basis of authorization) efficiently and securely based on authentication credentials is fundamental to a successful security implementation.

2. Authentication: Knowing Who You Are Dealing With

Authentication answers the question, "Who are you?" You, in this case, would be either a human being or some other computing entity such as a router or Web server. Answering this question requires some form of proof. The relative strength of this proof and its practicality in implementation are the two key issues security planners must deal with. Authentication is essential to security—knowing who or what you are interacting with strikes at the core of security

At one end of the spectrum we have the traditional username/password; on the other, stronger, but more complex, end of the spectrum, we have tokens, smart cards, and biometrics. Recall from Chapter 1 that authentication proof can be defined in terms of three components:

- What you know
- What you have
- What you are

So-called two-factor authentication uses two of these components. As you would expect, three-factor security leverages all three of them, and one-factor only one. A password alone would be a one-factor solution. The SecurID card mentioned in Chapter 1 is a two-factor solution.

Passwords are the least secure of the three methods, primarily because people are forced to remember so many of them and because much of the password-based technology is not particularly well implemented. Users tend to choose easy-to-remember (and thus easy-to-hack) passwords, and they keep them out in the open where they, and unfortunately others, can see them. If we addressed all of those issues, passwords wouldn't be so ineffective; however, we rarely do

---

AUTHENTICATION JARGON

When a client authenticates itself to a server, it is referred to as *client authentication*. In the other direction, it's called *server authentication*. When both the client and the server prove their identities to each other, it is referred to as *mutual authentication*.

so. A recent survey by CentralNic (www.centralnic.com) indicated that nearly half (47 percent) of its Internet users surveyed used their own nickname or the names of their partners, children, or pets for their passwords.

Moreover, people often reuse the same password on multiple systems—which wouldn't be as problematic if all passwords were managed by a single, well-secured, highly trusted entity. But let's say, for example, that you use the same password for your banking activities as you do to shop at Joe's CD Shack on the Internet; let's also assume that Joe has a limited security budget and an implementation to match. The result? Your banking world could come crashing down if Joe's site were hacked and the hacker subsequently invaded your banking account by guessing that you used the same password for banking as you did for Joe's CD Shack. Too few people consider this possibility when reusing passwords.

With increased reliance on public networks and the growing use of wireless technologies, which make eavesdropping on networks much easier, data is more at risk than ever. For example, many people believe their applications provide adequate protection for passwords transmitted over the network; in fact, most passwords are sent either unencrypted or very weakly protected. A hacker who breaks into any device that comes in contact with your traffic and then sets the LAN interface into promiscuous (sniffing) mode can read your passwords and anything else you haven't adequately encrypted that's sent over the LAN. Think of it as someone being able to listen in on your phone conversation. Vulnerability scanners and intrusion detection systems can check for weaknesses like Ethernet interfaces in promiscuous mode on your network, but you can rarely control every interface your data will travel through.

TCP/IP protocol applications such as the File Transfer Protocol (FTP), Hypertext Transfer Protocol (HTTP), Simple Network Management Protocol (SNMP), telnet (administrator terminal interface), and others offer little or no protection for passwords. For years now I've argued against doing any form of configuration using SNMP because of this. To protect passwords and sensitive data used with these applications, you must implement a secondary security protocol, such as SSH (Secure Shell), SSL (Secure Sockets Layer), or IPSec (IP Security), or take other restrictive measures. When you are administering routers and servers remotely, telnet and FTP should never be enabled without a protocol such as SSH. You should upload and download files using a secure protocol such as FTP with SSH. And for statistics gathering, if you choose to use SNMP for this, you should configure your router or server to accept SNMP queries only from the IP address of your network management server and limit your SNMP data to nonsensitive material.

Most of us now know to use SSL with HTTP (HTTPS) to transport information securely, but a common programming error often exposes passwords. HTTP basic authentication is the most common method of authenticating Web site visitors, but alone it provides inadequate password protection. When using SSL to secure a page for which HTTP basic authentication is configured, you must be sure to gather the password *after,* not before, you activate SSL in your HTML code. Otherwise, passwords will be sent in plaintext and not through the protected SSL session.

Tokens or smart cards (what you have) are combined with password or biometric technology to produce a stronger solution, the two-factor solution. Clearly, they must be combined to prevent losing our identity along with our smart card or token. That is, if someone picks up our lost token, he or she shouldn't be able to use it without also knowing the password or being able to pass the biometric test (e.g., have our fingerprint).

Biometrics require secure presampling of the physiological or behavioral component along with a device to sample it again when authentication is requested. The cost and administration of these two requirements have deterred some from deploying biometrics. If, however, a biometric solution is managed in a way that meets your business needs, certainly it can provide many advantages as one part of your authentication scheme.

Authentication isn't just about knowing who an individual is, John Doe or whoever; it may also require knowing the individual's attributes, such as his or her *role* in an organization (staff scientist, accounting administrator, etc.). *Role-based* and *attribute access control,* which we'll talk about more, are advanced forms of authentication and access control and can greatly simplify system security administration.

BIOMETRICS BACKLASH

Some opponents of biometrics argue that these technologies may encourage criminals who are willing kill or maim individuals in order to make use of a biometric body part to launch attacks on an enemy government or to gain access to high-value assets. Others argue that biometrics, such as fingerprints, may be reproducible if your fingerprint is "lifted" from some source and reproduced in such a way as to fool the biometric reader. All of this points out the necessity for using multiple factors. In summary, when choosing a biometric for the most sensitive assets (and such a high level of sensitivity might not apply to many organizations), think about the most extreme forms of attacks to which your organization might be prey. Obviously, when human beings are involved and there is a threat of physical harm, it's difficult to provide absolutely secure anything, including authentication through biometrics. This is why some government installations require multiple individuals to present multiple factors, some of which may include biometrics, for the most sensitive authorizations.

Imagine configuring a new employee once in all corporate applications according to his or her role, as opposed to individually configuring that person in each of your corporate applications one by one: This is the primary benefit of role-based authentication. For example, let's assume that everyone working in your organization's sales department requires access to specific systems. After assigning roles, you can then build your access control lists based on whether someone is in sales, as opposed to whether someone in particular, such as John Doe, should have access. Thus, if there are 40 people in sales, you can define one access control decision for a a set of applications, which essentially states "If in sales, you get access." Compare that to listing the 40 salespeople one at a time and defining 40 access rules, one for each.

Of course, this capability requires that your authentication and access control scheme accommodates the notion of a role. There are several ways to do this, including looking up the role attribute in the directory service or placing the role inside the authentication credential, such as inside a digital certificate. We will touch on role-based security and technologies such as digital certificates more in later chapters.

Directory services technology provides, among many things, a common centralized method of managing access control lists across a range of applications and operating system functions. The architecture should address the way the directory service is used for these functions, including rules of trust inheritance, resource naming, update frequency, and so forth. This will be discussed in future chapters as well.

The protection of authentication servers and related access control/authorization servers (e.g., directory servers) themselves should be adequately addressed within the architecture because, clearly, they are focal points affecting the operation of the business at large. The importance of this can be demonstrated by a real-life occurrence. Several years ago, a nationwide power outage caused a very large commercial network to be down for nearly two days. At the time, the public was told that the cause of the outage was a failed upgrade of network components. In reality, however, the administrative authentication servers for all network routers had been compromised by hackers. The hackers then modified the configuration of each router to render it dysfunctional and, finally, changed the password to one not known by the commercial network provider. Consequently, the network provider had to send people to each remote location around the country to perform a hardware reset on each router and then manually reenter the password (this was the only allowable recovery procedure when the router's main password was unknown). Clearly, the authentication server compromised (a RADIUS server) was not adequately protected.

3. Encryption: Keeping Information Away from Prying Eyes

Most organizations have information that needs to be protected from prying eyes using a mechanism stronger than cleartext storage and username/password access control. Encryption is a stronger process whereby only those having a specific key can unlock the data. This is differentiated from simply restricting access to it. If you access encrypted data, you still must have the key to unlock it. In contrast, if you access unencrypted (so-called plaintext data), you do not need a key. Encryption is added security. It's especially relevant when the information is moved from storage (for example, a hard drive) and sent across the network because over a network, unless you encrypt, anyone can potentially tap into your network transmissions and read them. This is especially a problem when your transmission includes usernames and passwords. As discussed throughout the book, the risks in network transmissions are much greater than even most "experts" realize; hence, network encryption may be called for more often than previously thought.

Encrypting information with keys does, however, add the burden of addressing key management policies and procedures, including required key lengths, encryption algorithms, key protection, key change procedures, security of keys, and key backup. We will look at encryption considerations in future chapters.

Wireless LANs in particular deserve special attention in a security plan because they are notorious for having very poor security measures. I could today, for example, drive up and down the streets of a major city and sniff out unprotected wireless LAN traffic in corporations all over. Whereas wireless LAN technologies should be deployed only with high-grade encryption, today most are configured with weak or no encryption.

4. Integrity: Hashing It Out

Protecting the integrity (incorruptibility) of information is a key component of a security plan. Hackers routinely modify configuration files, databases, programs, and so forth in order to cover their tracks and to wreak havoc on your business.

SYMMETRIC VERSUS ASYMMETRIC ENCRYPTION

There are two types of encryption, *symmetric* and *asymmetric*. With symmetric encryption, a single key is used to encrypt and decrypt the message. Therefore, the sender and recipient must agree on which key to use. If the key is compromised, the sender and recipient must agree on a new key. With asymmetric encryption, there are two different keys, one that is kept private and one that is made publicly available. *Public-key infrastructure* (PKI) technology provides a vehicle for asymmetric encryption by using two keys, one public and the other secret. Chapter 5 is dedicated to the topic of PKI.

TRIPPING UP HACKERS

For UNIX- and Linux-based operating systems, a tool called Tripwire has historically proven useful in detecting such modifications, though today there are other commercial products incorporating this and other, more advanced features. For online transactions and application-level access, SSL and SSH protect the integrity of data sent through it. IPSec can optimally provide this protection.

Information integrity checking is typically implemented through the use of a hash function. Hash functions produce a unique number called a hash, which is a pattern of ones and zeros based on data we provide to the hash function. The hash is typically small compared to the larger amount of data on which it is computed. The probability of getting the same unique hash produced for two different data inputs to a properly designed hash function is approximately zero—this is the fundamental property of a well-designed hash function. Intrusion detection systems compute the hash of various key system files and, if properly implemented, provide a means to securely compare the hash of the original system files with the hash of ones that may have been tampered with by a hacker. If the two hashes are not equal, then the files have been tampered with, and the intrusion detection system should sound an alarm.

Let's consider a few examples. Suppose you configure your UNIX system in a way that you view as secure. (Note: In this book, I refer to this securing process as *configuration management* (CM) and *lockdown*.) You have disabled services you don't need, disabled access on all protocol ports (e.g., TCP and UDP), except those you absolutely require, and so forth. Obviously, you have a vested interest in maintaining the integrity of this configuration. If a hacker comes and changes it, you'd like to be able to know that quickly and easily.

The same goes for an online transaction. You'd like to make sure that, for example, a hacker doesn't change your online order for 1 book to 100 books or the shipping address to theirs instead of yours. All of this relates to the ability to tell if data has been modified from its original intended form. Integrity checking provides that capability.

5. Nonrepudiation: Signing on the Dotted Line

When you write a check, sign a letter, or sign a contract, you are providing a means to prove that you agreed to a certain transaction or sent a certain message. The ability to prove that one party actually agreed to a transaction is known as *nonrepudiation*. To the extent requirements dictate a need for nonrepudiation, such as authorization of a purchase order, the security plan must address this.

6. Privacy: Separating Hype from Reality

Privacy has become the buzzword of our connected society, and privacy advocates garner a great deal of media attention with their "sexy" stories about how employees and consumers alike are in danger of privacy violations. Certainly, privacy is an important topic, one that deserves very close attention in terms of technology and, especially, in policies and procedures. It will also receive considerable attention in our security plan as one of our 28 security elements.

That said, I do not overhype privacy in this book. You will not, for example, see endless pages discussing the potential evils of browser cookies. Cookies, a popular privacy topic, are only one small part of the whole privacy picture. Instead, we will address the full range of policy, procedure, technology, and life cycle management issues associated with managing access to and maintaining the protection of private information and related infrastructures. We'll consider the privacy expectations of different people and identify organizational responsibilities in maintaining privacy, not just by managing what we do internally (as in what information we store about individuals and what those individuals know of it), but also how we protect highly private information from others through sound security planning.

7. Addressing, Protocol Space, Routing Plan, Filtering, and Disablement: Closing the Hacker's Route to You

As you're no doubt aware, all the devices in your network have addresses of one form or another. You may not be aware of a number of new important themes and notions with regard to how your address space, at both the application and the network layers, can be more aggressively organized to improve security.

Inherent in all modern networks is a hierarchy of addresses; just as telephone numbers are organized by country code, area code, and local exchange, your network addresses have a similar structure. In the world of IP, this is called *subnetting*. The way IP addressing is structured *within* an organization, not just at the firewall, can greatly influence security capabilities. You need to know which addresses belong where, and which ones don't, on each segment in your network. Most organizations fail to organize subnet space according to a security model; instead, they do it more from the standpoint of routing only.

To improve security, you need to create physically diverse (*switched*, as in Ethernet-switched) paths through your network and organize your addresses so that they are grouped efficiently within these paths. By controlling where addresses are and how they are organized, you make it easier to detect a hacker who doesn't belong. Hackers will spoof (fake) addresses and then flood your network with them, as in a denial-of-service (DoS) attack wherein packets contain bogus addresses. To protect against these and other exploits, you need to be able to carefully filter out (discard) packets that don't belong. If you do not organize your addresses adequately and you flood too many addresses on too many physical paths in your network, you will make it hard to perform filtering because it's harder to know what belongs and what doesn't. If you don't sufficiently organize your address space and, next, your protocol space, intrusion detection systems (IDSs) will more often sound false alarms at greatly increased probability.

Organizing your protocol space means that applications in your network are confined to specific physical switched segments; and on these segments we have also, as just discussed, organized our address space. By confining protocols to the segments on which they belong—such as isolating Web servers on their own segment using the HTTP protocol—we make life easier for the intrusion detection and vulnerability processes because, simply put, on those segments, if it ain't HTTP, it ain't right. The decision process is simplified. And if it is HTTP, your systems can provide greater focus on particular expected (and unexpected, thus conspicuous) HTTP behavior because intrusion detection systems are not burdened with monitoring everything else under the sun happening on that segment.

Network routers and switches determine how all these network packets with their addresses and protocols are moved through the network. But one characteristic of routers plays right into the hands of hackers: Routers do exactly what they're told. Given that routing is so important, you'd think routing protocols would have evolved with more security than they have. In fact, they are quite insecure, so it's relatively easy to hack a router by giving it false information. Historically, authentication between routers is very weak; also, the transport mechanism used to send routes between routers is, in most historical cases, weakly protected. Fortunately, numerous efforts are underway to begin to address secure routing protocols. As they become available, take a careful look at them. Evaluate the strength of your routing protocol in terms of the other fundamentals discussed here, and work to improve its security. In the meantime, ensure that your routing plan takes into account potential hacker exploits such as spoofing, malformed packets, and reconnaissance traffic that tries to determine which systems you have deployed. The best way to address these attacks in your routing plan is, simply, not to route this attacker traffic by discarding it as near to the source as possible.

MORE ON RECONNAISSANCE

Reconnaissance packets are snoop-style data packets sometimes sent at a very low/infrequent basis with the objective to, first, determine which systems you have installed in order to, second, craft a focused attack based on known vulnerabilities in your systems. These packets are sent purely to observe the system's response (the response may help determine what you have installed because different systems respond differently, as in variants of an operating system or Web server to a specific style of packet sent). In some cases, it's nearly impossible to stop this kind of traffic as it can appear as normal behavior; nevertheless, your architecture, including routing plan and disablement/filtering procedures (see the "Disablement, Information Path, and Information Control Mind-Set" sidebar), should take into account the capability to disable as many of these signature responses as possible and to detect them and correlate them when they are used as part of an overall organized/orchestrated attack on your systems.

THE DISABLEMENT, INFORMATION PATH, AND INFORMATION CONTROL MIND-SET

If you don't need it, disable it. The challenge is knowing what you don't need. That implies technical, business, and people know-how. If information does not have to be transmitted over a particular physical segment (an Ethernet segment, for example), then isolate it, and don't transmit it there. To date, too much focus has been on firewalling and intrusion detection, both very important but insufficient components of a security plan. If you don't isolate network traffic to only those physical segments where it absolutely must traverse , then your firewalls, intrusion detection tools, and other tools will be severely limited. Control the information you provide about your infrastructure. That means preventing applications and operating systems, as much as possible, from, for example, responding to network-launched reconnaissance attempts to determine which version of software they are running and which services they provide. Software and systems tend to respond in patterns that produce a "signature," allowing them to be identified. Be aware that whatever you can do to prevent a hacker from understanding your IT architecture, you should do it. The same goes for communicating it to people. From help desk administrators to vendors to IT managers, all of them should understand that your information infrastructure is confidential. Don't, for example, casually pass out network topology diagrams to partners or at conferences.

The best security engineers are constantly looking for opportunities to disable, which means uninstalling unneeded software on desktop computers and in servers, disabling features through configuration, and filtering out network traffic by making use of network routing, addressing, and protocol space organization. Firewalls play an important role in disablement and filtering.

A security architecture should specifically address disablement and filtering at every layer of the security stack. It should be done at every boundary of the network—Internet, intranet, desktop, server, networking device, switched Ethernet segment, firewall, proxy server, and so forth.

Disablement and filtering reduce the range of exploits hackers have available to them. It also protects you against DoS attacks because, by filtering and disabling, you cut off the DoS traffic flood sooner and leave fewer entities to be concerned with during a DoS flood.

8. Configuration Management: Tracking Changes

Many organizations perform little or no configuration management (CM) for the system files and configurations of their network components—that is, routers, firewalls, directory servers, proxy servers, applications, and so forth. Failing to maintain a history of what was running in the system at any point in time and to back up that history securely within the CM system makes recovery difficult; moreover, pinpointing which vulnerabilities may have been exploited at any given point in time may be impossible.

You should define policies and procedures for how desktop computers are configured (installed with software, configured on the network, and so forth). Describe exactly what software can and cannot be installed (an example of very dangerous software is included in the discussion of security element number 24, procurement).

On the server side, document policies and procedures for testing and patching systems. Keep software at a common revision level; test patches before applying them and do so carefully, according to testing, intesting, and staging guidelines (see security element number 26). Document exact revision levels, including patches, for all systems, including when a system was on which revision level so that logs can be correlated as needed in the event an intrusion or other security-related event must be investigated. This will allow you to correlate a potential intrusion with a particular software revision.

9. Content and Executable Management: Controlling the Flow

Content and executable management means, in part, controlling the flow of dynamic executable content (for example, computer programs), such as Java and ActiveX, email attachments, and Web content, such as multimedia content (for example, Macromedia Flash) through your network. The flow of content is controlled at the firewall, where it may be filtered. It may also be virus-scanned.

Proxy servers may also act as a *front man* for content, shielding internal devices from being exposed to a less protected or trusted portion of the network, such as the Internet at large. Consider the definition of the word *proxy*: to "stand in for" or "on behalf of." That gives a reasonable idea of what a proxy server does: It stands in for and acts on behalf of some server or application behind it, typically providing enhanced security and efficiency.

Content and executable management also means placing certain requirements on content—for example, in the case of dynamic executable content, *digitally signing,* or *code signing,* that code to validate its authenticity (that is, relying only on trusted digital signatures, the electronic equivalent of a trusted handwritten signature, on software that you have approved for use in your company).

MORE ON CODE SIGNING

Examples of code signing standards and products include Microsoft Authenticode for Microsoft ActiveX objects, Netscape Object Signing for signed Java objects executed within the browser, Java JAR code signing for Java objects within the Sun Java framework, Microsoft Visual Basic (VBA) code signing, and Macromedia Shockwave code signing.

10. Directory Services: Location Is Everything

Directory services control how resources are located and described and how access to them is controlled (including related authentication). General-purpose directory service standards are the modern means of achieving this for network, application, and operating system resources. These include standards such as the Lightweight Directory Access Protocol (LDAP), Novell NetWare, X.500, and Microsoft Active Directory. Single-purpose directory services, the Domain Name Service (DNS) as the principle example, are also used for resource location, as in the case of DNS and universal resource locator (URL) domain name address resolution.

Directory servers in general, such as domain name servers and others discussed in this book, give the hacker opportunities to route your information his or her way rather than yours. In Chapters 3 and 4, we will repeatedly revisit the many benefits of directory service technology while highlighting the need to secure it heavily.

11. Diversity, Redundancy, and Isolation: The Triple Threat against Hacking

To prevent a hacker from doing something simple that can grind your business to a halt, you need to think about diversity, redundancy, and isolation (DRI).

Redundancy means that you back up one component with another. Redundancy without diversity is unwise. Consider, for example, network connectivity for many corporations today: They typically have redundant links (one backing up another) in many areas of their network. However, nine times out of ten, these redundant links follow the *same physical path* along the underlying network provider's fiber—that is, the links are *redundant*, but they are *not physically diverse*. Therefore, when a cable is cut (accidentally or intentionally), both links, the online and the backup (redundant) one, go down. Therein lies the difference between simple redundancy and redundancy with diversity.

If, in our example, a fiber is cut, our network becomes *isolated*, meaning that we have lost all connectivity to the outside world. You need to procure physically diverse links, not just redundant ones, in order to maximize the reliability of your network.

Let's take another example of this: your firewalls, an issue I've raised repeatedly. Many companies have redundant firewall configurations; from a hacker compromise standpoint, if these firewalls are provided by the same vendor and thus have identical holes, they are by no means diverse. Instead, you might consider deploying firewalls from two different vendors, one behind the other, and be ready to take one or the other offline at any given time to address a vulnerability.

Preventing isolation, from a security standpoint, can also mean *separating* systems that, when compromised together, act to cause a complete security failure. For example, a database of credit card numbers stored on one machine without the names and expiration date associated with them is not terribly attractive to a hacker. And if you divide storage of credit card number, name, and expiration date on separate systems and implement redundant and diverse security mechanisms for each system, the hacker will have a harder time. You could link these systems by a unique identifier that would not be useful to hackers unless they attacked the system correlating the identifier to the individual, presumably a very heavily secured and monitored system. Recently, one company, an online software seller, went out of business because of the bad press it received following a hack of its credit card database. In hindsight, serious thought about the entire concept of multipart data storage, such as credit card data, might have been time well spent. How far you are willing to go with this or another implementation is a function of how much security you need and how much you can afford, as driven by the impact analysis described in Chapter 1. Unless you do that analysis and then think seriously about security, these types of approaches won't be used. Instead, as implementors of systems, you'll wallow in the unknown, accepting solutions and implementations without any real relationship to security impact.

12. Intrusion Detection Systems and Vulnerability Analysis: Monitoring in Real Time

Intrusion detection is a real-time analysis of the behavior and interactions of a computing entity to determine whether penetrations have occurred or are likely. An intrusion detection system (IDS)—typically a server running IDS application software—probes servers, workstations, firewalls, and routers and analyzes them for symptoms of security breaches. The IDS monitors for known attack patterns, determines if important system files have been tampered with (that is, verifies integrity), analyzes system logs (audit trails), and issues alerts based on violations of security policy.

RELATIONSHIP OF RECOVERY TO DRI

Recovery, the twenty-eighth and final security element, is related to DRI, but they are not the same. Incorporating diversity and redundancy and preventing isolation of core systems do not mean that you can necessarily recover from an attack. Recovery implies an architecture that takes advantage of diversity, redundancy, and isolation protection in order to keep things going. Contingency means you are somewhat prepared if your recovery plans fail. Rebuild may be part of the recovery process. When we address DRI in our security plan, we need to do simple things, such as test our recovery capability and implement contingency plans. We also need to devise, and then test the rebuild process.

HOW MUCH TO LOG

The amount of logging you do depends on storage space and processing power because intensive logging can consume significant resources and cause system instability. Anyone who tells you to log everything conceivable is not helping you. In the real world, such an approach is impractical. You need to anticipate what you need, in order to pinpoint the most relevant information to log.

A vulnerability audit (VA) is an analysis of system weaknesses. A vulnerability scanner (typically a server running vulnerability analysis software) may appear, from the perspective of the IDS, as a device attempting an intrusion. The vulnerability scanner tests the system by poking around as a hacker would and by checking system configurations the way an experienced administrator might when looking for errors and weak spots. Some scanners are aggressive enough to crash the systems they scan; test carefully before deploying one on your live network.

Vulnerability analysis and intrusion detection should be focused on components at all levels of the security stack and should include the desktop. System administrators may argue that analysis and detection are not needed behind the firewall because that area is safe. This is a very dangerous assumption. An IDS and vulnerability scanner should be implemented both behind your firewall and for those devices exposed to the open Internet.

Note that your IDS and vulnerability analysis tools can be configured to monitor components managed on your behalf by an external managed service provider such as outsourced Web hosting or a managed router. If you do this, coordinate your analysis with the service provider because your systems may appear as intruders to the provider's detection systems. If you are not doing vulnerability or IDS analysis on the managed systems, be sure their owners are. These third-party managed systems, if not properly secured, can prove an ideal jumping-off spot for hackers, who can gain leverage by using the trust arrangements you have for systems managed by a third party.

Your security plan should include a detailed discussion of how system logs will be accommodated at every layer of the security stack. You need to define what is logged and what isn't, how much is stored before it is archived or destroyed (you need to estimate storage requirements), and how logs will be correlated.

Your intrusion and vulnerability analysis architecture needs to address all forms of attacks and vulnerabilities, such as the following:

- Misconfigured systems that leave too many doors open (vulnerability)
- Attacks involving the delivery of malformed protocol requests; for example, a stream of intentionally corrupt TCP/IP control data packets that crash your systems (intrusion)

- Warning signs of an onslaught of packets from a denial-of-service (DoS) attack or worm (intrusion)

- Application inputs causing buffer overflows, which then allow for the execution of arbitrary code chosen by the hacker (both an intrusion and a vulnerability)

An often overlooked, but highly useful, approach to intrusion detection involves studying performance/utilization statistics and looking for trends. This can help you understand if, for example, you are under a DoS attack or if a hacker has made his or her way into your network. I'm reminded of a company (the world's third-largest corporation at the time) for which my group managed a private network. My group provided regular detailed network utilization statistics, and we had noticed a sudden change in network usage along a few of the links and thought it might be an intruder. The customer confirmed that there was absolutely no justification for this increased usage. In fact, an intruder was on the network and moving large amounts of data between systems.

If you detect a DoS attack, the minimum response is address and protocol disablement and filtering. DoS attacks take advantage of the fact that without adequate filtering, routers will deliver traffic wherever a hacker wishes, regardless of source IP address, destination address, or traffic protocol type. Systems can thus be overloaded and brought to a standstill. We all know we need to filter, but many of us think this should occur only at the firewall. Wrong. You should also configure routers that have the computing power to handle filtering to do so. And follow this essential principle: Disable any components you don't absolutely need, and cut off the traffic at the earliest possible point of entry. Other guidelines include the following:

- Establish a solid security escalation path with your Internet service provider (ISP) that lets you quickly notify its engineers to filter DoS-based traffic upstream, within the ISP's network. Ask your ISP about its procedures for coordinating filtering with its peering partners in response to DoS attacks. Don't allow yourself to be put on hold with a customer service rep during a DoS attack.

- Running systems close to the capacity of the CPU, the memory, the available storage, and the network bandwidth maximizes vulnerability to a DoS attack. Therefore, monitor resource usage within your system; look for suspicious increases in usage; and allocate sufficient spare capacity to accommodate sudden, unexpected increases in load. Though you may not be able to protect against the largest distributed DoS attacks this way, a hacker accessing a few computers and bombarding your system shouldn't necessarily be able to overwhelm your capacity quickly.

- Consider the deployment of anti-DoS tools within your network. These tools work to predict the onset of a DoS attack and help you take proactive steps to protect your network.

- Perform intrusion detection and vulnerability analysis at every layer of the security stack and on all computing elements, including the desktop, servers, network routers, and so forth.

- Give serious consideration to deploying desktop-level firewalls and intrusion detection systems because employees routinely violate policies or otherwise fall prey to malicious software that, when launched from their desktop, can affect not only them but also the rest of the corporate network. This is specially true for laptops because users often install their own software on these systems (despite your content and executable management policies that may prohibit this), and when connecting them to the Internet, laptops can be easily infected in one way or another.

- Watch over your intrusion detection and vulnerability analysis systems. Few things bring a hacker more joy than compromising your intrusion and vulnerability analysis systems. One common hack is to replace your version intrusion detection software with the hacker's own neutralized (ineffective) version of it. For example, those that use Tripwire and store the Tripwire executable and integrity files on the same system they are protecting represent ideal targets for this type of attack. Protect your intrusion and vulnerability analysis systems. Avoid administering your systems so that the protectors (intrusion detection and vulnerability analysis systems) fall to a hacker as easily, and at the same time, as the systems they are protecting.

The intrusion detection and vulnerability analysis architecture is reliant on tight policies regarding the manner (timeliness, chain of command, response method) in which intrusions and suspected vulnerabilities are addressed. Outline detailed procedures to take, in accordance with policies, to address intruders and suspected vulnerabilities. These policies and procedures should integrate tightly with incident response procedures.

13. Securing Software: Starting at the Source

For software you have deployed or have developed in-house, conduct a formal security review to assess its potential vulnerability. As part of this review, address any other policies and procedures relating to software disablement, protocol filtering, and protocols used by the software. Assess whether your vendor is able to keep up with needed security patches. On an ongoing basis, assess whether your vendor or your in-house development staff has demonstrated a reasonable track record of producing software that is less vulnerable to hacks.

Information stored in temporary areas (caches, temporary files) for performance or other reasons leaves nice holes for hackers to jump in. Memory management and buffer management are key to secure software design. Define policies for how software under your control, such as software you develop or have developed for you, functions relative to memory management. It should include procedures for deploying code-checking utilities that attempt to detect the kind of buffer exploits hackers employ to execute arbitrary programs on your hacked systems.

Within your operating system and application server environments, computer programs pass data (for example, transactions) back and forth among each other and, in doing so, choose to inherently trust each other, or not. The way that software processes trust each other—that is, the way trust is assigned, delegated, and inherited—is an important part of security and should not be overlooked. It affects how much control a hacker can have over your application or collection of applications and, eventually, business, based on compromise of a single process. If, for example, you have assigned your Web server process full trust (full permission to access everything within the computer) and a hacker compromises that Web server process, he or she will also inherit the permissions assigned to that process. Therefore, the hacker will have full permission to do what he or she wants on the entire computer. In this example, it behooves you to assign only minimal permissions, not all, to your Web server process.

14. Securing Time Services: Keeping Your Eye on the Clock

If you're wondering what time could possibly have to do with security, consider that many of your security systems fully rely on time synchronization among network devices. For example, Microsoft server environments (Windows 2000/XP) rely on a security scheme called Kerberos. Kerberos is used to authenticate you to all Windows resources in the network (file servers and so forth). If a hacker tampers with or otherwise destroys time services in the network, he or she destroys Kerberos and thus everyone's ability to reach servers and other resources on the network. For most businesses, that means action pretty much grinds to a halt. Also, public-key infrastructure (PKI; see Chapter 5) relies heavily on synchronized time so that your authentication credentials, called *digital certificates*, can be determined to be valid or not (to determine if they have expired).

Consider another, simpler example: the logs of your devices. These logs record the valid actions of users and administrators to keep track of security-related events and to track the actions of hackers. If hackers can modify or otherwise change time, they can effectively confound your ability to rely on time stamps in log records.

15. Staff Management: Managing Employees and Contractors

It's essential to know who you are bringing into your organization. That means you must conduct in-depth background checks. Most companies are far too lax in this area, and the result may be inviting a highly untrustworthy individual into a highly trusted position. Let me give you an example from my own experience. Years ago I was all set to hire a staff engineer for a position that would report to a manager in my organization. This engineer made it through all of the interviews, and human resources informed me we were ready to offer him the job. But just prior to presenting him the job offer, I decided to give him a call (he had indicated I could call him at his current work number if needed). I discovered he was no longer with his previous employer, which I found somewhat surprising because he gave no indication he would leave before getting an offer. I also noticed that his employer was not very talkative about the engineer's exit, I got the idea it had *not* been voluntary. I decided to dig further and, in the process, discovered some amazing information.

First though, my company's human resources department did, as a matter of course, request a background check (police, FBI) on new employees; in this case, it could often take as long as seven months to get the result from this applicant's city of residence. Clearly, the human resources department had not really completed the background check, as I had been led to believe. By the time I was done completing my own, I discovered the individual we were about to hire had lied in numerous places on his application, the most glaring being in regard to past incarceration—it turns out he had robbed a bank a few years earlier. I think you get my point.

Another important part of staff management is how you handle termination. If a staff member is in a sensitive position, with access to business-critical systems, do not unexpectedly terminate that person and continue to allow open and unmonitored access to critical systems. Obviously, termination should be an important aspect of your staff management policies and procedures, factoring in, of course, how tightly you want or need to run your organization. Just bear in mind that a great deal of system hacks are performed by disgruntled employees.

The Wrap-up Elements

Now that we have reviewed the core elements, we're ready to wrap things up. These remaining 13 elements take a closer look at details relating to the planning process that we have touched on when exploring the core elements, but we stand to gain by a final thorough evaluation.

16. Administration and Management: Watching Over the Enterprise

Obviously, how we administer and manage our systems is an important aspect of security. Today, as explained previously under number 2, "Authentication: Knowing Who You Are Dealing With," organizations often use the Simple Network Management Protocol (SNMP) to perform many management activities, from configuring devices to monitoring them. Likewise, administrators frequently use tools such as Telnet and FTP to update software and directly administer systems. These standard habits spell bad news for security without a plan and due care.

Recall from the previous discussion that TCP/IP protocol applications, such as FTP, HTTP, SNMP, telnet, and others, offer little or no protection for passwords, which means you must implement a secondary security protocol, such as SSH SSL, or IPSec, or take other restrictive measures. And when you are administering routers and servers remotely, telnet and FTP should never be enabled without a protocol such as SSH.

Another underpublicized vulnerability, where administration and management is concerned, is the Dynamic Host Configuration Protocol (DHCP), which is based on another protocol, the Boot Protocol (BOOTP). Both are widely used today in corporations and through dial-up connections to configure network-related parameters of devices including desktops, servers, and routers. Keeping in mind that influencing network behavior is just what experienced hackers are hoping to achieve, by compromising your DHCP servers, they can attempt to route information where they want it to go, as opposed to where you do. To preclude this sort of intrusion, you must make sure your security architecture addresses the security of DHCP servers and carefully monitors and controls their usage and operation; you must regularly verify that correct/expected configuration information is being delivered.

MORE ON DHCP AND BOOTP

DHCP and the protocol it is based on, BOOTP, dynamically deliver network addresses and configuration information to routers, desktops, servers—pretty much to any network-attached device. It's a "plug-and-play" standard, the kind that brings joy to hackers because while you plug, they play. DHCP and BOOTP rely on network broadcasts for everyone to hear, including the hacker, and these requests ask for configuration information. The last thing you want is for a hacker to provide configuration and addressing information to your devices, rather than your own trusted DHCP/ BOOTP server.

HOME ON THE LAN

A favorite hacker spot in large organizations is on the LAN, from which most network and application monitoring and configuration is performed by administrators—as in your network management center (NMC) LAN. Often this is the most trusted spot in your network, meaning that from there, a hacker can reach out to just about any device in your network. It's an ugly scene when hackers make their way onto a network management center's LAN. In one case, a carrier's frame relay network was compromised this way, proving false what many people today believe: that technologies such as frame relay are immune to the kind of risks found over the Internet. Also, many frame relay networks are themselves IP networks, whereby frame relay is transported over them. Don't be fooled into believing that dumbed-down technology such as frame relay will always make you safer. Simply, you can't "have security" with something like frame relay; you still need a plan, and you need to assiduously protect your LAN and carefully analyze intrusion detection and vulnerability. Disable everything except what your administrators need.

The point here is, administration and management mechanisms must be addressed as a fundamental part of the security architecture, not as an afterthought. In general, you need to make sure your security architecture is easily configurable to meet the security goals you establish. Do not hand over an unmaintainable, unconfigurable system to the implementation and operations team. Think about configuration up front, both automated and manual. Put policies and procedures into place as part of security life cycle planning and configuration management.

17. Interoperability and Standards: Working Together

The security architecture should address the interoperability of security-related systems and their adherence to standards. At the same time, it's important not to overdo it. Too often, the ultra-planner and absolutist enjoy making a meal of interoperability and standards, typically taking it to bizarre extremes such as overstandardization of what are otherwise small details or outlying situations. One excellent example of this is in the area of public-key infrastructure (PKI) technology, a topic to which Chapter 5 is dedicated. Ultra-planners flock to PKI because it offers so many opportunities for standards to be taken to bizarre extremes. On the surface, PKI is merely a sophisticated digital mechanism for securing information and creating a nonrepudiatable digital framework. But within it exists an entire new world of applications that can empower the population of a country, and next the world, to sign everything electronically that is today signed by hand.

It's within that unbounded world that the ultra-planner thrives. For example, while it's true that PKI offers the opportunity to provide a nonrepudiable framework to millions of people, is it truly necessary, for the purposes of our much smaller organization, that we conquer the million-person scaling problem right away and that we discover and implement every standard available to achieve that? No, but this is the very problem I have seen ultra-planners introduce repeatedly when relatively small-scale PKI deployments would do.

The objective is to achieve the maximum and most manageable security solution for your dollar and to get it into place quickly. It makes little sense to plan a security architecture that's so scalable, interoperable, and standards-based that it'll last well into the next century when our business cycles mainly operate from quarter to quarter. Balance is the watchword here.

18. Laws and Regulations: Staying Out of Trouble

Depending on where and how your organization operates, you may be required to adhere to laws and regulations that will affect how you plan security. These may include local, state, national, and even international trade regulations regarding allowable encryption and specific regulations for maintaining confidentiality of certain information. Therefore, you must write policies to describe specific, security-relevant laws and regulations with which your organization must comply and define procedures for implementing those policies. For example, some countries prohibit the export or import of certain encryption technologies. If you're a multinational company and plan to deploy an application using encryption to countries with such restrictions, then you must adhere to their laws.

19. Lockdown: Keeping Things Tight

In accordance with the security architecture, as part of the staging process, components in every layer of the security stack should be "locked down," meaning that a known set of security-focused configuration parameters and installed software (see also number 8, "Configuration Management: Tracking Changes") has been chosen for specific machines or classes of machines.

Laptops and any other portable computing entities must meet content and executable management and configuration policies and procedures so that they do not compromise systems within the corporate network by introducing network-borne, hostile software. For example, employees shouldn't be allowed to install anything they want on a machine connected to the corporate network. They should be instructed to follow guidelines (that is, policies and procedures) established by the security planning team. Otherwise, a portable computer, for example, can essentially become an unsecured system, hence an "intruder" upon being brought into work and connected to the corporate LAN.

20. Lost or Stolen Items: When Important Things Disappear

Some of the most effective hacks are launched from stolen or lost laptops, enabled, for example, because many people store default usernames/passwords on them. (Check yours out now: Perhaps your dial-up connection and email are both configured to automatically store and supply username and password.) One company specializing in security and secure hosting went out of business because of the the bad press generated by a serious hack made possible via a stolen laptop.

This security element is best addressed via policies that clearly set out the reporting procedure employees are to follow when they lose or note something missing—laptops, desktops, handhelds, badges, tokens, smart cards, or floppy disks with sensitive information. They should be instructed to report the incident to a designated security officer, who must act quickly to disable and reissue authentication and access control configurations. Policies in this category should describe what employees and security officers must respond to, how quickly, and the procedures for carrying out the appropriate response.

21. Managed/Outsourced Security: Working with Outside Security Vendors

An external organization (outsource) that manages any of your organization's information or infrastructure elements must be required to adhere strictly to policies you define that meet the minimum requirements of your internal security planning process. These policies should include procedures for reviewing and validating (practicing, testing) adherence to your minimum requirements and include metrics for measuring this adherence.

22. Performance: Security Takes Time

Because security measures such as firewalls, proxy servers, directory server lookups, logging, encryption, and real-time intrusion detection and vulnerability analysis all consume resources of one form or another, security can slow things down. Therefore, your security plan should try to anticipate the performance impact. An excellent way of doing this is to test up front under a realistic user load, then capacity-plan accordingly. For example, if you intend to increase event logging for a high-impact application, measure storage and CPU load before and after you increase logging; then compare the results and work to accommodate any increased load by increasing storage and CPU capacity as needed.

A SECOND OPINION

It's a good idea to have your organization's security policies and procedures, as well as the security plan, routinely reviewed by an independent trusted third party, one that is external to the organization. Such a review provides a fresh viewpoint on security. Security planning is too complex to entrust entirely to a single organization, even your own.

That said, slowing things down in the name of security isn't necessarily problematic unless it significantly affects business and the bottom line. That is, we can't take the attitude with security that it always comes at no performance cost to us. If implementing security means that high-impact application performance decreases and, at the same time, the company has no available budget to buy the needed hardware to speed things back up, you face a classic security trade-off. The historical response to this situation has been to reverse the security implementation because compromising on performance is something people haven't been willing to accept. But times have changed and, as a security planner, you need to work to sell security in such a way as to help people in the organization understand that this kind of performance sacrifice may be reasonable and that increased security is value, just as performance is value.

Of course, we shouldn't take this to extremes. I'm reminded of one PKI deployment in which so many CPU-intensive operations were required because of the paranoia of the security planners that it would take a user five minutes to log in to the system and, once logged in, the user would face intermittent delays of one minute or more as he or she was constantly re-authenticated to the system. In this example, the slightly enhanced security achieved by constantly re-authenticating the individual (in this case, through a CPU-intensive PKI digital signing operation) never seemed to me to justify this poor level of performance. Sometimes simple things can be done to improve security performance. In this PKI example, I suggested to the client that they develop an activity timer-based authentication mechanism whereby users would be re-authenticated only after a configurable timeout period, such as when the user didn't do anything for five minutes. Such inactivity might indicate that the user has walked away from his or her computer without first logging out. This suggestion, along with several other enhancements, dramatically improved the performance of the application while meeting security planning objectives.

23. Physical Security: Locking Up

In Chapter 1, I described how a hacker walked unimpeded into a company conference center to wreak havoc. An effective security plan will address overall building security, to include employee, visitor, and contractor access to the building and, once inside, any additional restrictions and controls needed to secure shared areas such as conference centers, conference rooms (where visitors or guests may be left unattended), data centers, and any other public-access areas.

You might decide to log physical access using a centralized building access system that would allow you to track any suspicious movement throughout the building. You might also, for example, choose to monitor physical access to sensitive areas by video and control access using combination locks, tokens, and biometrics. Keep in mind, though, that building access tokens can be lost and that many popular ones today use one-factor authentication. An example of a simple building access token would be the common proximity identification badge. Such access control is insufficient for areas that require higher security because employees lose badges but don't realize it for days. They then report the loss late to the security officer, giving a hacker plenty of time to make use of the badge. Combination locks are vulnerable because a casual observer can easily read the combination as someone enters it. To improve security, use two factors, such as a combination lock and a proximity badge. Add a biometric to improve things further. And don't forget to disable building access to all terminated employees.

When it comes to defining policies and procedures that apply to the physical security architecture, you need to address who is allowed access to where, based on employee role, new employee orientation, and terminated employee exit procedures. But your policies can't stop here. You also need them for all types of visitors and contractors including cleaning staff, repair people, clients, and customers. And don't forget: You need to provide policies and procedures for both business hours and "after hours."

24. Procurement: Be Discriminating

Procurement procedures can't be casual, along the lines of "Hey, that's a great freeware security program; let's download it." Freeware or any other ware might be fine, as long as you have a policy in place for where it can and cannot be used and a procedure for testing it and installing it.

I once downloaded a very interesting SNMP manager from the Internet to check out. I was a bit suspicious as I had noted it was coming from a part of an unknown developer and from a part of the world not particularly known for designing this type of software—not a problem in and of itself, but at the time I was aware that network-borne viruses were being aggressively developed there. After downloading this program and installing it, all of the firewall and IDS alarms on my test systems went wild. It seems this program was designed to take full network control over the computer and begin delivering content off the hard drive to a hacker.

WATCH THE DOOR

Sometimes, a physical security measure can be something as simple as watching the door. Once, while visiting a client, I noted that one of the doors in their highly secure data center closed very slowly and, in fact, didn't shut completely on its own. While walking down the hall, I asked one of my company's engineers to see if he could reenter the room without the required biometric. He could. Needless to say, we quickly alerted the client. The point here is, test anything connected to security. Don't get burned by something as simple as a door not closing properly. It makes little sense to put all these safeguards in place only to have them, essentially, fly out the door.

The point is, you've got to know the source of your infrastructure components and, then, you have to test them. Consequently, your policies and procedures for this security element involve testing and review by a team of subject matter experts, who are responsible for ensuring that software like the one I just described isn't unwittingly unleashed on your network.

25. Support Interface: Protecting Confidential Information

All organizations have employees and contractors who have access to confidential information, everything from detailed information on how to administer infrastructure components to an employee's Social Security number. Typically, these include help desk staff, customer support representatives, human resources employees, and others. All employees with such access must understand how to handle this sensitive information. This is accomplished by writing very specific policies and procedures that help support staff understand how to handle sensitive and confidential information and high-impact system administration. Next, an aggressive training program for support interface policies and procedures needs to be put in place. As noted in number 27, "Training: Achieving Security through Education," support interface policies and procedures should also be practiced during scheduled drills.

26. Testing, Integration, and Staging: Get It Right before Betting the House on It

Deploying a complex system without first testing and staging (that is, simulating a real environment) is like performing surgery on a patient without sterilizing the instruments. One of the most serious mistakes you can make in implementing a security plan is to connect a new machine to a live network without first staging and testing it. Unfortunately, this is what most people do. Bluntly put, you cannot build a secure system that is connected to a live network because while you're securing it, a hacker could be taking advantage of the vulnerabilities you have yet to lock down.

Systems must be staged and built offline on isolated networks, those not connected to anything but other systems being built. You need policies and procedures that detail how to test, stage, and deploy software on your network. Then you must test systems before you deploy them. For example, if you decide to implement a vulnerability analysis system, do not simply set the thing loose on your live network. They have been known to crash live systems. Test first. The same goes for just about anything else affected by security. After you have tested, deploy, but first on a limited basis if possible; collect information, then make a decision whether to complete the deployment or return to the lab for further testing.

27. Training: Achieving Security through Education

No security plan is complete without a policy that makes ongoing training mandatory for general staff, contractors, and security staff. A training program should incorporate classes, presentations, formal training, posters, and any other mechanisms that will reinforce to employees the importance of security. The training program should also define procedures for carrying out this training, the objective being to practice the security strength of your organization and thus the effectiveness of this training. You should conduct role-playing drills, for example, to simulate a hacker attempting to convince a help desk employee to provide a password to a system. The following is an example from my own experience.

I called a company specializing in security to make a change to my account. Instead of first asking me for my account number and then my password (which they need to make changes), I was asked only to "please provide your password." Seeing this as an opportunity, I shot back, "But that makes no sense; many people could have the same password as I do." Apparently my question rattled the company representative a bit. She then provided—without my asking—the full names of five people who had the same password as mine. She wanted to prove that if I had simply given her my password without making such a point of it, she still could have determined my name. She indicated this by telling me that she intended to ask for my name after I provided my password. In this way, she explained, she could ultimately narrow down who I was. I suppose the idea here was that no two people would ever likely have the same password. What a complicated, contrived, inefficient, and, most importantly, insecure scheme, and what a poorly trained support representative. I thanked her for providing the password for five other people.

This is a good example of how a poorly trained employee, working with a poorly designed infrastructure, can easily get rattled and provide information he or she shouldn't—in this case, potentially very damaging information.

28. Recovery: Getting Back on Track

Finally, we come to recovery. Obviously, you need to be able to recover from a security incident. To do that, you should include contingency planning as part of your security effort, in case things don't go as expected. One of the most important aspects of a recovery plan is a solid backup/restoration plan. Unfortunately, many organizations run backups but *never* practice restoration. Restoring often fails because data, programs, and so forth are correlated, and if you restore one thing but not something else, often the entire system is broken. You need to have a backup and restoration plan that takes into account data dependencies of all kinds, from business data to configuration information used within your machine that you may need to restore.

That said, it's important to be aware that repairing, as opposed to rebuilding, a hacked system is dangerous and a nearly impossible task. Why? Because you don't know exactly what the hacker did. Therefore, part of your restoration activity is to know how to rebuild a system, from scratch, to a certain level, apply any needed patches in response to the security compromise, then carefully determine what—if any—data can be restored back over that machine. Obviously, hackers modify data to their advantage, so a security plan that considers this is necessary. An IDS can help here, assuming that the IDS itself wasn't compromised and that what it reports can be relied on, as it can help point us to things that have been tampered with. Still, this is a messy process that requires detailed knowledge of data dependencies. Therefore, your backup plan has to clearly state exactly what will be backed up, including system files and configuration data, not just information relevant to the business process itself. It must state how often data will be backed up and whether full backups or incremental backups will be performed. Also, because hackers have a way of destroying anything they can access online, remember that highly reliable online storage systems aren't enough. You need backups of systems, and these backups need to have physical disconnection and storage away from the real-time systems.

An important aspect of a backup plan is to store media *off-site* at a secure location. It seems like common sense to do this, but I repeatedly find clients who do not perform off-site backups. They just don't take this risk seriously enough. Fire, theft, flood, or vandalism can cost a company its ability to survive. I'm reminded of a technology company whose building was burned down by the employees of a competitor. The company went out of business because it didn't maintain off-site backups; all of its backups were in the burned building.

In your recovery policies and procedures, detail the steps required to implement the recovery and contingency plan. These policies and procedures should include mandatory, regularly scheduled drills to practice recovery and contingency procedures. Then, address any problems discovered during these drills through revision of associated planning documents and processes.

Conclusions

It should be clear from these first two chapters that security planning is a multidimensional effort. It touches every aspect of our organization—people, business, and technology. A security plan that works is one that addresses real-world issues in a balanced fashion and, at the same time, is well organized. In the next two chapters, we combine our security template and 28 security elements, forging them into a powerful tool you can use to write your own security plan. In Chapter 3 we'll focus on the fundamental security elements, and in Chapter 4 we'll walk through the core and wrap-up elements. Those two chapters also include the security worksheets you'll use to complete your own security plan.

Using the Security Plan Worksheets: The Fundamentals

In this chapter, we begin the process of completing the security worksheets that will serve as your guide throughout the security planning process. The worksheets contain an important starter set of questions and pointers. When you address them conscientiously and plan accordingly, the result will be a comprehensive security plan. Note that many of the questions demand more than a simple yes or no or a one- or two-sentence response. Certain questions point to the need to develop a detailed technical plan of some kind or to write related polices and procedures.

From Here to Security

The goal of this chapter and the next is to ease you into increasingly more effective, rigorous, and complete security planning. Note, I say *goal*: In truth, you may not feel that you are being eased into anything, as this is an exhaustive and rigorous process. I can assure you, though, that after going through it and absorbing a reasonable amount of its material, you will be rewarded. You will have a truly holistic and well-rounded view of security planning. You will, in short, be ready to develop your own plan, one that truly works.

CUSTOMIZING AND OBTAINING ELECTRONIC COPIES OF THE WORKSHEETS

Feel free to customize these worksheets to include more questions and pointers related to your particular needs. Electronic copies of the worksheets included in this book are available from the Web site maintained by the author at www.criticalsecurity.com or from the book's companion Web site at www. wiley.com/compbooks/greenberg.

It's a good idea to start this process simply by writing notes in your worksheets. For example, you might write your thoughts on what's needed, next steps to meet those needs, whom you might ask to complete part of the worksheet, or how you might assign responsibilities at your next security team meeting. Over time, the worksheets can serve as a central repository, providing links to any related plans, policies, and procedures. For example, when a worksheet directive reads something to the effect of "Write policies and procedures for doing XYZ," you can simply place in the worksheet itself hyperlinks to where those policies and procedures are stored within your configuration-management system.

Organization of the Worksheets

As you learned in Chapter 2, the 28 security elements are divided into two groups: 15 core elements, 6 of which are considered "fundamental," and 13 wrap-up elements. In this chapter, we will apply the full rigor of our security template to the 6 fundamental security plan elements; in Chapter 4, we will do the same for the remaining 9 core elements. The 13 wrap-up elements are handled differently because, as explained in Chapter 2, these are summary elements tightly linked to the core elements; that is, they will serve more as a final checklist as we complete our security plan, to help us catch anything we've missed. Therefore, we don't need to go through the entire security template for these elements, as we do for the core elements. Instead, each of the wrap-up elements is listed in its own section at the end of Chapter 4.

By way of review before we get started on the worksheets, let's consider what we've accomplished so far:

- We compared approaches for successful and unsuccessful security planning.
- We reviewed the security planning template.
- We familiarized ourselves with the 28 security elements that are necessary to an effective security plan.

Now we can begin the process of joining the security elements to our template. For each of the six fundamental core security elements, five worksheets are provided, directly correlating with our security template. The first worksheet, Quality Management (see Worksheet 3.1), is somewhat different from the other four. It is "generic," in that it applies equally to all security elements. You can, of course, modify the worksheet to meet your particular needs. In some cases, you might find it useful to develop several different customized quality management worksheets depending on the needs of your organization. But in all cases, you will want to complete at least one quality management worksheet for every security element. To help you fill out the Quality Management worksheets, look at Table 3.1, where column 2, Security Plan, details how to address each item in column 1.

Each of the other four worksheets is preceded, first, by a summary and, second, by a special figure called Key Relationships. The summary provides a simple recapitulation of the important issues to keep in mind as we examine the particular security element. The Key Relationships figure summarizes the top four security elements tied to the one currently undergoing study. Following the summary and the Key Relationships figure is a series of guidelines, categorized to correspond to the template, outlined as follows:

Quality Management

Security Stack

- Physical
- Network
- Application
- Operating system

Life-Cycle Management

- Technology selection
- Implementation
- Operations
- Incident response

Business

- Businesspeople
  - Employees
  - Customers
  - Owners
  - Suppliers
  - Partners
- Information
- Infrastructure

Selling Security
- Executive
- Middle Management
- Staff

There is, necessarily, a certain amount of overlap in these guidelines. For example, under Business, we examine the security element first from the perspective of information, then from the perspective of infrastructure. Why? Because our objective is completeness; we don't want to miss anything. By taking an alternate view on a problem, we often discover something new about it. We're looking for what we might have missed. Think about it: This is precisely what the hacker does—he or she looks for what we might have missed. As I said in Chapter 1, security is a way of thinking, and we need to think it through better than our adversary.

Table 3.1   Quality Management

QUALITY MANAGEMENT	SECURITY PLAN
Revision number	Uniquely identify each revision of the security element worksheet plan with a number (e.g., revision 2.1).
Revision date	Include the date the revision was made.
Change summary	Record changes made for each revision (i.e., maintain a revision history). For each revision, ensure that an adequate peer review is conducted.
Author(s)	Document the name(s) of the author(s) of this element of the security plan. This refers to those who actually wrote the plan, *not* the managers who, for example, oversaw the effort.
Owner	In most organization's this will be the manager or team leader who is coordinating the input of the authors of the plan.
Configuration-management status	Configuration-manage the state of all documentation, system configurations, hardware, and software relating to the security element. For more on this, refer to the Configuration Management security element worksheet in Chapter 4.

Table 3.1   Quality Management *(Continued)*

QUALITY MANAGEMENT	SECURITY PLAN
Budget	Our security expenditures begin with a budget driven by our impact analysis. The budget represents an up-front estimate of the cost to implement a particular aspect of the security plan. Obviously, sometimes our estimates aren't precise—sometimes we're over-budget, sometimes under. The purpose of this quality management metric is to track, over time, how close we are able to stay to our original budget estimate. You should track your original budget estimate over time and periodically as determined by your organization, such as monthly, and you should note the current amount of money spent thus far. Finally, you should project what you think the new budget will be, based on what you now know. For example, if you allocated $10,000 for a security element plan and have spent $8,000 and you're not nearly complete, then it's reasonable to expect that your projected budget may be over $10,000 unless you can find some way to reduce cost.
Schedule	Track how closely you stay on schedule as the implementation of your security plan proceeds; after the implementation is complete, record how accurate your initial estimates were.
Business value metrics	How does security bring value to your organization? How does it detract from it? Establish a set of metrics for measuring the business value of this element. These metrics are directly related to the way security is "sold" within your organization. For more on this, refer to the Selling Security worksheets in Chapter 4.
Training effectiveness	Track participation and effectiveness of security training programs. One way is to run security audits and drills (simulated security incidents) to verify that people and technology respond as intended. Track attendance and work to measure the effectiveness of training relating to this security element. The security worksheets provided in this chapter and the next frequently provide suggested security auditing and drill approaches. You can customize this quality management worksheet to include metrics for those approaches.

(continues)

Table 3.1 Quality Management *(Continued)*

QUALITY MANAGEMENT	SECURITY PLAN
Coordination	Define key handoff deliverables and organizational interfaces for security life-cycle management. Security planning requires coordination and handoff of responsibilities across multiple groups, both internal and external to your organization. Define key handoff deliverables and organizational interface and coordination requirements for security element life-cycle management.
Incident frequency	If an organization is overrun with security incidents, then it stands to reason that it may be doing something wrong. Therefore, we need to keep track of incidents. Maintain a count of the total number of incidents relating to a particular security element.
Incident Impact	By keeping track of incident frequency, we are well on our way to using quality metrics to drive improvements in our security plan. If we associate incidents with potential deficiencies in our security element plan, then we can learn from our mistakes, revise our plan, and reduce the number of incidents going forward. We accomplish this by calculating an incident impact for each recorded incident. If the impact of the incident on the organization is exceptionally high, we work to reduce it by revising our plan. If we have many high-impact incidents, then we know we need to make more aggressive changes to our security plan. Using the impact analysis variables introduced in Chapter 1, we can estimate the impact of a given incident on our organization. For each incident the security planning team should estimate the following: 1. Relative value of information or infrastructure component(s) compromised during the incident (V) 2. Degree of public exposure from the incident (P) 3. Denial-of-business effect of the incident (DoB) 4. Ease of attacking the given information or infrastructure components associated with the incident (E) A value of 0 through 25, as in our impact analysis, can be assigned to each of these variables for a particular incident. After assigning these values, they can, as before, simply be summed up. An incident impact value of 100 means the incident had the highest possible impact and thus is a "showstopper" for the organization. On the other end of the spectrum, incident impact values near zero are far less important.

Table 3.1   Quality Management *(Continued)*

QUALITY MANAGEMENT	SECURITY PLAN
Incident response time	A security incident has a timeline associated with it. First, the incident is discovered in some way, such as by an alarm from your intrusion-detection systems or an alert from a software vendor indicating the software you're running has a significant vulnerability associated with it. Let's call this first event *incident discovery*. Note that if you are forced to patch a system in response to such a software vulnerability notification from a software vendor, this should also be tracked as an incident. More on that in a moment. Returning to our timeline, after the incident has been discovered, the next significant moment occurs when the incident response team actually responds and assigns a resource to solve the problem. Call this second event *incident response*. Clearly, as an organization managing the quality of the incident response process, we want the time between incident discovery and incident response to be as short as possible. Third, we have the moment at which the organization believes the incident has been resolved and associated vulnerabilities removed. Call this third event *incident resolution*. Our objective is to minimize the time between incident response and incident resolution. Finally, the incident response team needs to file an incident report and record these quality management metrics. Call this final event *incident report*. For every incident, all of these times (discovery, response, resolution, and report) should be recorded in your quality management worksheet.
Incidents caused by problem software	Track how frequently you must patch systems to prevent incidents. Too many patches are a sign of a poorly implemented security product, service, plan, process, or procedure. For example, if your company uses an application sold by company XYZ, and if you are patching the application every other day as a proactive response to newly discovered security holes, then, arguably, company XYZ is doing a poor job of writing secure software. Your quality management process needs to track that. Developers of these problem applications must be held accountable. Define a metric to record the number, severity, and difficulty of responding to these incidents. This metric may also reveal problems within your security plan, such as the need to introduce additional levels of protection for difficult-to-secure applications.

(continues)

Table 3.1 Quality Management *(Continued)*

QUALITY MANAGEMENT	SECURITY PLAN
Incident response false-positives	The purpose of this quality metric is to remind us to keep a count of the total number of incident false alarms—the number of times we think we have an incident but, in reality, don't. As will be discussed when we complete the intrusion detection and vulnerability analysis (IDS/VA) worksheets in Chapter 4, if we have too many incident false alarms, then we have a problem in our overall security plan that we need to address. Record, report on, and analyze the number of false-positives reported. Continually fine-tune your plan to reduce the number of false-positives while reducing the impact of security incidents on the organization that aren't detected.
Performance	Define how you measure, report, and analyze the performance impact of security measures on key systems. Often security slows things down. It may also speed things up if, for example, manual processes can be automated thanks to the increased comfort level and, in some cases, increased functionality offered by your security plan. Measure, record, and perform trend analysis on key performance-affected systems relating to each security plan element. There are many tips in future worksheets for potential performance measurements you might make as you implement your security plan. Integrate here those performance measurement tips that apply to your particular organization.
Audits and drills	When you run audits and drills relating to your security plan element, you should assess the success or failure of the audit or drill. Because each audit and drill is unique, you should customize this quality management metric for your particular security element plan. As with performance, tips are provided throughout the worksheets indicating when audits and drills might be most beneficial.
Suppliers, quality, and service-level agreements	Show how you establish, measure, and analyze security quality according to any service-level agreements (SLAs) that have been established internally or with suppliers and partners. For example, if you have agreed with your Web-hosting supplier that you will experience no more than one security incident every six months, and the duration, from incident detection to incident resolution, should be no more than four hours, then track your supplier's performance to see if it is living up to the agreement.

Table 3.1 Quality Management *(Continued)*

QUALITY MANAGEMENT	SECURITY PLAN
Plan violations	Record when individuals or technology violates your security plan; analyze related trends. These violations are themselves incidents; however, they are special types of incidents. When we have many of them, we typically have a training problem in our organization. Track incidents such as the use of unauthorized software. Record how many occur over a set time (e.g., number of violations per month). Work to reduce violations over time; if they are not reduced, determine if more training and education are required or if the underlying security element needs to be revised so that it can be more easily adhered to.

You will notice that every worksheet has an Impact Analysis Summary. This is where you should list any impact analyses that relate to this security element and particular area of planning. In order to keep things simple, I recommend that you assign each of your impact analyses a unique identifier (ID), which you can then put in the first column labeled Impact Analysis ID. In the second column, you place the original impact value (before the current version of your security worksheet was implemented). In the Percent Improvement column, insert the percentage of impact improvement you expect after implementing your worksheet. For example, if, before implementing your plan, the expected impact was 80 and, by implementing your plan as described in your worksheet, you expect an improvement of 50 percent, then your new impact value would be 40 (see Table 3.2).

Table 3.2 Impact Analysis Summary

IMPACT ANALYSIS ID	BEFORE PLAN	PERCENT IMPROVEMENT	NEW VALUE

Quality Management Worksheet

REVISION NUMBER	REVISION DATE	CHANGE SUMMARY

Author(s)

_____
_____
_____

Owner

_____
_____

Configuration Management Status

Budget   Plan: .....   Current: .....   Projected: .....

Schedule

_____
_____

Business Value Metrics: How does security bring value to your organization?

_____
_____

Training Effectiveness: Track participation and effectiveness of security training programs.

_____
_____

Coordination: Define key handoff deliverables and organizational interfaces for security life-cycle management.

_____
_____
_____

Worksheet 3.1   Quality Management.

Incident Frequency: Describe how you will measure, issue reports, and analyze trends for the occurrence of security incidents.

_____

_____

_____

Incident Impact: Explain how you calculate, issue reports, and analyze trends for assessing the impact of incidents.

_____

_____

_____

Incident Response Time: Describe how you measure, issue reports, and analyze trends in response time to incidents.

_____

_____

_____

Incidents Caused by Problem Software: Track how frequently you must patch systems to proactively avoid incidents.

_____

_____

_____

Performance: Define how you measure, report, and analyze performance impact of security measures on key systems.

_____

_____

_____

Audits and Drills: Develop a plan for assessing the success or failure of audits and drills.

_____

_____

_____

Suppliers, Quality and Service-Level Agreements (SLAs): Show how you establish, measure, and analyze SLA performance.

_____

_____

_____

Plan Violations: When individuals or technology violate your security plan, record, report on, and analyze related trends.

_____

_____

_____

Worksheet 3.1   Quality Management. _(continued)_

NOTE The Impact Analysis Summary is also included in the Selling Security worksheet. When preparing to sell your security plan, you can list all of the related impact analyses in your summary.

Each of the worksheets also contains a checkbox that you fill in when you have completed the Quality Management worksheet for the security element currently under discussion. This is a simple way to track whether you have completed or updated your quality management worksheets.

Filling in the Fundamental Security Element Worksheets

As a reminder, the six fundamental security elements are:

- Authorization and access control
- Authentication
- Encryption
- Integrity
- Nonrepudiation
- Privacy

The discussions of these elements here follow the order in which they were presented in Chapter 2; this will make it easier for you to refer back to the information there should you need to refresh your memory as to the definition of any of these important elements.

Authorization and Access Control

Summary

Once you know the identity of someone or something via authentication, the next question to answer is this: What is the person or process authorized to do? Remarkably, many systems deployed today are deficient in this regard when seen through the eyes of hackers. Simply by not fully developing our access control plan, we enable hackers to gain access, for example, to destroy a system completely or modify it at will.

The most common mistake we make is to assume that access control applies mainly to human beings and to the resources routinely within their view. In fact, software processes within servers (such as a Web server process) also belong in the category of access control. That is, how many organizations inventory the operating system permission-levels they've assigned to processes? Few do, but it's extremely important to do so. Not only is it important to clearly identify to whom or what we are granting access, but also to define exactly what requires access control in the first place.

Access Control Matrix and Role-Based Access Control

The easy solution is to say you'll perform access control everywhere. That then raises the challenge of developing a means to manage all this access control. This task can become quite burdensome unless our authentication scheme is standardized and well architected and unless we use a little finesse and sophistication in managing access control lists in the first place, as with directory service technology. To help in this undertaking, I want to introduce two important concepts:

- Access control matrix
- Role-based access control

Throughout this exploration of the worksheets, you'll see the term *access control matrix* used in the worksheet instructions, as in "Define an access control matrix." This matrix refers to a table wherein the first column contains the entity to which access control rights are assigned and the second column contains the rights.

Role-based access control is based on the presumption that if we know who someone is, we might also be able to know what his or her role is in the organization—for example, an accounting manager or human resources administrator. The latter are *roles* and are the same for anyone and everyone who fills that role. Think about the power of role-based access control: We can provide access control to people based on their roles, not on an individual basis. In that way, we can configure access control just *once* in the system for, say, all accounting managers rather than configuring it individually for each and every accounting manager in the company. Wherever access control is discussed in this chapter and Chapter 4, you can—and should—consider the notion of role-based access control and make an effort to architect it into your security solution.

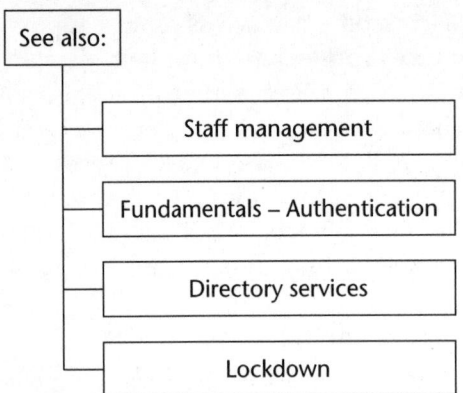

Figure 3.1 Authorization and access control.

Security Stack

Use Worksheet 3.2 here.

Here are the guidelines for filling out the Security Stack worksheet for the authorization and access control security element:

PHYSICAL

Build an access control matrix for all physical resources.   This includes buildings and rooms in buildings offering access to high-impact infrastructure such as servers and repositories of sensitive paper-based information. Relative to rooms, try to group them by areas of sensitivity.

Include all people in your matrix.   If you are going to allow customer access to conference rooms, limit access to the corporate network from those rooms. Otherwise, a "customer" might just download a few things one day over lunch or dinner when you're not looking.

Define how access is controlled.   Identify the means of authentication (for example, badge, proximity card, biometric, passcode) used to determine which access rights have been assigned. Determine where access control can be assigned based on roles. Too many large companies issue a single type of proximity access card for their entire building. There is no concept, with such badges, of someone being allowed access to one part of the building but not another. A better approach would be to organize individuals into functional roles and to restrict their access to those areas they typically need. Access to high-impact physical areas, such as where high-impact servers and other electronic infrastructure are housed, should be heavily restricted.

Security Stack Worksheet for Authorization and Access Control

IMPACT ANALYSIS ID	BEFORE PLAN	PERCENT IMPROVEMENT	NEW VALUE

Quality Management worksheet completed for this element? (check box) ☐

Physical

Build an access control matrix for sensitive physical resources including rooms, buildings, safes, closets, and so forth.

_____

_____

_____

Go back over your access control matrix and verify that you have addressed each of the businesspeople groups.

_____

_____

_____

Define, within your access control matrix, specific authentication mechanism requirements, as in badges and biometrics

_____

_____

_____

Identify opportunities to assign fewer access rights where they are not needed.

_____

_____

_____

Network

Define a network segmenting plan that supports your access control requirements.

_____

_____

_____

List all points of entry into your network.

_____

_____

_____

For each point of entry, define how access control is enforced at entry. Look for opportunities to further restrict access.

_____

_____

_____

Worksheet 3.2   Security Stack Worksheet for Authorization and Access Control.

For each point of entry, define how user access is controlled as attempts are made to move through the network. One approach to controlling this access is through source IP address filtering, for example.

_____

_____

_____

Application

Investigate approaches for reducing the number of logins required by your users by looking for common single sign-on access control opportunities.

_____

_____

Consider how you can use a directory service to manage access control more effectively across your applications.

_____

_____

Carefully write an access control matrix for all application resources including application processes, configuration files, databases, and general data files.

_____

_____

Identify opportunities to assign fewer access rights where they are not needed.

_____

_____

Operating System

Similar to your application access control matrix, write another matrix for operating system processes and resources.

_____

_____

Identify opportunities to assign fewer access rights where they are not needed.

_____

_____

Turn off, disable, and uninstall as many unneeded operating system functions as possible, keeping only what you need.

_____

_____

_____

Worksheet 3.2   Security Stack Worksheet for Authorization and Access Control. _(continued)_

NETWORK

Partition the network with access control in mind and focus on the point of entry.   Typically, access control to the network itself is partitioned according to who people are and, if we're more sophisticated, how they entered the network (by looking at any source addresses in packets, as opposed to just filtering based on destination). Dial-up users may, for example, gain access only to restricted areas of the network. Or users in product development might not have a network route to the finance portion of the network. This type of access control is often enforced by network address filtering, whereby, using our example, address ranges assigned to finance people would be in a different range from those assigned to development folks, and network routers would filter out traffic to prevent product developers from accessing finance servers. If, for some reason, finance had an application to which product developers or others required access, it could be placed in a special predefined *shared area* of the network set aside for such interorganizational applications.

APPLICATION

Design with a directory service to prevent authentication overload.
Imagine an organization where the average employee has access to seven corporate applications. Imagine the poor administrator who must configure specific authorization privileges to each user in the system for each of those applications. Now imagine *your* organization because odds are that this may come close to describing the situation there. Count the applications most users access. Fortunately, with the proliferation of directory services and role-based authentication and access control, we are moving away from this high-volume access control configuration and into a more manageable common repository and management scheme. (Directory services are discussed repeatedly in the remaining chapters. Also see the glossary and "For Further Reading" at the end of this book.)

Don't stop at individuals.   You must be careful when granting access control permissions to application software processes. Remember that we talked about the danger of giving too many permissions to a Web server process, or any other software process for that matter. The primary reason for this is that, if a hacker manages to compromise just one process that has been granted too much access (such as in full, unbridled, supernatural rights on your server), the hacker then has full control of the server. If the process doesn't require such broad access rights, restrict them at the operating system level.

SUPERNATURAL EVIL: CHMOD 777 AND YOUR WEB SERVER

For those of you familiar with the UNIX or Linux operating systems, you may be familiar with the *chmod* command, which allows you to assign permissions to a given file. Suppose you use chmod to assign rights to a file that is your Web server program—for example, the file *my_Webserver_program.exe*. When you assign rights to that file with chmod, the program will run as a process under UNIX/Linux and will assume the rights you have assigned to it. Suppose further that you issue the command *chmod 777 my_Webserver_program.exe*. The 777 in UNIX/Linux means, "Give me absolutely every form of control I could possibly want on this computer." You can think of that simply as *supernatural control*. If a hacker performs a buffer exploit on your Web server process (see the Secure Software security element in Chapter 4 for more details on buffer exploits), then he or she gains the rights you assigned to your Web server. In this case, those would be supernatural rights. In such an event, you have a very serious security incident on your hands. Avoid it by assigning fewer rights to the Web server process. An experienced system administrator is capable of determining which rights are needed and which ones aren't. Often, when troubleshooting or when being just plain lazy, we assign 777 supernatural rights to files in order to get things working quickly. This is a bad move from a security standpoint.

OPERATING SYSTEM

Address operating system access control in your security plan.   As just noted, operating system process-level (executable permission) access control is very important. If you perform an audit of how it's currently being done in your organization, you may discover it's the first time anyone has even asked the question on any comprehensive basis—not counting, of course, a hacker who is planning to make his or her way through your systems in the future. Relative to operating system access control in general, it is assigned to individuals, groups of individuals, roles (depending on your operating system), all executable files, data files, configuration files, and resources. The files used by the operating system itself are assigned permissions, not just application files; review how these permissions are assigned.

When it comes to rights, think "less is more."   Remember, give the fewest rights, the minimum required.

Do not use default access control configurations without first thoroughly reviewing them.   Do not become a victim of vendor support cost-reduction tactics, for whom "on" is easier than "off." Vendors routinely ship their products with too much access allowed—too much enabled—to save time and money in support costs, the thinking being that if capabilities are enabled right out of the box, they tend to work for all users whatever their needs. The problem is that they also work for the hacker. Therefore, when it comes to access control, keep in mind that your requirements may be different from those of the software provider.

Think open standards and interoperability for access control.   Operating system vendors have increasingly come to realize that if they control authentication and access control and extend it to the applications (a logical and good thing), they have a long-term hold on you (typically a bad thing) because authentication and access control configuration and administration represent a heavy investment not easily replaced by something new. The answer is open standards and interoperability for access control. Directory service standards such as LDAP pave the way for this.

TIP These worksheets are also available in an electronic format from the Web site maintained for this book. Using the electronic versions, you can further customize the worksheets to meet the particular needs of your organization. You can obtain them from the Web site maintained by the author at www .criticalsecurity.com as well as that maintained by the publisher, www.wiley.com/ compbooks/greenberg.

Life-Cycle Management

Use Worksheet 3.3 here.

Follow these guidelines for completing the authorization and access control life-cycle management worksheet:

TECHNOLOGY SELECTION

Consider all your options.   Once upon a time, you had no choice when it came to access control technology. You were confined to whatever access control your application vendor implemented, usually different for each application and, in a few circumstances, integrated into an operating system capability. Thankfully, those days are gone. Today, you can choose from a proliferation of directory service technologies, all allowing for the offloading of access control decisions to a centralized and standards-based application called the directory server. Ask yourself how interoperable and scalable the access control scheme is.

Life-Cycle Management Worksheet for Authorization and Access Control

IMPACT ANALYSIS ID	BEFORE PLAN	PERCENT IMPROVEMENT	NEW VALUE

Quality Management worksheet completed for this element? (check box) ☐

Technology Selection

Survey your security stack and determine where you have a true choice in open standards-based access control technology.

_____

_____

_____

Develop directory service access control requirements, and choose directory service technology meeting them.

_____

_____

_____

Look for opportunities to integrate access control management and processing across the security stack.

_____

_____

_____

Identify technology that eases the burden of managing and administering access control.

_____

_____

_____

Implementation

Identify each and every default (as in out-of-the-box) access control decision and either change it or accept that this is what you want.

_____

_____

_____

Implement so that access control is realistically manageable. Develop policies and procedures that are realistic.

_____

_____

_____

Worksheet 3.3   Life-Cycle Management Worksheet for Authorization and Access Control.

Emphasize administrator access control planning. Assign administrator access rights sparingly.

_____

_____

_____

Operations

Identify ways to reduce the complexity of access control system operations, ease administration and management.

_____

_____

_____

Incident Response

Provide the incident response team with a rapid access disablement capability.

_____

_____

_____

Develop access control incident response procedures in close coordination with staff management processes.

_____

_____

_____

Worksheet 3.3   Life-Cycle Management Worksheet for Authorization and Access Control. *(continued)*

Focus on integration.   Work to integrate access control straight through the entire security stack, to include the physical layer. Envision a day when employees are given smart cards with their pictures on them and maybe biometric readers embedded on the cards. Imagine those same cards facilitating authentication and access control for every layer of the security stack. This vision of a single smart card used for access control throughout the entire security stack is a good one for you to keep in your mind as you plan. I believe that such a card will become a reality. In fact, within the United States Department of Defense (DoD), a program known as the Common Access Card (CAC) is achieving exactly that—one card used for all forms of access and authentication, from physical access control to buildings and military bases to application access control.

IMPLEMENTATION

Disable default configurations.   In terms of implementation, the biggest hole introduced with access control is that of the default configuration. Administrators routinely take a good architecture and botch it by leaving in default rights instead of deleting all of them and consciously configuring what they know is right. What I said earlier in regard to operating systems applies here as well: Vendors ship products to minimize support calls, meaning that they enable as much as possible. Again, the problem with this is that if it works out of the box for you and other users, it also works for the hacker.

Streamline administration and management.   As mentioned earlier, comprehensive access control can quickly become difficult to manage. Make sure you implement the system with all ease-of-administration features available and evident to the operations group. Implement so that the operations group is set up for success, not failure. This means recognizing that keeping a steady hold on access control list configuration and management is a difficult task requiring a well-implemented system coupled with realistic policies and procedures.

OPERATIONS

Operate access control-related systems with an understanding of the risks.   The more you centralize the access control decision, the more opportunities you provide for it to fail or to be targeted by a hacker. Define an operations plan with policies and procedures that respect the impact of access control on the organization in order to keep the system secure and running.

Minimize complexity; focus on ease of administration and management.   Aside from managing the uptime of access control, operations staff must take care not to undermine it by misassigning access privileges. Be sure the system administration and management interfaces are designed so that operations staff can truly manage the system without mountains of complexity.

INCIDENT RESPONSE

Set up for rapid disablement.   The incident response team has to be able to quickly disable access to an individual, role, any application or group of applications, or network. The implementation and associated policies and procedures should allow for this.

Coordinate with staff management. In accordance with the staff management security element, access control should be granted and disabled consistently and with adequate logging. Logging is very important because those logs can assist in incident response should a security concern arise.

NOTE The Business worksheet for all security elements has three components: Businesspeople (categorized as Employees, Customers, Owners, Suppliers, and Partners) and Information and Infrastructure.

Business

Use Worksheet 3.4 here.

BUSINESSPEOPLE: EMPLOYEES

Organize employees into roles. Define access control rights for these roles in terms of applications, resources, and the network components they use. Even if you can't perform role-based access control in an automated fashion, you'll still benefit from documentation and a plan that reflects the fact that, usually, no employee is a "one-off" when it comes to access control rights. Rather, employees can be grouped into certain roles, and in those roles they typically have common access control needs.

Emphasize administrator access control. Emphasize administrator access control and fully define this matrix. Include any administrators who are also suppliers/contractors. This guideline is important because administrator access control applies to a smaller group of people so we often think of them last. Unfortunately, it's the first set of access control rights a hacker goes after, and he is often enough successful. Again, disable all default access control settings and carefully log and control administrator access controls to high-impact infrastructure.

BUSINESSPEOPLE: CUSTOMERS
Identify and categorize customer access control needs. Do the same thing for customers as you did for employees. If applicable, group them by roles such as "distributors" and "end consumers."

Business Worksheet for Authorization and Access Control

IMPACT ANALYSIS ID	BEFORE PLAN	PERCENT IMPROVEMENT	NEW VALUE

Quality Management worksheet completed for this element? (check box) ☐

Employees

Find ways to organize employees into roles and develop access rules based on those roles.

_____
_____
_____

Customers

Group customer access control requirements as you did employees. See if opportunities for role assignment exist.

_____
_____
_____

Owners

Identify high-impact information and property particularly sensitive to owners.

_____
_____
_____

Develop a sound and demonstrable access control plan around infrastructure particularly sensitive to owners.

_____
_____
_____

Suppliers and Partners

Write an access control plan for any electronic information exchange and business-to-business networking you do with suppliers.

_____
_____
_____

Worksheet 3.4 Business Worksheet for Authorization and Access Control.

Identify any information and infrastructure excessively vulnerable due to supplier or partner access control practices.

_____

_____

_____

Information

For a complete viewpoint, develop an access plan in terms of discrete information and not necessarily infrastructure.

_____

_____

_____

Identify where information is being managed by the wrong application, one preventing appropriate access control.

_____

_____

_____

Infrastructure

Look at it another way and, this time, reverse your thought process and define access in terms of infrastructure.

_____

_____

_____

When looking at infrastructure, again pay close attention to administrator access rights and minimize them.

_____

_____

_____

Worksheet 3.4   Business Worksheet for Authorization and Access Control. *(continued)*

BUSINESSPEOPLE: OWNERS

Protect owners by understanding their particular sensitivities.   Owners have a vested interest in seeing that solid access control is put into place. They are particularly sensitive regarding access to financial information or other sensitive intellectual property of the organization that can have a rapid watershed impact should it be shared at the wrong time and/or with the wrong people.

BUSINESSPEOPLE: SUPPLIERS

Define any access control mechanisms applicable to suppliers.   If, for example, you trade over a shared business-to-business virtual private network (VPN), carefully plan how you will achieve secure access control for applications shared by all businesses. Define how systems that have nothing to do with shared applications will be shielded and secured.

BUSINESSPEOPLE: PARTNERS

Acknowledge the limits of trust.   We sometimes let our guard down too far with partners. While trust is key to a successful business partnership, unbridled trust is simply unwise. Partners may become competitors, and relationships go south. The most common scenario is that an organization establishes a new form of partnership. Everyone is very excited, and an edict comes down to get systems and people working together. Unfortunately, the implementation quickly devolves into an either-or scenario wherein a partner is either given unbridled access to everything, as if he or she is an employee, or gets nothing at all. This happens because the concept of partner access control is not considered when most systems are originally deployed. Avoid this problem by thinking about it up front. Think about which security stack components might involve sharing of some kind with outside partners. Plan for a special partner/shared network segment, and develop an access control plan around it.

BUSINESS

Think about business, first, in terms of information.   Think of access control in terms of information and not necessarily applications, resources, doors, or network segments. This will enable you to plan a better solution. In some cases, you may discover that information is being managed by the wrong application. For example, a planner could list all information used to complete a customer order. He or she could then look at each application involved with this customer information. In some organizations, there could be a dozen or more applications involved in a given customer order. Is access control to customer information, in all of these applications, uniformly implemented? What are the access control requirements for this information? These are the types of questions a security planner should answer when considering information and access control.

Think about business, second, in terms of infrastructure.   This means emphasize administrator access. The alternate view of information access control is infrastructure access control. This is how we typically look at the problem. We consider an application or a file server and then implement access control around it. As part of infrastructure access control, be sure to fully plan administrator access control to all infra-structure components.

Selling Security

Use Worksheet 3.5 here.

Selling security requires knowing what your audience needs to hear to embrace security measures. Here are some guidelines to follow when selling security to executives, middle management, and staff, respectively.

Executives.   Explain to executives that a well-architected access control system will save the company money on administration costs. It will enable the company to add new employees more easily and to quickly and easily remove terminated employees' access rights in a controlled and well-documented fashion. Such a system will also make it possible to introduce new applications that enhance business productivity at lower cost because there will be no need for a separate administration process for each one that springs up.

To supplement these statements, offer examples of applications that are important to the company and that could have been brought online sooner and more safely with a better access control plan. Point out that fewer steps will be needed to add an employee to the system and that, as the company grows, its administrative costs will be better controlled. Give specific examples of how future applications involving partners and suppliers might save the company money and enable it to compete more effectively; add that all this will be achievable with a properly designed access control scheme.

Middle management.   Identify for middle managers specific business processes and staff activities that involve assignment, reassignment, and general usage of access control. Point out how quickly new employees can be added when they join the company or when there is a reorganization. Focus on aspects of security stack access control that can be quantified in terms of well-defined business processes to which a staff manager can relate. Talk in terms of better performance, more secure access, and lowered impact exposure.

Staff.   Most staff members know the frustration of having to wait before getting configured for access to some resource important to their job. They typically see this process as one involving an administrator giving them a login account to an application they need to use. Explain to staff that the security plan will reduce the amount of time required to be granted access to new applications. Explain how system security will be enhanced and how, in the future, administrative delays may be reduced.

Selling Security Worksheet for Authorization and Access Control

IMPACT ANALYSIS ID	BEFORE PLAN	PERCENT IMPROVEMENT	NEW VALUE

Executive

Walk through a business process improvement example such as adding a new employee or quickly terminating a problem one.

_____
_____
_____

Demonstrate how administrator costs are reduced through simplified access control management.

_____
_____
_____

Demonstrate a quantifiable reduction in impact from the risk of hackers compromising poorly designed access control systems.

_____
_____
_____

Point out that partner/supplier relationships may be streamlined, saving time and money, in the future.

_____
_____
_____

Middle Management

Walk through specific processes that involve assignment, reassignment, and general usage of access control.

_____
_____
_____

Show how specific processes will be improved with your new access approach such as adding a new employee.

_____
_____
_____
_____

Worksheet 3.5   Selling Security Worksheet for Authorization and Access Control.

Provide a chart highlighting improved performance, more secure access, and lowered impact exposure.

_____

_____

_____

Staff

Show how much faster it will be for them to, for example, be configured for access to an application they may need.

_____

_____

_____

Demonstrate how their own security is enhanced by further assurance that only authorized users gain access.

_____

_____

_____

Show how their daily work could be impacted by a poor access control scheme.

_____

_____

_____

Worksheet 3.5   Selling Security Worksheet for Authorization and Access Control. *(continued)*

Authentication

Summary

To begin the summary for the Authentication element, I want to tell you about an actual situation that points out the seriousness of dealing properly with this security element. I once had the misfortune of working with a senior engineer in a network group who, at the time, was the only holder of usernames and passwords for all core backbone network components. In a meeting during which he became frustrated, he stated loudly, "I am the only one who knows the usernames and passwords for this network. Therefore, I'll decide what goes on it and doesn't. If I get hit by a car tomorrow, this company will be minus one network." Keep the implications of that threat in mind as you read through this security element as well as the Staff Management security element in Chapter 4.

Know Where Trust Is Required

Knowing who or what is on the other end of any interaction is a fundamental aspect of security. When evaluating your security architecture, ask yourself exactly where an authentication determination is made and how it is performed, how strong the authentication mechanism is, how manageable it is for users and administrators, and how consistently it is implemented.

One simple way to begin is to take a step back and ask, "Where is trust required?" Trust is required for access to buildings, rooms, equipment, people, networks, applications, and information.

Focus Your Architecture

Based on your organization's impact analysis, you determined that some things require more trust than others. Now focus your authentication plan first on those highest-impact items. If the trust level required is high, make sure your authentication plan addresses that. If it's low and there are lots of people requiring access, consider making it easier to be authenticated.

Architecturally, authentication is achieved through three system functions:

Through registration. Essentially, this is the act of granting trust to an individual or entity (as in giving it a username/password or other credential).

Via the act of validation. For example, this involves validating that user in real time, such as requesting his or her username/password and validating it somehow.

By managing and maintaining the authentication systems. Examples of authentication systems include Kerberos, used with Microsoft Windows (from Windows 2000 onwards); RADIUS authentication servers, used within dial-up networks; electronic mail servers that authenticate users; and others. These systems should be managed and maintained according to the security planning elements in this book.

Your security plan should address each of these functions. It should identify where and how authentication credentials are stored and compared to those entered by the user. For example, many users store their electronic mail username/password on their desktop computer. From there it is typically delivered automatically to their mail server, which then compares the username/password to its own database. The most common electronic mail protocol used today is called the Post Office Protocol (POP). POP authentication sends usernames and passwords in the clear—in other words, unencrypted and in plain view of the hacker.

Let's suppose for a moment that a hacker doesn't manage to steal your POP username and password from the network even though doing so is easier than it should be. Maybe he or she will simply steal your laptop. Most of the time, we store our POP mail usernames and passwords permanently on our computers. In this way, if our laptop, for example, is stolen, so is access to our email and any assigned capabilities and rights.

Once hackers can fully impersonate an individual via email, they can typically pull off a wide range of attacks—not to mention fraudulent transactions of one kind or another. For example, if the email username and password of a Web administrator is stolen, a hacker could potentially reassign the company's Web site address to some other Web site by impersonating the Web site administrator, thereby effectively hijacking the company's Web site and potentially tricking customers visiting the company Web site into giving up sensitive information. In other words, they could reroute www.your_company_Web_site .com to the hacker's own Web site. It may look the same as yours, but it may be nowhere near as well intentioned.

Be aware that the manner in which authentication credentials are stored, transmitted over the network, and compared to those entered by the user greatly influences system vulnerability. Authentication mechanisms such as Kerberos use a sophisticated mechanism for authenticating over the network, never sending the username and password in the clear. Other mechanisms, such as POP email authentication, as well as others previously mentioned including FTP and telnet, send the username and password in the clear. In general, the objective for any security plan is to standardize on as few authentication systems as possible, ideally just one. Next, standardize the act of authentication, and combine the fundamentals of authentication, as discussed in Chapter 1, namely what you know (username/password), what you have (tokens, smart cards), or what you are (biometrics).

Deal with the Basics

When it comes to authentication, dealing with the basics refers to following these guidelines:

- For passwords, address concerns such as programatically enforcing the strength of passwords and password aging (making users change their passwords at certain intervals). In username/password-based systems, increase the time between username/password attempts in order to prevent dictionary attacks (repeated random guesses) at a username/ password.

- Temporarily disable accounts after some preconfigured number of failed attempts (such as 10).

- Ensure that applications time-out their authentication after periods of inactivity so that, if a user walks away from his or her terminal for an extended period of time of inactivity (for example, 20 minutes), that user should be required to log back in on return. This helps to prevent unauthorized users from making use of unattended computers that have been previously logged in to applications requiring authentication.

- Minimize the number of passwords a user must remember. Plan for "single sign-on," whereby a single well-secured authentication credential (such as a username and password) enables access to multiple applications.

- In most corporations, access to applications is managed by many groups, such as human resources, finance, engineering, and so forth. Address how these different groups authenticate an individual and how they coordinate with one another. Make sure these decisions are reflected in staff management policies and procedures. For example, human resources should do full background checks to adequately authenticate a new employee.

- When users are granted first-time access to an application (they are, for example, given a username/password), record the date and time of this event; streamline technical procedures for removing that access should the employee leave the company (and record the date/time of that event as well).

- Have intrusion-detection systems (IDSs) audit failed authentication attempts. Notify the security administrator if an unusual number of failed attempts are encountered (such as greater than seven attempts).

- Enable rapid disablement in case tokens, smart cards, or passwords are misappropriated (lost, accidentally divulged, and so forth).

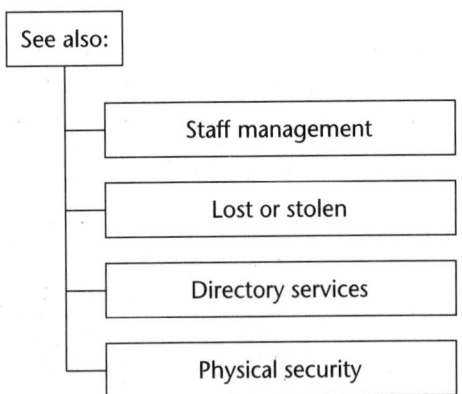

Figure 3.2 Authentication.

IMPROVE YOUR SOCIAL SKILLS

While online, I frequently read through posts on security-related newsgroups and mailing lists. I'm amazed at how effectively hackers use social engineering techniques on people who are responsible for security. In spite of all the warnings, too many people, even those involved in security, are so eager to help that, in the end, they end up helping the hacker.

Many times I've read seemingly harmless posts on these newsgroups that receive a great deal of response from named (i.e., not anonymous) list participants. A very common one is to ask for help in selecting secure passwords. It goes something like this: "I'm having a hard time coming up with strong passwords for my firewall. Could someone give me tips on how to generate strong, yet easy-to-remember passwords?" If you're thinking nobody would fall for this, that everyone would realize the person asking the question was trying to see if he or she could get clues to crack newsgroup participant passwords, you'd be wrong. In one instance, I saw about 30 responses to a post just like this; for example: "Well, I pick my favorite football player and add a number to the end of his name."

The point is, when you give up this kind of information, you narrow the universe of password possibilities down to a smaller set. Admittedly, the set may still be large, but if the hacker combined the range of responses and followed up with a few more one-to-one questions such as, "Oh, by the way, what is your favorite football team?" the hacker would have what he or she was after. It's also just a good way for hackers to find out who's "soft" in the area of divulging information; then they acquaint themselves further with those people.

Security Stack

Use Worksheet 3.6 here.

PHYSICAL

Identify and assess how people are authenticated for access to physical facilities.   The most obvious example is the use of badges for building access. Too few companies scrutinize this process. Don't be one of them: Go through the whole "people process" as delineated here.

Start with the hiring process for employees and consultants.   Identify how you determine that these individuals are who they say they are. Most companies perform too few cross-checks to accumulate consistent information.

Security Stack Worksheet for Authentication

IMPACT ANALYSIS ID	BEFORE PLAN	PERCENT IMPROVEMENT	NEW VALUE

Quality Management worksheet completed for this element? (check box) ☐

Physical

Identify and assess how people are authenticated for access to physical facilities.

_____

_____

_____

Define how your hiring process (staff management) authentication process relates to physical facilities authentication.

_____

_____

_____

Look for any specific loopholes in your physical authentication procedure for customers, suppliers, and partners.

_____

_____

_____

Identify how the three core functions are best performed for physical security such as for building access control: (1) registration; (2) validation; and (3) managing and maintaining authentication.

_____

_____

_____

Network

Identify all points of entry into your network. Build an authentication plan around the three core authentication functions.

_____

_____

_____

Closely assess the strength and manageability of authentication technology for each network point of entry.

_____

_____

_____

Define how devices (not people) authenticate to one another, for example; servers and routers (routing protocols). Assess the strength of your approach.

_____

_____

_____

Worksheet 3.6   Security Stack Worksheet for Authentication.

Write and implement an effective administrator authentication plan. Identify weaknesses and quickly address them. Consider the use of tokens and biometrics for strengthened administrator authentication.

_____
_____
_____

Application

Specify steps you are taking, now or in the future, to achieve a secure single sign-on architecture.

_____
_____
_____

Define your default password disablement policies and procedures.

_____
_____
_____

Assess the relative strength of authentication technology, policies, and procedures for high-impact applications.

_____
_____
_____

Identify and evaluate how the three core authentication functions are carried out across applications.

_____
_____
_____

Operating System

Correlate your authentication approach to your access control matrix.

_____
_____
_____

Describe technologies used to manage authentication at the operating system level and assess their strength.

_____
_____
_____

Identify and evaluate how the three core authentication functions are carried out across operating systems.

_____
_____
_____

Evaluate how well your operating systems support single-sign-on with application and networking components.

_____
_____
_____

Worksheet 3.6   Security Stack Worksheet for Authentication. *(continued)*

Do the same thing for companies you work with and their employees, whether customers or partners.   If it's a small company you've never heard of, perform some kind of due diligence before you start signing nondisclosure agreements (NDAs) and giving up information. Never forget: These people can enter your buildings; hence, they have the keys to the kingdom.

Remember the three authentication functions.   Plan for the three system functions of the authentication system, as discussed in the summary, for every element of the security stack.

NETWORK
Identify all points of entry into your network and build a plan around them.   Possible points of entry include these:

- From within an office building
- For multisite companies, between remote sites
- For those providing remote dial-in access, access via the Internet or private dial-in networks
- Business-to-business network access

Your authentication plan should take into account each possible entry point. Network addresses can be assigned differently (via DHCP, for example) to network devices based on their point of entry. An address, when assigned to a network device, is called the *source address*. Because source addresses can be assigned differently depending on point of entry, you can effectively control network access based on it. For example, if a user dials into the network and he or she is assigned an address (a source address) in a certain address range, then you can restrict users within that address range so that they may be allowed to access only particular applications in the network, not all of them. You achieve this by filtering out network packets with addresses in that range for those applications they should not be allowed to get near. Such filters can be configured within your network routers, for example. Note that this is not a strong form of authentication, but it is, instead, a good example of how your standard authentication mechanism and address filtering can be combined to make it harder for a hacker to reach deeper into your network.

Deploy technologies such as SSL, SSH, and IPSec, as well as more advanced authentication protocols, to improve security.   As discussed in Chapter 2, many people have a false sense of security about how well protected their passwords are when sent over the network. You should know better by now.

Don't authenticate just people.   Your authentication plan should, of course, identify how individuals are authenticated for access to network resources. But what about how network components are authenticated to each other? This is a very weak area for many networks deployed today. For example, today, your network routers typically perform little if any authentication on routers to which they connect. This allows a hacker to potentially deliver malicious routes to one of your routers. Work is going on now within the Internet standards groups to enhance router-to-router authentication mechanisms. As they become available, you'd be well advised to implement them.

Remember: Administrator authentication is fundamental. Your network authentication plan must specify how network administrators authenticate to network components (such as routers). The plan should assess how secure these mechanisms are. To protect administrator authentication credentials, use protocols previously discussed in this book, such as SSH. In addition, because administrators are in control of high-impact systems, it is often well worth considering the use of tokens and/or biometrics as part of your administrator authentication implementation.

APPLICATION

Move toward a single identity for application authentication and network authentication. Historically, the mechanism used to authenticate individuals for access to the network has been separate from that used to authenticate them for access to an application. Increasingly, these two mechanisms are becoming one and will also include physical authentication. Plan to integrate, over time, all authentication mechanisms into one well-secured, single-sign-on solution.

Institute a default password disablement policy. Administrators are notorious for leaving default authentication configurations in place, allowing hackers to access applications (and operating systems) using default usernames and passwords. Don't allow this.

OPERATING SYSTEM

Define authentication levels, then audit. Classically speaking, operating system authentication gives you access to resources controlled by the operating system itself, such as files on file servers, printers, and any network facilities controlled by the operating system. Define the levels of authentication required for access to these resources (see also the access control matrix discussed as part of the Authorization and Access Control security element). Audit your organization to determine what has been overlooked or too loosely managed.

Integrate. Increasingly, as just mentioned, operating system, application, and network-level authentication will become one thing, so steer your plan in that direction over time.

Life-Cycle Management

Use Worksheet 3.7 here.

TECHNOLOGY SELECTION

Do your homework.   When selecting technology, study carefully how each of the three authentication functions are performed and highlight strengths and weaknesses.

Think about the future.   Select technology that will not impede you significantly, over time, from integrating your authentication architecture to accommodate a common authentication mechanism at every layer of the security stack (that is, single sign-on across your security stack).

Factor in ease of use.   Design your authentication plan within the context of the people who work in your organization; anticipate their willingness (or lack thereof) to adopt new authentication mechanisms. That means you must consider ease of use of the authentication mechanism and portability of authentication credentials (as in things people remember versus things people must carry). Keep in mind that their willingness will be influenced by the effectiveness of your security sales pitch, which we'll talk about in a moment. In any event, decisions on authentication mechanisms must be made within the context of your impact analysis. As effective security planners, it's balance that we're after—balancing out business, the reality that people are involved, and technology. That is, while user convenience is important, so is maintaining sufficient security. A strong security mechanism that nobody uses is, of course, not helpful, nor is a weak one that's highly convenient.

IMPLEMENTATION

Hope for the best; plan for things to go wrong.   The key to implementation is securing, partitioning, and backing up authentication-related server components.

Take into account user needs and behavior.   What will you do if a user loses his or her username/password or is locked out due to too many incorrect authentication attempts performed by the user or a hacker? Be sure to address implementation fundamentals, such as authentication credential recovery.

Life-Cycle Management Worksheet for Authentication

IMPACT ANALYSIS ID	BEFORE PLAN	PERCENT IMPROVEMENT	NEW VALUE

Quality Management worksheet completed for this element? (check box) ☐

Technology Selection

Assess authentication technology for manageability, vulnerability, ease-of-use, integration, and logging capabilities.

_____

_____

Assess the scalability of authentication technology within your organization and with customers, suppliers, and partners. Will your system scale up and perform well as the number of users increases?

_____

_____

Analyze failure and attack scenarios, and determine the technology response and the impact on the organization.

_____

_____

Specify technology support for one-, two-, and three-factor authentication.

_____

_____

Define how credential strength (as in password strength) is enforced.

_____

_____

Implementation

Define how authentication systems are partitioned, backed up, and locked down.

_____

_____

Worksheet 3.7   Life-Cycle Management Worksheet for Authentication. *(continues)*

Consider user needs such as recovery from lost password, token, or a locked-out account from excessive failed logins.

_____

_____

_____

Develop training and education plan for administration of authentication systems.

_____

_____

_____

Operations

Specify policies and procedures for operations staff so that they can support a user having difficulties with any of the three core authentication functions.

_____

_____

_____

Define tools available to operations for isolating authentication problems to specific system components.

_____

_____

_____

Incident Response

Define the steps and technology needed for the incident team to access who/what/when/how logging information.

_____

_____

_____

Describe policies, procedures, and technology for rapid authentication credential disablement of an individual, group, or device (e.g., server or router).

_____

_____

_____

Worksheet 3.7   Life-Cycle Management Worksheet for Authentication. _(continued)_

Implement training and education procedures.   Administrator training and education on authentication systems are key because these systems are fundamental to the security infrastructure.

OPERATIONS

Design a system that makes operations safe, consistent, traceable, and recoverable.   No doubt about it, authentication systems are very policy- and procedure-intensive. Thus, operations groups need an authentication system that allows them to realistically enforce the organization's authentication-related policies and procedures. This means having an easy way to reset authentication credentials if a user forgets his or her password, securely backing up systems, and having a realistic means of recovery should things go wrong.

INCIDENT RESPONSE

Know who, what, when, and how.   The authentication system's logging capabilities, as discussed in Chapter 2, are fundamental to incident response. The incident response team needs to know who authenticated to what and when. Logging systems should include a record of time (this is also discussed in the Secure Time security element in Chapter 4), IP/network addresses used during authentication, number of failed attempts, and systems for which access was attempted.

Be able to disable immediately.   The incident response team must be able to quickly and easily request immediate disablement of authentication for any individual or, if applicable, group(s) of individuals. This should include administrator access for any administration accounts used at all levels of the security stack.

Business

Use Worksheet 3.8 here.

BUSINESSPEOPLE: EMPLOYEES

Group employees in a way that makes sense for your organization, such as by business unit and job function.   Determine if there are unique authentication requirements for each of these groups. For example, you may choose to monitor authentication logs more closely for employees having access to higher-impact applications.

Review your security impact analysis to identify individuals in the most sensitive positions.   In nearly all cases, system administrators fall into this realm because of their power within the context of the security stack implementation.

Consider convenience.   Keep in mind that all people are affected by the convenience (ease of use) of the more advanced authentication credential mechanisms you choose to include in your plan (such as a biometric). If the mechanism is convenient, you'll achieve buy-in; if it isn't as convenient, you need to focus on selling the business benefits of the solution.

BUSINESSPEOPLE: CUSTOMERS

Define who, how, and when customers will be authenticated.   Consider your impact analysis as it relates to any failures in customer authentication. Here's an excellent example of the damaging effect of not having a strong customer authentication plan including training, policies, and procedures: While testing security relating to the hosting service of an Internet service provider (ISP), the third largest at the time, I simply called on the phone and said, "I'm from company XYZ (a customer of the ISP), and I'd like to have the Web site service canceled." The customer service rep did not ask for any identification other than what is publicly available from the WhoIs record for the site (the record maintained by companies such as VeriSign). The customer service representative simply took the information I gave, immediately agreed to disable the Web site, and then actually did it. The point here is that this customer service agent shouldn't have been able to instruct anyone to disable the Web site without first authenticating to whom they were talking.

BUSINESSPEOPLE: OWNERS

Consider the viewpoint of the owners, to include stockholders or other stakeholders, on the authentication process.   For example, authenticating individuals authorized to issue press releases for the organization (such as those relating to financial condition) can be quite important from their perspective. Bogus press releases have been issued on behalf of several organizations, causing significant loss.

BUSINESSPEOPLE: SUPPLIERS

Consider all forms of shared access.   Your suppliers may also need to be authenticated by your systems. In some cases, you may allow them full or partial access to security stack elements. Define all scenarios applicable to your organization, and address them in your plan.

BUSINESSPEOPLE: PARTNERS

Determine how you will authenticate the individuals that fall under the rubric "partner."   Companies form partnerships with companies and government organizations routinely. How do you authenticate these various individuals you are dealing with? How do you even know, for example, that the IRS auditor in your accounting office really works for the IRS and isn't an agent for a competitor or a foreign government? Or what about those people working for an "investment group" interested in buying your company? Are they real, or are they just trying to pump you for information? As far as "real" partners are concerned, in the course of doing business, we may authenticate them at part or all of the security stack. Define how this is accomplished within your security architecture.

BUSINESS: INFORMATION

Authenticate from the viewpoint of information versus applications. Another way to identify authentication requirements is to look across your organization to determine what the authentication requirements are for the information itself, as opposed to looking at the problem in the aggregate, from an application-by-application or server-by-server basis. For example, consider an application, look at its information elements, then consider what you believe should be the authentication requirements for the individual information elements. This may drive you to, for example, redesign some of your applications to require different types of authentication for access to certain kinds of information.

BUSINESS: INFRASTRUCTURE

Keep infrastructure authentication requirements in perspective.   The traditional approach is to relate authentication requirements to each individual infrastructure component. That explains our authentication experience today—we authenticate one or more times to the network, once to the email server every time we check our mail, and many times over, once for each of our many corporate applications. And so it goes that, for our planning, we do, of course, need to identify all infrastructure components to which we must authenticate and plan accordingly. But as has probably become clear to you now, this isn't the best approach. We need to, instead, plan for one very strong authentication mechanism for all of our infrastructure. Our perspective should be to strengthen and reconcile all of these individual authentication mechanisms into one highly managable and usable solution.

Define the administrator-level authentication requirements to all infrastructure components.   The administrator-level authentication architecture for infrastructure components is one of the most neglected areas of many organizational security plans; not surprisingly then, it is also one of the most frequently hacked components. Hackers seek administrator access to systems before they seek any other. It simply gives them more power.

Business Worksheet for Authentication

IMPACT ANALYSIS ID	BEFORE PLAN	PERCENT IMPROVEMENT	NEW VALUE

Quality Management worksheet completed for this element? (check box) ☐

Employees

Identify opportunities to group authentication requirements by organizational roles such as job function or business unit.

_____

_____

_____

Identify unique authentication requirements for individuals in sensitive positions such as system administrators.

_____

_____

_____

What authentication ease-of-use (such as a reduced number of usernames and passwords) features are most valued by employees in your organization?

_____

_____

_____

Customers

Define the who, what, when, and how authentication requirements for customers of your organization.

_____

_____

_____

Owners

Identify any high-impact authentication requirements that might be driven by owner sensitivities, such as authentication for access or distribution of sensitive financial information to the public.

_____

_____

_____

Worksheet 3.8   Business Worksheet for Authentication.

Describe any other events particularly sensitive to owners that have an authentication component to them.

_____

_____

_____

Suppliers and Partners

Describe any authentication requirements relating to suppliers and partners—think carefully about where they may be needed.

_____

_____

_____

Information

Describe authentication requirements from the perspective of information rather than applications. Identify high-impact information that may require stronger authentication policies and procedures.

_____

_____

_____

Infrastructure

Describe authentication requirements from the perspective of infrastructure, but keep in mind the objective of single-sign-on.

_____

_____

_____

Specifically address administrator authentication requirements for infrastructure components.

_____

_____

_____

Worksheet 3.8   Business Worksheet for Authentication. *(continued)*

Selling Security

Use Worksheet 3.9 here.

EXECUTIVES

Provide examples of what may cost money.   Your security plan may call for investment in new authentication technologies such as smart cards, enhancements to servers and software, upgrades to applications, biometric readers, and so forth. Executives will want to know exactly how much these investments will cost.

Selling Security Worksheet for Authentication

IMPACT ANALYSIS ID	BEFORE PLAN	PERCENT IMPROVEMENT	NEW VALUE

Executive

Present all costs related to enhanced authentication technologies in an up-front fashion.

Emphasize potential workflow and efficiency gains from enhanced authentication trust, integration, and ease-of-use.

Demonstrate a quantifiable reduction in organizational impact from hacked authentication such as impersonation.

Middle Management

Identity very specific business processes that are strengthened through enhanced authentication.

Walk through benefits, step-by-step, and simulate different authentication attacks in relation to business processes.

Staff

Highlight how improved management of identity protects staff members. Provide specific examples.

Describe the trade-off between strength of protection and ease-of-use. Describe any day-to-day benefits.

Worksheet 3.9 Selling Security Worksheet for Authentication.

Explain how the plan will affect business operations. Execs want to know if system implementation will affect general business operations. Be prepared to answer this.

Clearly present the benefits in terms executives can understand. Fortunately, there are many benefits. First, simplifying and strengthening the authentication process opens the door to more enhanced workflow systems that can rely more heavily on the systems for trust. For example, paperless purchase order processing may allow for better tracking and control of expenditures in real time and may reduce administrative costs. Better authentication opens the door to future capabilities such as nonrepudiation, the ability to sign things electronically. Try to quantify real potential for dollar savings achieved through enhanced authentication efforts by identifying potential follow-on money-saving system and business process enhancements. Provide examples of how the existing system is vulnerable and how this represents a certain degree of risk to owners, employees, and so forth. For example, the fact that all employees must remember and manage an average of seven username/password combinations weakens security and encourages them to use weaker ones they can remember or to write down difficult-to-remember passwords and put them in the wrong places, such as pasted on top of their desks and monitors.

Demonstrate a reduction in quantifiable impact. For these and other impact-related issues, refer back to your security impact analysis and describe how impact variables will be reduced, thus working to protect owner (as in shareholder or stakeholder) value.

MIDDLE MANAGEMENT

Describe exactly what will happen and why, and clearly lay out business process-focused benefits. Describe how any changes to the current authentication mechanism will affect existing business processes. Describe the benefits of reduced impact and the potential for increased workflow efficiency in terms of daily discrete tasks. Be specific. Executives want a higher-level description of improvements, but middle management needs concrete, specific examples with a little more detail.

Walk through the system, step by step, and demonstrate the benefits. Simulate attacks if needed.

Walk through how authentication is done now and will be done in the future. Use a very specific task that is commonly performed by an employee or customer. Simulate how a hacker could compromise the existing system. For example, if usernames and passwords are sent in the clear over the network today but are protected by the new authentication system, put a network sniffer (the equivalent of a phone tap) on the network and reveal how easy it is to take a username/password right off the network in the current system but not in the new one. While the nontechnical staff may not know what they're looking at, the mere act of showing, at least once, their passwords on a network sniffer may have the desired effect on those you need to convince.

STAFF

Highlight how improved management of their identity protects them. Talk about the trade-off between protection of their identity and ease of use. Describe day-to-day benefits.

Explain how their work will be safer from hackers and, ideally, how much easier it may be to use the new authentication scheme.   Here, too, choose specific examples of information important to them and show them how improved authentication technology protects that information. Put it in concrete, understandable terms. At the same time, don't scare them too much about the existing system.

Encryption

Summary

The encryption security element involves two processes: the encryption itself and the associated management of keys. Encryption is the act of scrambling data so that, even once accessed, its usefulness is limited to those who have the encryption key. If you don't have the encryption key, the encrypted data is useless to you. You probably know all this. But do you know the answers to these questions as they relate to your security plan?

- How do you determine, in a consistent manner, what will and will not be encrypted?
- Which encryption method(s) will you use?
- How will you manage encryption keys?

These are all important questions that need to be addressed to make encryption workable on a large scale.

Encryption is not simple; if it were, we could and would encrypt everything. But there are administrative, performance, and functional factors that need to be orchestrated in order to implement encryption in a convenient way such that it doesn't significantly interfere with routine business activities and, at the same time, offers real effectiveness. In our plan, we will focus on the management—the what, how, and when—of encryption.

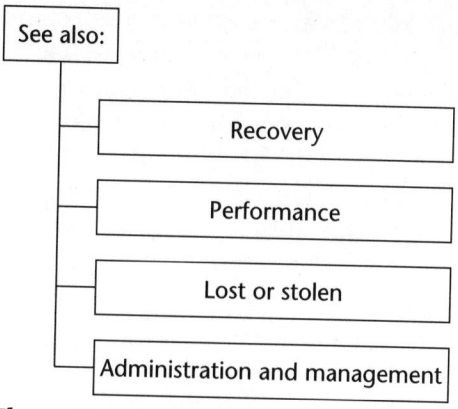

Figure 3.3 Encryption.

Key management—the life-cycle management of encryption keys—is a show-stopping aspect of your encryption architecture. Public key infrastructure (PKI) technology (described in detail in Chapter 5) provides a way to ease the management of encryption keys.

One of the downsides of encryption is that sometimes keys become inaccessible by accident or through a malicious act. An important aspect of encryption may be therefore, depending on your corporate policies and procedures, the ability for a designated corporate security staff member to decrypt information encrypted by an employee or contractor. This capability is called *key escrow* or *key recovery*.

Security Stack

Use Worksheet 3.10 here.

PHYSICAL

Decide where to put your keys. In terms of encryption, the physical security stack has to do with physically managing the encryption keys that enable you to "unlock" the encrypted material. As just noted in the summary, the benefit of encryption is that, theoretically, it prevents intruders from reading the encrypted material because they don't have the key. In practice, without proper management, the key may be lost or misappropriated (by a hacker), in which case encryption would only cause more problems. So the question becomes this: Where do you put your encryption keys for safekeeping?

- *On a smart card?* Portable tokens such as smart cards provide a great deal of benefit for encryption because you can store a long encryption key on the card (such as your PKI private key), enabling you to take it with you wherever you go. You can also password-protect the key so that only you can gain access to it. (But, note, you must use a strong password, one not easily guessed.) Moreover, many smart cards can be configured to disable themselves automatically after some number of incorrect password attempts. And, finally, many smart cards can be configured so that the key is generated directly on the smart card and never leaves it. This means that hackers cannot gain any access to the key unless they know your password; and hackers get only a few tries at guessing it before the smart card automatically disables itself. Smart card management systems can make a one-time copy of your key when the card is initially configured if you need to implement key recovery. Smart card management systems must, of course, be heavily secured—in fact, often it's practical to not connect them to any network whatsoever (that is, to completely isolate them).

- *On my hard drive?* If you can't carry your encryption keys around with you on a smart card, you must store them somewhere. Generally, this means physically storing a very long key on your hard drive. This also means you can't take your key with you to another machine unless you copy it onto some physical media such as a floppy disk. That key will itself be encrypted with a special shorter key (a password) that you can remember. The problem with this approach is that, because your key is stored out in the open, on the hard drive, and it is itself protected with a weak key (your password), a hacker could work to decrypt your key through what's called a *brute-force* attack, to break the encryption algorithm. You can't do this with a smart card configured to never allow the key to leave the card because the hacker can't even get close to the encrypted key without first knowing your password. And if the hacker guesses that password incorrectly just a few times, as previously mentioned, the smart card disables itself. Smart cards, or any hardware device storing keys and offering similar security characteristics, offer many advantages over key storage on a hard drive or floppy disk.

Devise a plan, one that addresses key recovery.   Your plan should address how keys are created, where they are stored, and what happens if a key is lost or otherwise made unavailable by someone with not-so-nice intentions. Key recovery, the ability to recover a key from a physical storage location should it become unavailable through its primary mechanism, is an important part of your security plan. Unfortunately, key recovery opens another can of worms relating to an individual's privacy and the presumed control he or she has over his or her own key material. If the key being stored is an individual's private key, then someone can impersonate the individual by forging his or her digital signature (this is discussed in more detail under the Nonrepudiation security element later in this chapter).

NETWORK

Know where and when to encrypt.   There's a difference between encrypting information while it is in transport across the network and storing that same information in its encrypted state on either end of the connection (on the client, the server, or both). If a hacker taps into your network and tries to read your encrypted information, he or she will be unable to read it. If, however, the hacker breaks into the client or server and the information is not encrypted there, as in *not* stored and encrypted on the hard drive, the hacker will be able to read the information there. Therefore, encryption has what's called a *statefulness* associated with it— that is, the *state* of information encryption while in transport and the *state* while that information is stored. Encryption of information while in transport is a simpler problem to solve than keeping it encrypted long term. For transport, we can more easily establish encryption keys dynamically, and we can change them frequently without human involvement. Furthermore, we can delete the keys after information has been received by the network device. Technologies for network-level encryption include SSL/TLS, IPSec, and SSH. If, on the other hand, you want to read encrypted information stored on your hard drive, you usu-ally need a little help with the keys. As previously discussed, those keys need to be stored on your hard drive, on a floppy disk, or on a hardware device such as a token.

In all cases, encrypt wireless network links.   Whether you are using a wireless Ethernet inside your office or a handheld computer with a wire-less network connection, you need encryption if you want to avoid get-ting quickly hacked. As mentioned in Chapter 1, the laziest of hackers can read all of your sensitive wireless transmissions behind your firewall if you don't implement encryption. Furthermore, a hacker can typically join right in on your network, wirelessly. The security impact of this is devastating, and currently too many companies have this vulnerability. As for wireless handheld devices, these too offer enormous security challenges without encryption. Many of these devices allow all corpo-rate email to be forwarded to them. Without encryption, and with weak forms of email authentication, your email accounts and all of your mes-sages can be easily hijacked by a hacker. Finally, these handheld devices are themselves not well secured. I discuss this increasing risk in the final chapter of this book, when we consider the future of security and hacking in general.

Choose between encryption on individual network devices and end-to-end.   Some network approaches allow for encryption specifically between networking devices themselves (for example, between two routers), whereas others are oriented toward end-to-end encryption between the client and server applications. An excellent example of an encryption protocol for networking devices is the IP Security (IPSec) protocol. Through IPSec, the notion of a *security association* (SA) is introduced. An SA is something you define between any two network devices, allowing you to request that certain security features be implemented, such as encryption, authentication, and integrity checking. You can mix and match SAs between devices. For example, you can configure one IPSec encryption SA from a device on the Internet to your firewall. Your firewall can then decrypt the network transmission. Another separate encrypted SA can be established between your firewall and some internal network device. This approach allows for the firewall to inspect the contents of the network connection. This offers security benefits because, as a security planner, you need to be concerned with the network traffic coming in and out of your organization. Some argue, however, that this approach to encryption is dangerous because the firewall acts as a man-in-the-middle; as such, if a hacker breaks into the firewall, then all sensitive network transmissions can be read, even those that were encrypted. SSL/TLS, on the other hand, does not allow for a man-in-the-middle attack. Most organizations today allow fully encrypted SSL/TLS sessions to go straight through their firewall without inspection, allowing a fully encrypted end-to-end connection between a host on the Internet and a Web browser within the corporation and behind the firewall. This offers the benefit of not allowing for a man-in-the-middle attack because the firewall cannot decrypt the SSL/TLS session. Therefore, this approach does not allow the firewall administrator to see what's going on inside the network transmission. Some organizations implement an SSL proxy server, which basically makes the proxy look, to the outside world, as if it is the Web browser inside the organization (the SSL proxy emulates a Web browser running SSL). There are various approaches to implementing SSL proxies, but many of them have the disadvantage of putting information in the clear within the corporate network or disabling advanced features of SSL, such as the ability to authenticate SSL clients with digital certificates (a feature not commonly used today but that may become more popular in the future.) You need to decide, based on your own security policies and impact analysis, how encrypted network traffic should flow in and out of your organization.

Security Stack Worksheet for Encryption

IMPACT ANALYSIS ID	BEFORE PLAN	PERCENT IMPROVEMENT	NEW VALUE

Quality Management worksheet completed for this element? (check box) ☐

Physical

Describe how keys are physically managed, to include keys stored electronically on stationary or removable media.

_____
_____
_____

Define how tokens, smart cards, rooms, and buildings housing encryption keys are physically protected and access controlled.

_____
_____
_____

Describe how passwords used to protect keys are secured. These should be secured as if they are keys themselves.

_____
_____
_____

How does your security plan address key recovery from a physical standpoint? Where are keys backed up?

_____
_____
_____

Network

Develop network encryption requirements. Differentiate between purely in-transport encryption and on-disk encryption.

_____
_____
_____

Describe how network encryption protocols, including SSL/TLS, SSH, and IPSec, are used to protect sensitive traffic.

_____
_____
_____

If public-key infrastructure (PKI) technology is used, specify how digital certificates and private keys are managed.

_____
_____
_____

Worksheet 3.10   Security Stack Worksheet for Encryption. *(continues)*

Plan for the network encryption protocol impact on firewall, proxy server, caching, and load balancing systems.

_____
_____
_____

Application

Determine what applications may require encryption, and define needed encryption statefulness.

_____
_____
_____

Identify existing application-level encryption mechanisms and key management approaches.

_____
_____
_____

Develop a plan for the how, when, where, and why of encryption at the application level.

_____
_____
_____

Differentiate between file-level and data-level encryption approaches relative to your requirements.

_____
_____
_____

Operating System

Determine operating system-level encryption requirements such as encryption of sensitive system files.

_____
_____
_____

Identify encryption technologies within your operating system that may be used at the network and application levels.

_____
_____
_____

Assess the strength of the key management mechanism used for file system encryption at the operating system level.

_____
_____
_____

Worksheet 3.10   Security Stack Worksheet for Encryption. *(continued)*

Differentiate between these approaches in your security plan.   Your security plan should reflect an understanding of where data in transport is encrypted and where it is not and what the related impact is.

Consider the effect on your intrusion-detection systems.   Encryption within the network can affect your ability to perform intrusion detection because intrusion-detection systems cannot read encrypted network traffic nor decipher hacker signature behavior that is indicative of an intrusion or potential intrusion.

APPLICATION

In your plan, specify the what, why, how, when, and where of encryption at the application level.   That means determining what you want to encrypt, why you believe it should be encrypted, how you will do it, when you will encrypt/decrypt, and finally where the encrypted and decrypted information will be stored. We already considered different encryption approaches as they relate to the network, noting the general difference between encrypting information as it moves through the network versus encrypting it for long-term storage on a computer. When we look strictly at the application layer, we are able to consider certain approaches that provide some of the best of both worlds. An excellent example of such an approach would be encrypted electronic mail. To keep a hacker out of email, you need to encrypt it. Encrypted email allows information to be encrypted, long term, on a computer's hard drive; at the same time, it can be used across the network. The two most popular secure mail standards are Secure MIME (S/MIME) and Pretty Good Privacy (PGP). S/MIME support is built into most popular email software such as Microsoft Outlook, Netscape Messenger, and Lotus Notes. S/MIME relies on the use of a PKI; therefore, those that use it must have a digital certificate and a secure mechanism to store and protect their private key. Secure key storage mechanisms include a smart card or, with the disadvantages previously noted, a hard drive or floppy disk. Other example application-level approaches to encryption include database encryption, directory server encryption, or encryption of the data used by a general application of some kind. With these approaches, a key is somehow managed within the application. Often, with these approaches, software vendors offer you relatively weak but easy-to-administer solutions and very strong, but more difficult-to-administer, PKI-based encryption approaches. For the strongest encryption approach, a stationary hardware cryptographic device that can securely hold the private key is required. Because applications have detailed knowledge about the information they manage, they are in a better position than the operating system (discussed next) to streamline encryption decisions such as when information should and should not be encrypted and decrypted.

OPERATING SYSTEM

Encrypt in the operating system.   Perhaps the most obvious example of operating system encryption would be file system-based encryption. In this case, the operating system manages the encryption keys used to encrypt files on the hard drive. Generally speaking, file system encryption does make hacking more difficult; but, because the operating system is inherently limited in the assumptions it can make about the use of information, encryption at the file level, rather than at the individual application-managed data component level (as in a field in a database or an email message), results in more security vulnerabilities than when encryption is performed at the application level. Operating system-level encryption tends to result in more information being left in the clear more often and with fewer safeguards.

Life-Cycle Management

Use Worksheet 3.11 here.

TECHNOLOGY SELECTION

Focus on encryption algorithms enough to understand the consensus view on their strength.   Often, when selecting encryption-based technologies, people start by developing an understanding the strength of one encryption algorithm versus another. They become lost in a sea of terms relating to key length, randomization, RC this, DES that, and so forth. Strength, and making sure algorithms you choose remain strong or are updated over time for strength, is indeed important and something your security plan should address. At the same time, you don't need to turn yourself into a full-fledged cryptographer in order to plan a security solution; in fact, if you do, you run the risk of missing the forest for the trees. You can obtain a consensus view by doing simple research on the Internet. (If you are interested in learning more about cryptography in general, check out the references in "For Further Reading" at the back of this book.)

Estimate performance of encryption algorithms and key management schemes.   This requires addressing very important and relevant topics that affect your implementation and the day-to-day practicality of encryption: key management, including recovery, statefulness of encryption (in transport, at the application, in the operating system), and how encryption is integrated into your application and the network. While many encryption algorithms are surprisingly efficient, some encryption plans, when all elements are considered, including public key and private key operations associated with dynamic secret key negotiation, introduce some kind of performance burden that should be quantified and managed over time. You can assess this by running your application under load without encryption and measuring computer CPU utilization and qualitative application response time. Next, turn encryption on and perform the same measurements. Finally, compare the measurements.

Select your encryption technology so that it can be integrated in the intended way, with your intrusion-detection and vulnerability analysis systems.   As mentioned earlier in the discussion on encryption at the network layer and IPSec, SAs, and SSL/TLS, encryption can introduce challenges to your intrusion-detection and vulnerability analysis systems.

Select key storage and management solutions.   Fundamental to technology selection are the ease, convenience, and scalability of the key storage and management mechanisms. Using PKI implies a significant infrastructure investment (see Chapter 5). Hardware storage of keys and smart cards also introduce considerable overhead. Keys stored on floppy disks and hard drives decrease security. There is no easy solution here, so you will have to drive your decisions based on your impact analysis and security budget.

IMPLEMENTATION

Carefully monitor system performance over time.   Do this as you phase in your deployment of encryption; include CPU loading, system response times, and measures of system stability (uptime). Perform measurements before and after encryption is enabled. Validate any performance assumptions you make over time by regularly reviewing performance statistics as encryption is more heavily used.

OPERATIONS

Give the operations group a solid method of dealing with key management.   Include retrieval of backup keys, should they exist, resetting of keys (unencryption with old key, re-encryption with new key). Or, better yet, design a comprehensive operational architecture that simplifies life, wherever possible, based on a well-implemented PKI architecture and simplified key management plan.

INCIDENT RESPONSE

Ensure that the incident response team knows, to the extent possible, what has been encrypted, when, by whom, and how.   This demands strong logging capability within your encryption architecture. If your corporate privacy policies and procedures allow for it, this team should be able to make use of key recovery mechanisms to look at data encrypted by a suspect employee or contractor. For example, the team may want to look at encrypted electronic mail stored on a company desktop computer. In order to do that, your organization would need to implement a key recovery mechanism when issuing digital certificates for S/MIME. The team may also need the ability to request that new keys be used as part of the encryption process in the event they believe the keys of one form or another have been compromised. Also, the incident response team should have a process to respond to outside legal entities, as in regulatory agencies or the government in general, should they be requested as part of an investigation to provide access to information that is encrypted.

Life-Cycle Management Worksheet for Encryption

IMPACT ANALYSIS ID	BEFORE PLAN	PERCENT IMPROVEMENT	NEW VALUE

Quality Management worksheet completed for this element? (check box) ☐

Technology Selection

Evaluate integration options, key management, and performance of the encryption tools you choose.

_____

_____

Determine how well reviewed and publicly scrutinized the implementation is as one measure of quality.

_____

_____

Select encryption algorithms and key lengths considering the current industry consensus on strength and performance.

_____

_____

_____

Implementation

As you phase in encryption, carefully measure any user-perceived performance degradation.

_____

_____

Measure system response time, CPU loading, and system stability as you implement.

_____

_____

Worksheet 3.11   Life-Cycle Management Worksheet for Encryption.

Operations

Define policies and procedures for key management including generation, backup and retrieval, and resetting.

_____

_____

_____

Incident Response

Team needs to be able to know what has been encrypted, when, by whom, and how to the extent possible.

_____

_____

_____

The ability to respond may be limited if the company does not implement a key recovery mechanism.

_____

_____

_____

The team should have the ability to request that new keys be generated for potentially compromised systems.

_____

_____

_____

The incident team should be prepared to respond to law enforcement should a request be made to access information that is encrypted.

_____

_____

_____

Worksheet 3.11   Life-Cycle Management Worksheet for Encryption. _(continued)_

Business

Use Worksheet 3.12 here.

BUSINESSPEOPLE: EMPLOYEES

Categorize and identify encryption requirements for employees based on their organization roles.   Consider how employees collaborate when writing your encryption plan. That is, your plan may need to take into consideration the fact that many individuals in specific roles in the organization require access to the same collection of encrypted information, or at least to be able to exchange it in an encrypted manner when not otherwise stored in a protected server environment.

Business Worksheet for Encryption

IMPACT ANALYSIS ID	BEFORE PLAN	PERCENT IMPROVEMENT	NEW VALUE

Quality Management worksheet completed for this element? (check box) ☐

Employees

Categorize and identify encryption requirements for employees based on organizational roles.

_____

_____

_____

Address any specific encryption requirements that are driven by the need to allow group collaboration on information.

_____

_____

_____

Educate employees on the importance of remembering and protecting keys and passwords used to protect keys.

_____

_____

_____

Customers

Identify customer information that is particularly sensitive to the company or considered private for an individual as candidates for encryption.

_____

_____

_____

Develop an encryption plan for sensitive and private customer information.

_____

_____

_____

Owners

Consider encryption as a means for protecting corporate assets and drive requirements accordingly.

_____

_____

_____

Worksheet 3.12   Business Worksheet for Encryption.

Identify any laws in your country or multinational laws, if applicable to your company, relating to the import, export, or use of encryption.

_____

_____

_____

Specifically consider the need to encrypt sensitive financial information that is considered company confidential.

_____

_____

_____

Suppliers and Partners

Identify information exchanged with suppliers that may have hidden value to competitors. Consider encryption needs.

_____

_____

_____

Consider the use of encryption with partners as one way to drive home the importance of protecting intellectual property.

_____

_____

_____

Information

Consider encryption needs from the perspective of information and not networks, applications, and servers.

_____

_____

_____

Infrastructure

Take the inverse view and look at encryption needs for infrastructure and not information.

_____

_____

_____

What new infrastructure components are needed to implement encryption per your requirements?

_____

_____

_____

Worksheet 3.12   Business Worksheet for Encryption. *(continued)*

BUSINESSPEOPLE: CUSTOMERS

Protect private customer information held by your organization.   One common method to achieve this is through encryption.

BUSINESSPEOPLE: OWNERS

Help owners to protect corporate assets, operate in accordance with the law, and manage public perception.   Encryption of anything relating to assets, such as intellectual property and financial matters, is of particular importance to owners.

BUSINESSPEOPLE: SUPPLIERS

Consider integrating important suppliers into your encryption plan where practical.   You may need to exchange information privately with your suppliers, such as those providing high-volume raw materials to your organization. Keep in mind that information about your organization's buying habits can be of great value to those gathering information about your company. They may be able to predict how well your company is doing and thus affect, in some negative way, for example, the value of your stock. Or they may be able to predict your next big product or service. What you buy says quite a bit about what you are planning and where you are at. This is an often overlooked area of security.

BUSINESSPEOPLE: PARTNERS

Encourage the concept of security and property with your partners.
One way to do this is to drive them toward implementing security mechanisms around any sensitive information you exchange with them. One of the biggest security holes in organizations is created through partnerships because most organizations don't have any requirements for how partners protect their sensitive information, other than through the signing of a nondisclosure agreement or other partnership agreement that highlights legal requirements but says nothing about operational and procedural expectations—other than that "something should be done."

BUSINESS: INFORMATION

Identify high-impact information that needs to be encrypted.   Organize information according to business functions in your organization, such as accounting, human resources, product management, and so forth.

BUSINESS: INFRASTRUCTURE

Determine how your infrastructure is affected and what new requirements exist to implement your security plan.   Performance, key management, reliability, security of key management components, quality of encryption implementation, and operational interfaces are all fundamental aspects of your encryption plan.

Selling Security

Use Worksheet 3.13 here.

EXECUTIVES

Draw comparisons.   Referencing your impact analysis, give examples of existing company information routinely sent and/or stored in the clear (unencrypted) today. Demonstrate how easily it can be compromised. Associate a cost with that loss. Describe how a sound encryption plan reduces potential impact. Show a path toward increased savings and efficiency by allowing transactions conducted manually today to be implemented electronically in the future.

MIDDLE MANAGEMENT

Give specific examples of how encryption is integrated into the workflow process, either transparently or overtly by employees and management.   Help managers understand any productivity impact from encryption, then point out the benefits, such as the ability to conduct sensitive transactions electronically that are done by hand today. Staff members may be required to play a role in key storage and management, as would be the case if, for example, they needed to carry a key with them on a smart card or floppy disk. If so, then managers need to be aware of this so they can factor in any required training and support.

STAFF

Spell out exactly what they need to know about encryption and/or where they actively need to engage it.   In the event that employees need to be aware of encryption at all, such as if they are required to carry a smart card, then they need to be sold on the value of encryption in a manner similar to middle management: Communicate the value of the decreased impact and the potential for the automation of future tasks that are today performed manually due to electronic security concerns. Prepare staff for any training, policies, and procedures they may need to be aware of if they must manage keys.

Selling Security Worksheet for Encryption

IMPACT ANALYSIS ID	BEFORE PLAN	PERCENT IMPROVEMENT	NEW VALUE

Executives

Provide examples of high-impact information routinely sent or stored unencrypted today. Show risks and impact.

_____

_____

_____

Be specific on potential losses to the organization. Demonstrate with a network sniffer, for example, a compromise.

_____

_____

_____

Show a path toward increased efficiency and savings by allowing sensitive manual transactions to be safely automated.

_____

_____

_____

Clearly describe how impact is reduced, resulting in lowered potential dollar losses to the organization.

_____

_____

_____

Middle Management

Give specific examples of how encryption will be integrated into the workflow process.

_____

_____

_____

Demonstrate a potential future application implemented manually today that may be automated safely with encryption.

_____

_____

_____

Worksheet 3.13   Selling Security Worksheet for Encryption.

Staff

Spell out exactly what staff members need to know regarding encryption: usage, policies, and procedures.

_____

_____

_____

Demonstrate how their daily work is better protected with encryption by showing how it can be hacked without it.

_____

_____

_____

Worksheet 3.13   Selling Security Worksheet for Encryption. *(continued)*

Integrity

Summary

It's stating the obvious to say we should care about the integrity of information and infrastructure we rely on. If, say, a hacker reconfigures a server so that he or she can read or control your processes or procedures—for example, changes one of your sales orders to ship to him or her instead of to your customer or tampers with your company's financial information—we experience a renewed awareness of the value of integrity. Fortunately, we can implement technology to ensure the integrity of our information and infrastructure.

We also need to be aware of the integrity of our physical access controls. For example, if it's particularly easy to tamper with a stolen or expired visitor's or employee's badge to make it easier for a hacker to gain physical entry, then we will want to address the integrity checks inherent in our office badging system.

To achieve electronic information integrity, we can invoke complex mathematical algorithms, in conjunction with cryptography, to provide us with a means of verifying the integrity of information. This process is called *hashing*. Intrusion-detection systems (IDSs), employed to determine if a hacker has modified or tampered with system files, make use of hash algorithms. The Secure Sockets Layer (SSL), Transport Layer Security (TLS), and Secure Shell (SSH) protocols also implement network-level integrity checking, as does IPSec as an optional feature.

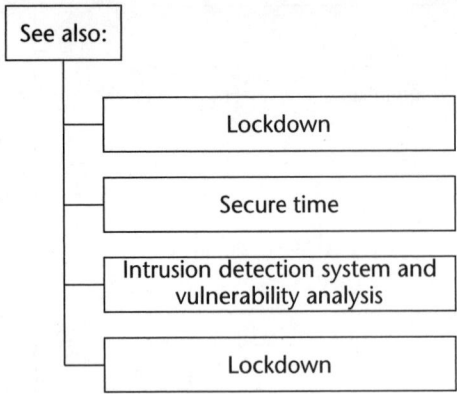

Figure 3.4 Integrity.

Other examples of the importance of the integrity security element include the following:

- The integrity of systems files and logs is crucial to effective incident response.

- Integrity of time sources, addressed by the Secure Time security element (see Chapter 4), is important to protect against a range of hacker attacks such as on your Kerberos authentication mechanism.

- Intrusion-detection systems make extensive use of integrity-checking mechanisms.

Security Stack

Use Worksheet 3.14 here.

PHYSICAL

Verify the integrity of access control systems for your company's building(s), including badging for employees, visitors, and contractors. Assess how easily someone can gain access to a secured area with a tampered badge. For any crucial paper-based processes, assess how integrity is enforced on high-impact items.

NETWORK

Define when, where, and how sensitive information is transmitted over the network.   Sensitive high-impact information includes confidential intellectual property or key financial information. Assess where secure transport protocols, such as SSL, TLS, SSH, IPSec, and similar standards, can be used to ensure integrity.

Distinguish between network- and application-level integrity.   This is very important. Network integrity checking ensures only the integrity of information while in transit over the network. Once that information is received and stored at the destination, the application and operating system control integrity, not the network. If you want to maintain complete end-to-end integrity, you have to implement integrity mechanisms at *both* the network and application levels.

APPLICATION

Use application-level integrity mechanisms.   Application-level integrity mechanisms work to maintain the incorruptibility of information managed within client and server applications. For example, if your electronic mail application implements the Secure MIME (S/MIME) protocol (most popular ones do), then integrity of your email can be ensured. Implementing application-level integrity-checking mechanisms in conjunction with other security measures such as encryption often, as in the case of S/MIME, demands that a broader cryptographic infrastructure be deployed in your organization, namely a public-key infrastructure (PKI).

Maintain integrity of software.   Code signing is the technique used to ensure the integrity and nonrepudiatability of the software you use or distribute. Code signing is addressed as part of several related security elements, including Nonrepudiation, Content and Executable Management, and Secure Software.

OPERATING SYSTEM

Use an IDS for verification.   As already explained, intrusion detection makes use of an integrity-checking mechanism to determine if a hacker has modified important system files for his or her own (destructive) purposes. After you have locked down your system, you should implement an integrity-checking mechanism to verify that a hacker hasn't unlocked it or that an administrator hasn't inadvertently introduced a change to your standard lockdown configuration.

Security Stack Worksheet for Integrity

IMPACT ANALYSIS ID	BEFORE PLAN	PERCENT IMPROVEMENT	NEW VALUE

Quality Management worksheet completed for this element? (check box) ☐

Physical

How prone to tampering is your building physical badging system? Can, for example, employees spot a fake or tampered visitor's badge? For this and building access control in general, write a policy and procedure for employees to report a concern over unauthorized visitors, be it a suspected fake badge or no badge at all.

_____
_____
_____

For any sensitive, high-impact paper-based processes, assess how integrity is enforced for high-impact items.

_____
_____
_____

Network

Document integrity mechanisms employed for high-impact information today, especially when sent over public networks.

_____
_____
_____

Develop a plan to incorporate integrity-capable network protocols such as SSL/TLS, SSH, and IPSec.

_____
_____
_____

Specify any adjunct platform technologies required such as public-key infrastructure (PKI) technology.

_____
_____
_____

Application

Identify high-impact information having application-level (as opposed to only network-level) integrity requirements.

_____
_____
_____

Worksheet 3.14   Security Stack Worksheet for Integrity.

Design with application integrity mechanisms such as S/MIME and digitally signed files and stored data.

_____

_____

_____

Specify any adjunct platform technologies required such as public key infrastructure (PKI) technology.

_____

_____

_____

Assess the need for code signing (e.g., Active-X, Java JAR signing) for software you develop or use.

_____

_____

_____

Operating System

Pay special attention to key system logs that paralyze your incident response team if corrupted by a hacker.

_____

_____

_____

Plan for an aggressive implementation of the integrity-checking capabilities offered by your intrusion detection system.

_____

_____

_____

Worksheet 3.14   Security Stack Worksheet for Integrity. _(continued)_

Life-Cycle Management

Use Worksheet 3.15 here.

TECHNOLOGY SELECTION

Protect the integrity-checking mechanism itself.   Physical-level integrity technology includes techniques such as using holograms on badges or biometrics to uniquely identify an individual. Perhaps the most important aspect of any integrity-checking mechanism you choose is its resistance to tampering by a hacker. Integrity checking at the application level is often combined with other security measures, such as encryption and digital signing. In such a case, the scope of your technology selection may be broadened to include, at the same time, technology to support encryption.

Life-Cycle Management Worksheet for Integrity

IMPACT ANALYSIS ID	BEFORE PLAN	PERCENT IMPROVEMENT	NEW VALUE

Quality Management worksheet completed for this element? (check box) ☐

Technology Selection

Evaluate physical integrity technologies, such as holograms, watermarks, and biometrics for visual badging/ID cards.

_____
_____

Based on your network architecture and security mind-set, choose where network integrity checking is most important.

_____
_____

For the integrity checking technology you deploy, verify that it has features to protect itself from tampering. See Implementation.

_____
_____
_____

Implementation

Plan for how you will implement integrity systems to prevent a hacker from easily tampering with the systems themselves.

_____
_____

Describe how you will carefully implement security for related technology such as PKI.

_____
_____
_____

Operations

Define policies and procedures to detect and respond to high-impact integrity compromise.

_____
_____
_____

Worksheet 3.15 Life-Cycle Management Worksheet for Integrity.

Develop an atmosphere of "trust but verify" relative to suspicious logs that are not themselves integrity-checked.

_____

_____

_____

Train staff (policies and procedures) to not disrupt the integrity of information monitored by intrusion detection systems.

_____

_____

_____

Incident Response

The incident team should know in advance what logs and system files are integrity-checked and what are not.

_____

_____

_____

For those systems that are not integrity-checked, the incident team should implement a "trust but verify" approach.

_____

_____

_____

For sensitive related components such as PKI, the team needs a solid plan to assess the integrity of underlying components because your integrity mechanisms may rely on your PKI.

_____

_____

_____

Worksheet 3.15   Life-Cycle Management Worksheet for Integrity. *(continued)*

IMPLEMENTATION

Ensure that your integrity-checking scheme is well implemented.   Too many aren't. For example, organizations routinely implement systems that compute a hash snapshot (remember, a hash is used to determine whether something has changed) and then store that snapshot in a vulnerable system, thereby making it possible for a hacker to replace that snapshot with his or her own (modified) version. Another popular hacker approach is to replace your integrity-checking software with his or her own modified version. When you run your integrity-checking software, you think you're running yours, but it's the hacker's. No surprise, the hacker's version does not detect tampering; thus, the illicit activities go undetected.

OPERATIONS

Verify that your operations group can clearly identify violations.   When monitoring sensitive, high-impact infrastructure or information, your operations staff must know how to easily recognize when that infrastructure or information has been violated.

INCIDENT RESPONSE

Consider integrity checking part of your logging architecture, as well as your system files.   If the logs and system files, on which the incident response team is relying to determine what has happened, how to immediately respond, and who may be responsible, are easy to tamper with (that is, their integrity is in question) then their job is more difficult. Of course, we can't perform integrity checking on everything, such as all logs, given the state-of-the-art in technology; nevertheless, integrity checking should be part of your logging architecture as well as your system files. The incident team has to know what "level of trust" they can assume for a given log they are analyzing. Did the log come from the system that was compromised or some other system? Was there any type of integrity checking enabled for the log? What about the system files being analyzed during incident response: Which ones were integrity checked? Which ones were not? The incident team must associate a *confidence factor* with any information they use as part of the incident response process.

Business

Use Worksheet 3.16 here.

BUSINESSPEOPLE: EMPLOYEES

Give employees mechanisms to report suspicious transactions.
Where possible, enable employees to report if the integrity of important information seems out of the ordinary. This relates as much to policies and procedures as it does to program user interfaces and training. For example, if employees make use of S/MIME for secure mail, the software they use will report to the user when the integrity of a mail message is in question. Employees should be trained to understand exactly what their mail software is telling them with regard to the integrity of the mail they receive.

BUSINESSPEOPLE: CUSTOMERS

Instill confidence; earn trust.   Customer confidence in your organization depends heavily on whether they can trust that you can maintain the integrity of a sales order or other service. If, say, a customer asks for 100 widgets and you deliver 1,000 due to a system glitch or hack, then that customer may lose confidence in you. Public perception, as quantified by your impact analysis, is therefore affected. Customers expect you to maintain the integrity of their transactions and of any information you hold about them. The last thing you want to have to do is to inform all your customers that you've been hacked and that you need them to reenter everything.

BUSINESSPEOPLE: OWNERS

Understand owner sensitivities.   Owners require integrity when it comes to the organization's financial information . They also care very much about public confidence, which is easily shaken by an incident where important information that the company relies on has been tampered with.

BUSINESSPEOPLE: SUPPLIERS

Know who and what you rely on to do business.   The integrity of information provided to you by high-impact suppliers is important. To ensure integrity, implement policies and procedures that identify those suppliers from whom the integrity of information may have a significant effect on your organization and work to implement integrity measures in coordination with them.

BUSINESSPEOPLE: PARTNERS

Establish technical approaches to exchange information with high-impact partners.   As with suppliers, if you routinely exchange high-impact information with partners or rely heavily on each other's infrastructure, then you should develop a plan to ensure the integrity of the information you exchange.

BUSINESS: INFORMATION

Prioritize information by integrity requirements.   Following this guideline is a very effective way to prioritize your security integrity plan. The prioritization will often become clear when looked at in conjunction with your security impact analysis.

Business Worksheet for Integrity

IMPACT ANALYSIS ID	BEFORE PLAN	PERCENT IMPROVEMENT	NEW VALUE

Quality Management worksheet completed for this element? (check box) ☐

Employees

Identify those integrity mechanisms that require employee knowledge or intervention.

_____

_____

_____

Train employees to use integrity mechanisms. Tell them when to use them and how to detect tampering with them.

_____

_____

_____

Establish policies and procedures to define when, where, how, and why integrity mechanisms should be employed.

_____

_____

_____

Customers

Be prepared to reassure customers by explaining to them the integrity mechanisms you put in place.

_____

_____

_____

Identify any "extreme" sensitivities your customers may have relating to information integrity.

_____

_____

_____

Define your plan for ensuring the integrity of customer-sensitive information.

_____

_____

_____

Worksheet 3.16 Business Worksheet for Integrity.

Owners

Identify particularly sensitive integrity concerns for owners. Examples include financial information and information released to the press.

_____

_____

_____

Develop a plan to ensure the integrity of information sensitive to owners.

_____

_____

_____

Suppliers and Partners

Identify high-impact information from suppliers and partners that warrants integrity checking.

_____

_____

_____

Develop a plan, with interoperable technologies, policies, and procedures, to implement needed integrity.

_____

_____

_____

Information

Prioritize integrity requirements and an integrity plan for high-impact information.

_____

_____

_____

Infrastructure

Develop an integrity plan including intrusion detection for high-impact infrastructure components.

_____

_____

_____

Worksheet 3.16   Business Worksheet for Integrity. *(continued)*

BUSINESS: INFRASTRUCTURE

Inventory how integrity is maintained for high-impact infrastructure component files.   The integrity of infrastructure components themselves, such as operating system files, application configuration files, and so forth is very important. An architecture for achieving integrity includes a quality intrusion-detection system, in conjunction with a sound log management plan, and implementation of cross-checking where applicable to validate sanity of configurations.

Selling Security

Use Worksheet 3.17 here.

EXECUTIVES

Demonstrate the dangers of tampering.   Tampering with information is something anyone can understand. Provide a demonstration for your executives of how easily today key financial or other high-impact organizational information can be modified by a hacker. Show such an intrusion step by step; and, if possible, do a mock-up of the entire scenario using a real application. But a word of caution: Keep it real. Make it clear that your demonstration isn't contrived, but that it reflects a real risk. Bring out your impact analysis and show the costs involved with lowering the potential impact by following the specific plans you've laid out.

Highlight added value.   Show specific examples of how the organization can save money by further automating an important process that can now be implemented with greater confidence because of your integrity architecture.

MIDDLE MANAGEMENT

Do a before-and-after comparison.   Specify the business processes that will be affected by the implementation of your integrity architecture. Demonstrate the reduced potential impact with your new architecture based on your impact analysis. Show how future business processes may be streamlined by taking advantage of the proposed integrity architecture.

STAFF

Describe features and benefits of the integrity architecture in terms of day-to-day activities.   If the integrity plan will be entirely transparent to staff members then, typically, they simply don't care about it. If, on the other hand, the change requires their involvement, from performing better sanity checks on information as they go about their business to implementing complex secure email processes, you need to convince them this is valuable, as it will prevent the risk and embarrassment of being hacked.

Selling Security Worksheet for Integrity

IMPACT ANALYSIS ID	BEFORE PLAN	PERCENT IMPROVEMENT	NEW VALUE

Executives

Walk through a high-impact scenario, using a real application and business process, where tampering occurs.

_____

_____

_____

Clearly show the potential losses, drawn from your impact analysis, when information or infrastructure is tampered with.

_____

_____

_____

Provide examples of how future business processes may be enhanced from improved trust and reliance gained from advanced integrity checking.

_____

_____

_____

Show how the impact to the organization is reduced, and thus high-value losses avoided, through improved integrity.

_____

_____

_____

Middle Management

Show how specific business processes will be affected, if at all, by your integrity plan.

_____

_____

_____

Walk through, step-by-step, the benefits and simulate different integrity attacks in relation to business processes.

_____

_____

_____

Worksheet 3.17   Selling Security Worksheet for Integrity. *(continues)*

Show how future business processes may be streamlined with the benefit of integrity-checking technology. Give a specific step-by-step example.

_____

_____

_____

Staff

If the integrity plan requires staff to perform new tasks, such as use secure email, encourage them to see the value.

_____

_____

Provide specific examples of how tampering can affect their daily work. Show how your plan reduces the risk of this.

_____

_____

_____

Worksheet 3.17   Selling Security Worksheet for Integrity. _(continued)_

Nonrepudiation

Summary

The ability to dependably record the electronic equivalent of a handwritten signature and associate that securely with a transaction or flow of information is quite powerful, from a security standpoint as well as from a workflow perspective (as in digitally signing documents that today require handwritten signatures). The operative words here are _dependable_ and _secure_. To date, the most powerful technology for achieving nonrepudiation electronically is through the use of PKI technology. But the integration of PKI technology with business-focused, transaction-based applications has historically been a non-trivial task. At the same time, it offers a great many benefits. (See Chapter 5 for more on the topic of PKI.)

PKI-based strong nonrepudiation often demands the use of some kind of handheld token or smart card, or for a server for which nonrepudiation is performed regularly, a heavily secured stationary token. These tokens hold the private key used to sign information digitally. Two of the biggest challenges to building a powerful nonrepudiation architecture are portability of handheld tokens—being able to carry them conveniently—and the capability to read from and write to them securely, as needed.

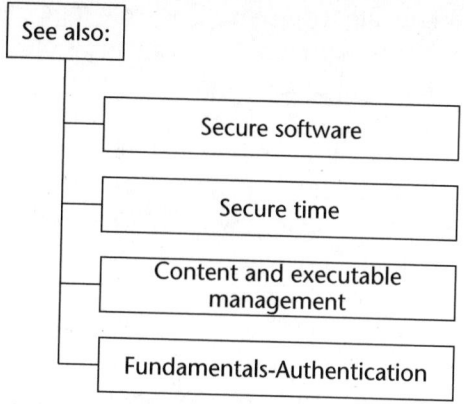

Figure 3.5   Nonrepudiation.

Security Stack

Use Worksheet 3.18 here.

PHYSICAL

Provide a comprehensive and integrated security strategy up/down the security stack; enlist state-of-the art technologies where appropriate. Historically, nonrepudiation in the physical world, such as it was, came in the form of building badges and handwritten sign-in logs. Today, frequently, those forms of authentication are being supplemented with biometrics and other, newer technologies. PKI and smart cards specifically provide this binding in a highly secure manner. Increasingly, smart cards are available that integrate building access, network, application, and operating system nonrepudiation as needed, thus providing the bridge between the electronic and physical worlds.

NETWORK

Define network-level nonrepudiation.   At the network level, nonrepudiation becomes significant within two contexts: (1) where a network device performs some action with another and that action has some kind of nonrepudiation characteristic associated with it; and (2) a human being authenticates to a network device (such as a firewall) and some type of nonrepudiation event is associated with that.

Distinguish a network-level nonrepudiation event from an application-level event.   For example, the SSL/TLS protocol supports the capability for one end of the connection to authenticate to another. The exchange involves the digital signing of sample data as part of the authentication. It's arguable that on either end, or both, the digitally signed sample could be stored along with other information and deemed some form of nonrepudiation event. Though I have not seen an implementation of SSL/TLS doing this today, nothing precludes it from being done. Even if nonrepudiation were implemented in this way, we would still be left with the nonrepudiation of a connection that occurred. This has nothing to do with the nature of the transactions that occurred over it—for example, did you really authorize the purchase of 1,000 pairs of socks instead of 100 over that connection? There's no way of knowing; all we know is that a connection was established by an individual and a digital signature verified that. Therefore, while nonrepudiation of a network event can be quite valuable, it's not the same as nonrepudiation of a specific application-level transaction, such as approval of a specific order for goods or services. This latter example can be provided by application-level nonrepudiation.

APPLICATION

Carefully study those applications offering some form of nonrepudiation to determine costs and achievability.   Application-level nonrepudiation typically means that each end of the application interaction—client and server—has the capability to securely authenticate to one another, after which an electronic mechanism exists to record that a specific application-level event has occurred and to bind this event in some nonrepudiatable manner. Application-level nonrepudiation for specific transactions typically implies tight PKI-based integration. Some vendors offer wraparound applications that integrate with the application and operating system, thus simplifying this integration. Perhaps the simplest form of electronic nonrepudiation is secure, digitally signed email. The S/MIME email protocol provides this capability and is integrated with most popular email clients. Making use of it requires digital certificates and PKI.

Consider the significance of time (time stamping).   Nonrepudiation often introduces the notion of time (so-called time stamping of a trans-action). That is, when you sign a contract today, for example, you usually write the date as well. The same goes for the digital equivalent: We want to know when something was signed securely. This brings us to the need for secure time. (The Secure Time security element is discussed in Chapter 4.)

Security Stack Worksheet for Nonrepudiation

IMPACT ANALYSIS ID	BEFORE PLAN	PERCENT IMPROVEMENT	NEW VALUE

Quality Management worksheet completed for this element? (check box) ☐

Physical

Define, for this and every element of your security stack, what you consider to be strong, acceptable, or weak nonrepudiation.

_____

_____

_____

Assess the strength of nonrepudiation in any physical processes such as handwritten logs and building access control.

_____

_____

_____

Write a plan to improve nonrepudiation for physical processes as driven by your impact analysis.

_____

_____

_____

Network

Assess if you have any nonrepudiation requirements for users authenticating to your network, such as in VPN access.

_____

_____

_____

Develop your own policies for what you consider strong, moderate, and weak nonrepudiation.

_____

_____

_____

Application

As driven by your impact analysis, identify applications needing nonrepudiation.

_____

_____

_____

Worksheet 3.18   Security Stack Worksheet for Nonrepudiation. *(continues)*

Specify the nature of the applications as either, or some combination of, transactional or session-based.

_____

_____

_____

Pay close attention to usability and cost parameters as you develop your plan. Nonrepudiation can become difficult and costly.

_____

_____

Develop policies and procedures for any required code signing such as Authenticode or Java signing (see also the Content and Executable Management security element discussed in Chapter 4).

_____

_____

_____

Operating System

Identify any new features available within the operating system that may leverage nonrepudiation such as the digital signing of system files and configurations.

_____

_____

_____

Worksheet 3.18   Security Stack Worksheet for Nonrepudiation. *(continued)*

Establish the authorship of software; implement code signing.   Code signing, discussed in more detail in several other security elements presented in this book (for example, Content and Executable Management) allows software to be signed digitally. In this way, you can be assured that the software you're executing has, in fact, been written by the software publisher you thought wrote it and has not been tampered with and modified by a hacker.

OPERATING SYSTEM

Enable nonrepudiation at the operating-system level.   This is a new concept. I can imagine many potential benefits to enabling a nonrepudiation feature set within the operating system. As of this writing, though, no widely available operating systems implement nonrepudiation in a particularly interesting way. In terms of future features, perhaps a future operating system might force administrators to digitally sign any system configuration changes they make and could attempt to implement some type of secure signature verification mechanism. This may work to restrict the kinds of changes that hackers can make. Furthermore, keeping track of administrator changes through digital signatures could also enhance the tracking of changes made to systems as part of the configuration-management process.

Life-Cycle Management

Use Worksheet 3.19 here.

TECHNOLOGY SELECTION

When selecting PKI-enabled nonrepudiation technology, focus on how well it integrates, or can be integrated with, your applications. Determine its manageability. Recognize that if components of your PKI are compromised, your nonrepudiation architecture may be compromised as well.

Beware of interoperability overkill. Historically, interoperability has been a major topic of discussion as it relates to nonrepudiation and PKI. As security "realists," we must view interoperability as important while focusing on solving business problems, as opposed to engaging in debates about academic standards. The point is not to overdo it. (Again, see Chapter 5 on PKI.)

IMPLEMENTATION

Implement cleanly. Regardless of the technology chosen, if we are sloppy in how we implement nonrepudiation technology, we can't count on it for much of anything. If, for example, we implement a PKI but have weak protection of the digital signing keys, we weaken our architecture overall.

Identify areas of weakness relating to our implementation. This means determining how our particular implementation may be compromised, then locking down systems to minimize these compromises. For example, if we are PKI-enabled, then we must plan for how private keys are stored and accessed by applications (both well-intentioned applications and those of a hacker).

Life-Cycle Management Worksheet for Nonrepudiation

IMPACT ANALYSIS ID	BEFORE PLAN	PERCENT IMPROVEMENT	NEW VALUE

Quality Management worksheet completed for this element? (check box) ☐

Technology Selection

Identify steps for minimizing up-front technology cost and complexity for simple nonrepudiation applications.

_____

_____

_____

Carefully examine nonrepudiation user software interfaces (such as the S/MIME user interface of your mail software) so that people in your organization can make effective use of your nonrepudiation design. That is, how will users be able to know when information they have received has been correctly digitally signed?

_____

_____

_____

Implementation

Establish policies and procedures that reflect the strength of nonrepudiation you intend to achieve. Strong nonrepudiation means a tight ship.

_____

_____

_____

If you use PKI, establish a suite of PKI-related policies and procedures including CA and signing key management.

_____

_____

_____

Identify specific training requirements for nonrepudiation systems implementation, operation, and for users.

_____

_____

_____

Worksheet 3.19   Life-Cycle Management Worksheet for Nonrepudiation.

Operations

Train operations staff to understand the particular sensitivity and security requirements for nonrepudiation components.

_____

_____

_____

Nonrepudiation based on PKI requires careful signing key life-cycle management. Provide operations the tools and training for this.

_____

_____

_____

Incident Response

Identify the relative strength of any nonrepudiation information relied on by the team. The veracity of nonrepudiation information should, ideally, not need to be questioned by the incident team; however, when a system has been compromised, careful checking needs to be performed.

_____

_____

_____

Define how the team will access any evidence relating to a nonrepudiation event they must investigate.

_____

_____

_____

Worksheet 3.19   Life-Cycle Management Worksheet for Nonrepudiation. *(continued)*

OPERATIONS

Give the operations group the tools and training to administer and make use of the nonrepudiation architecture.   Build in safeguards to plan to prevent operators from accidentally destroying nonrepudiation records. Strong nonrepudiation technology, such as PKI-enabled nonrepudiation, has historically required substantial infrastructure deployment, new administration and management responsibilities, and a specific focused integration effort at the security stack layer in which it will be used—whether physical-, network-, application-, and/or operating-system-level integration or all of them.

INCIDENT RESPONSE

Grant the incident response team full access to logs, databases, and any evidence of a nonrepudiable event relating to an intrusion.   The team also needs to understand what "assurance level" the team can assume for an event—that is, how nonrepudiatable the event really is.

Business

Use Worksheet 3.20 here.

BUSINESSPEOPLE: EMPLOYEES

Identify nonrepudiation requirements for sensitive actions taken by employees, as driven by your impact analysis.   Examples include large purchase authorizations, exchange of highly confidential information, or approval of significant company-wide product or service decisions. Another example would be digitally signing a new release of the company's software (see also the Secure Software and Content and Executable Management security elements in Chapter 4).

BUSINESSPEOPLE: CUSTOMERS

Identify customer expectations and review your plan and impact analysis to identify areas where nonrepudiation can be improved.   Customers expect to have certain nonrepudiable evidence relating to transactions they conduct with your organization. The classic example of nonrepudiable evidence, from a customer's perspective, is a receipt and order number. Find out how easy such things may be to compromise—how easy, for example, would it be for a hacker to undermine your commerce process?

BUSINESSPEOPLE: OWNERS

Meet owners' expectations about nonrepudiation.   Owners expect events such as release and manipulation of financial information, key public relations information, and other crucial informational events to be traceable and to have some notion of nonrepudiation associated with them. It's not uncommon these days to read or hear headline stories about a company for which fraudulent activity has occurred regularly and for which there was a very poor, nonrepudiatable audit history. In short, when public accountability is important, so is nonrepudiation.

Business Worksheet for Nonrepudiation

IMPACT ANALYSIS ID	BEFORE PLAN	PERCENT IMPROVEMENT	NEW VALUE

Quality Management worksheet completed for this element? (check box) ☐

Employees

Define what type of actions would benefit from nonrepudiation such as purchase authorizations or any sensitive approval.

_____

_____

_____

Customers

Define customer expectations relative to nonrepudiation evidence relating to the transactions they conduct with you.

_____

_____

_____

Determine how nonrepudiation evidence is maintained today for customers, and assess if it is sufficient based on impact analysis.

_____

_____

_____

Assess if there are ways to improve customer service and workflow with nonrepudiation such as automating manual processes.

_____

_____

_____

Owners

Develop a nonrepudiation plan to address high-impact information of specific interest to owners.

_____

_____

_____

Look for opportunities to save money and enhance workflow with nonrepudiation.

_____

_____

_____

Worksheet 3.20   Business Worksheet for Nonrepudiation. *(continues)*

Suppliers and Partners

Identify how nonrepudiation may be used to improve accountability between organizations.

_____
_____
_____

Determine specific interoperable technology requirements for supplier and partner nonrepudiation.

_____
_____
_____

Information

Identify what, where, when, and how nonrepudiation can be implemented effectively for high-impact information.

_____
_____
_____

Infrastructure

What new infrastructure components are required to implement nonrepudiation in your organization?

_____
_____
_____

What infrastructure components benefit from nonrepudiation? For example, administration events for high-impact components.

_____
_____
_____

Worksheet 3.20   Business Worksheet for Nonrepudiation. *(continued)*

BUSINESSPEOPLE: SUPPLIERS

Identify organizational requirements to record events that were authorized and approved.   For example, if a supplier promises to provide a crucial component for your product/service but doesn't commit in a nonrepudiable way, and if you have no record of this transaction, you may have less recourse. As you manage the security of your supply chain with suppliers, consider implementing a nonrepudiation mechanism.

BUSINESSPEOPLE: PARTNERS

Consider an electronic architecture that, at least in part, enables a nonrepudiable framework for partner activities.   Such activities include approval of press releases, control and exchange of confidential information, and agreement on steps and related partnerships. Sometimes the simplest approach is to use secure email, such as with the S/MIME protocol.

BUSINESS: INFORMATION

Identify all key high-impact information elements in your organization and assess associated nonrepudiation requirements.   Again, it's common to look first at applications and servers, and not strictly at information elements. There are benefits to viewing information only, as part of your plan development.

BUSINESS: INFRASTRUCTURE

Consider all of the infrastructure components required to implement nonrepudiation.   To broadly implement nonrepudiation, you need to implement a PKI in some way, either completely internally or through some combination of internally and externally managed security services (such as through managed PKI services provided by a certificate authority such as VeriSign).

Selling Security

Use Worksheet 3.21 here.

EXECUTIVES

Illustrate for executives a high-impact application wherein a hacker or insider effectively executes a fraudulent act that would otherwise have been prevented with nonrepudiation architecture.   Show how a visible high-impact infrastructure business process, product, or service provided by your company can be violated by a hacker taking advantage of the lack of a nonrepudiation architecture.

Illustrate enhanced workflow.   Show how tasks previously performed manually may now or in the future, as a result of laying the nonrepudiation groundwork, be implemented at significantly lower cost and with better service (speed, information availability) with nonrepudiation architecture. A classic example of this would be a process that today requires a handwritten signature but that tomorrow could make use of nonrepudiable electronic signature.

Selling Security Worksheet for Nonrepudiation

IMPACT ANALYSIS ID	BEFORE PLAN	PERCENT IMPROVEMENT	NEW VALUE

Executives

Show a real example of a fraudulent authorization or spoofed email message.

_____
_____
_____

Emphasize potential workflow and efficiency with nonrepudiation by converting paper processes to electronic ones.

_____
_____
_____

Demonstrate a quantifiable reduction in organizational impact from fraud by introducing nonrepudiation.

_____
_____
_____

Middle Management

Identity very specific business processes that are strengthened by nonrepudiation.

_____
_____
_____

Walk through, step-by-step, nonrepudiation benefits, and simulate different fraudulent attacks in relation to business processes

_____
_____
_____

Show carefully what additional steps, training, technology, and overhead will be introduced with nonrepudiation.

_____
_____
_____

Show impact reduction by demonstrating a specific business process and associated loss due to fraud that could be otherwise prevented with nonrepudiation.

_____
_____
_____

Worksheet 3.21   Selling Security Worksheet for Nonrepudiation.

Staff

Highlight how nonrepudiation protects staff by protecting them and the organization from fraud. Provide specific examples.

_____

_____

_____

Describe the day-to-day benefits that nonrepudiation may bring, such as automation of unpopular manual processes.

_____

_____

_____

Prepare staff for any specific training and technology required to implement your nonrepudiation plan.

_____

_____

_____

Worksheet 3.21   Selling Security Worksheet for Nonrepudiation. *(continued)*

MIDDLE MANAGEMENT

Highlight before-and-after workflow impact.   Compare the disruption and fraud caused by the lack of nonrepudiation capabilities to improvement of existing processes from enhanced automation and security provided by a nonrepudiation architecture.

STAFF

Show value-adds of nonrepudiation architecture.   Identify how the new architecture will add value to employees' day-to-day tasks by reducing the probability of fraud carried out in their name and by allowing them, now or in the future, to securely automate tasks they perform manually today.

Privacy

Summary

I've said it before, but it bears repeating: Security is as much about education as it is about anything else. Nowhere is this more evident than with regard to the Privacy security element. Most of the major debates over privacy have to do with those we *choose* to interact with, including merchants and our employers. In making choices to engage with someone, we infer and imply some level of trust; thus, our privacy becomes an issue of communicating expectations between the other party and ourselves.

There are two basic dimensions to privacy: appropriate steps taken to protect private information from hackers and steps taken by an organization to assure those with whom they have a relationship that their private information will not be "abused" by the organization or anyone working for or with that organization. Guiding how an organization, employer, merchant, or even the government guards our privacy is about trust, education, and agreement. In the case of a merchant-customer relationship, the customer is entering into a trust-based relationship with the merchant when he or she gives a credit card number, address, and so forth and trusts the merchant to provide the product or service paid for with that credit card. What merchants do with browser *cookies*, a major privacy concern, in this is less relevant than most think at this point. It's how the merchant guards your privacy overall in accordance with its policies and procedures that ultimately determines security. In short, it's the relationship that's most important.

One very real security problem is the use of so-called e-monitoring software, which employers use to scan employee email, chat messages, or snapshots of Web pages browsed, without telling the staff they are doing so. It is of paramount importance that companies that use such tactics publish a privacy policy that informs employees of the practice. Increasingly, this will be a matter of law, not simply good corporate citizenship.

This set of worksheets addresses how we can put technology into place that allows us to guard privacy in accordance with our policies and procedures.

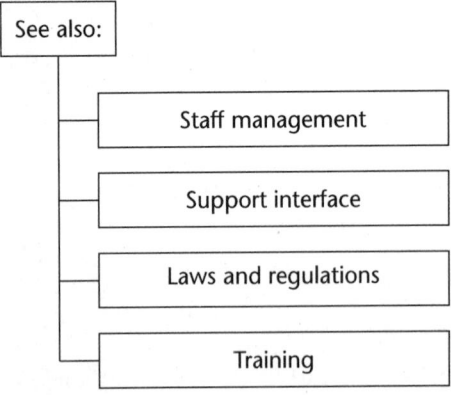

Figure 3.6 Privacy.

Security Stack

Use Worksheet 3.22 here.

PHYSICAL

Walk through key areas in your company and observe how information can be absconded to violate the privacy of individuals or organizations. Let me explain this by way of example. A year or so ago I signed in for a visitor's pass at the front lobby desk of a defense contractor. I filled out a 3 x 5-inch index card that included a range of private and sensitive information including my Social Security number, date of birth, place of birth, and the like. In short, it asked me to provide all the information needed to pull off an identity theft easily. After completing the card, I gave it to the receptionist, who took it and put it into a plastic index card holder on her desk. This card holder was kept out on the desk all day long in plain view, attended and unattended. I asked her if she locked up the cards at night. She responded, "No, but I do put them into this drawer sometimes. It doesn't matter, nobody knows what they are." Really? Another front-desk privacy weak link is company sign-in sheets for visitors. These sign-in sheets are often kept in plain view, where anyone can routinely scan them and learn, for example, with whom the company may be planning on doing business or who is interviewing for a job. In general, these sign-in sheets are a bad idea for many reasons. Instead, visitors should register individually at the front desk, and their registration information should be well-protected. The point is, whether it's front-desk information or other printed or audible information you have or may share with someone, think about privacy in deeper terms.

NETWORK

Define what administrators are allowed and not allowed to do.   Administrators have the ability to routinely monitor Internet browsing patterns, email exchanges—pretty much any electronic exchange—that traverses the corporation's network connections, for suspicious activity. E-monitoring technology, firewalls, and proxy servers provide an ideal means for all of this. Therefore, you must plan your technology in such a way that no administrator can easily violate individual or organizational privacy policies. This starts by having well-understood and well-documented privacy policies and procedures for employees and administrators.

Define acceptable browsing.   Give employees clear policies and procedures that state where on the Web they may browse on company time. Define company values; for example, that they may not visit Web sites engaging in illegal activities or the display of pornography.

Security Stack Worksheet for Privacy

IMPACT ANALYSIS ID	BEFORE PLAN	PERCENT IMPROVEMENT	NEW VALUE

Quality Management worksheet completed for this element? (check box) ☐

Physical

Perform a visual walk-through in your company, and observe how information can be combined to violate privacy.

_____

_____

_____

Carefully examine all front-desk/reception area procedures including sign-in, badging, and information gathering.

_____

_____

_____

Institute policies for simple things such as erasing white boards and clean desk policies for private information.

_____

_____

_____

Network

Define any e-monitoring policies and procedures, and clearly communicate them to all affected people.

_____

_____

_____

A hacker is as much a privacy violation as an overly aggressive company. Design network security with privacy in mind.

_____

_____

_____

To the extent you can, isolate extremely private information onto a well-known group of well-secured network segments.

_____

_____

_____

Worksheet 3.22   Security Stack Worksheet for Privacy.

Application

Reconfigure or (re)design applications to deter intentional misuse of private information.

_____

_____

_____

Attempt to logically partition private information to reduce its value should one application be hacked and not another.

_____

_____

_____

Determine any way in which your applications unwittingly combine information to violate your security policy.

_____

_____

_____

Identify existing applications and design new ones to "clean up" after themselves to avoid leaking private information.

_____

_____

_____

Operating System

Review and revise your operating system access control matrix so that it addresses your privacy objectives.

_____

_____

_____

Identify administrator errors that easily unravel privacy. Develop technologies and procedures to reduce potential errors.

_____

_____

_____

Worksheet 3.22 Security Stack Worksheet for Privacy. *(continued)*

Implement an overall security architecture that protects information privacy according to the impact analysis plan.   If an organization, for example, sends sensitive customer records in the clear over the Internet, then the organization has not adequately taken steps to protect the privacy of customer information. Your security privacy plan may delineate between the relative privacy of parts of your network behind and in front of your firewall(s)—though I generally caution against making such "relativity" assumptions. From my point of view, high-impact applications *always* need protection over any part of your network. If, however, you decide to make these assumptions, you might, for example, choose to encrypt network transport of sensitive private information going over the Internet but not from within your firewall.

APPLICATION

Design applications to protect private information from hackers and to prevent abuse of private information by the organization. Applications protect information by incorporating other security planning elements such as access control and encryption. Applications abuse information by unwittingly sharing private information and by making use of information that the organization's privacy policies and procedures would otherwise disallow. For example, let's say your organization has access to more detailed information about a given customer than he or she has directly provided you (such as from a mass-marketing consumer database or a partner or supplier database): This does not mean you are free to combine this information with what you already have and to sell it or even use it to service the customer unless the customer has granted permission. The right to do this, or not, is determined by your organization's privacy policies and procedures and the permissions granted by your customers.

Design applications to prevent the violation of private information as defined by the organization's privacy policies. "Backdoor" information sharing or information-tracking tactics and inappropriate aggregation of private information represent examples of such poor design choices.

OPERATING SYSTEM

Coordinate access control and privacy management. At the operating system level, access control and privacy management are tied closely together. Lack of operating-system-level security provides tremendous opportunities to violate privacy by enabling unauthorized access to private information held in places such as files, directories, databases, and in memory. A breakdown of access control leads to a breakdown of privacy. Moreover, operating systems that are either misconfigured or poorly implemented, leaving information from one user accessible to another, also represent a threat.

Life-Cycle Management

Use Worksheet 3.23 here.

TECHNOLOGY SELECTION

Write privacy requirements for all technology implemented as part of the security stack.   These requirements are driven by your privacy policies and procedures. The key here is to think about privacy up front, during technology selection and implementation. The same idea can, of course, be applied to existing technology that you're auditing from a privacy standpoint. Remember that nearly all technology has the potential to violate privacy in one way or another, regardless of whether its design has anything to do with privacy in the first place. Carefully test technology that is implemented within your security stack for privacy holes. Carefully review test plans and results so that you are reasonably assured that privacy is maintained in accordance with your requirements.

IMPLEMENTATION

Implement safeguards to prevent privacy from being violated, as driven by your organization's policies and procedures.   In implementation and operations, the customer service interface to any organization (be it the front desk or the support desk) is a common place to find a weak spot in privacy implementation. Customer service organizations, as one example, routinely violate the privacy of those they service by sharing information they shouldn't. Often this happens because the technology has been implemented in such a way that they have too much access to information without appropriate safeguards. For example, customer service representatives should not be able to access private customer information without first securely entering authentication information received from the customer into their workstation. The customer's private information, and the ability to act on that information, should not be available to the representative until the customer authentication is successful.

OPERATIONS

Operate systems in accordance with established privacy policies and procedures.   Your plan should incorporate operational training so that users know what they should and should not do.

Life-Cycle Management Worksheet for Privacy

IMPACT ANALYSIS ID	BEFORE PLAN	PERCENT IMPROVEMENT	NEW VALUE

Quality Management worksheet completed for this element? (check box) ☐

Technology Selection

Privacy should be written as a general requirement for all security stack components. Define steps to achieve this.

_____

_____

_____

Identify technology that is flexible enough to meet the needs of your organization's privacy policies and procedures.

_____

_____

_____

Perform an audit of existing security stack technology, and bring it in-line with your privacy policies and procedures.

_____

_____

_____

Aggressively look for "privacy holes" in any security stack technology you consider. Identify high-risk technology.

_____

_____

_____

Implementation

Develop privacy training programs for customer service and support groups; instill privacy policies and procedures.

_____

_____

_____

Determine ways to make privacy difficult to accidentally violate by those with sensitive information access.

_____

_____

_____

Worksheet 3.23   Life-Cycle Management Worksheet for Privacy.

Test the privacy of your organization by developing, as part of your implementation plan, an ongoing privacy audit plan.

_____

_____

_____

Carefully tie your authentication implementation to your privacy implementation—they are inseparable. By doing this, you will prevent inadvertent sharing of private information with the wrong people.

_____

_____

_____

Operations

Write an operational training plan, based on privacy polices and procedures, for handling sensitive private information.

_____

_____

_____

Develop a testing plan to validate privacy. For example, call customer support and attempt to gather private information as a hacker would.

_____

_____

_____

Incident Response

Identify how the incident response team will access logs, both physical and electronic, to assess privacy violations.

_____

_____

_____

Be prepared for an individual or industry objection to your policies and procedures. Form a privacy committee.

_____

_____

_____

Plan for incident team and public relations (PR) coordination should a privacy violation/concern threaten public image.

_____

_____

_____

Worksheet 3.23   Life-Cycle Management Worksheet for Privacy. _(continued)_

INCIDENT RESPONSE

In response to a suspected violation of privacy, enable the incident response team to log information to validate what has happened to the extent possible. Also enable the team to disable systems quickly, if necessary, and to chart a path of recovery. For example, if a credit card database is compromised, the incident response team should have the means, through technology and policies and procedures, to immediately and securely transmit the numbers of those compromised credit cards to their issuers so they can be disabled. If privacy has been violated because an employee did not follow published policies and procedures, this should also be reported to the incident response team. Such violations, along with all other incidents, should be tracked as part of the quality management process. If enough privacy policy violations occur, this may indicate a need to retrain employees.

Business

Use Worksheet 3.24 here.

BUSINESSPEOPLE: EMPLOYEES

To protect the privacy of employees, educate them as to what they can expect relative to privacy; implement technology in accordance with your organization's policies and procedures. Technology that impacts employees includes software and systems used by the organization to monitor what they're doing in real time and historically (for example, e-monitoring technology).

BUSINESSPEOPLE: CUSTOMERS

Respect customer privacy. Organizations typically maintain considerable information on their customers (which here is defined to include departments, other organizations, or classical end customers), and they care very much about what technology you put into place to safeguard their privacy. A sample customer privacy outline is provided next.

BUSINESSPEOPLE: OWNERS

Implement technology that safeguards the privacy of your highest-impact information. Owners will be especially concerned with maintaining the privacy of customers, suppliers, and partners because not doing so not only can hurt these people, but also can cause considerable public embarrassment for the company.

SAMPLE PRIVACY POLICY OUTLINE

This policy outline is tailored to customers; however, you can adapt it for any of the businesspeople in these worksheets—employees, owners (as in shareholders), suppliers, and partners.

A. *Collecting information.* Define any and all information you collect on customers.

B. *How information is used.* Describe what you do with the information you collect, such as using it to make customers aware of products and services they may be interested in.

C. *Why we share information.* If you share any information outside of your organization, explain why you do so. For example, if you're a bank that issues credit, you may share information with credit-reporting agencies.

D. *Information we share.* Describe the information you share.

E. *Who information is shared with.* State whether you share information only with companies with which you are affiliated or if you share information to a broader group of companies such as those selling any kind of product or service you think the customer would be interested in.

F. *Your choices regarding information sharing.* Explain what choices the customer has with regard to information sharing and how they can communicate those choices to your organization.

G. *Former relationships/archival.* Define what happens when your relationship with the company ends.

H. *Security procedures.* Make a high-level statement indicating what safeguards you have put in place to help ensure the protection of private information.

I. *Questions or comments.* Provide an email address or contact for answering questions.

Integrate privacy policies with related agreements written by your company such as Terms of Use for your product or service.

BUSINESSPEOPLE: SUPPLIERS

Require suppliers to implement technology to safeguard the privacy of your organization's information as driven by its privacy polices and procedures. Coordinate with them to achieve this. Conversely, you may hold information relating to them that you must safeguard.

BUSINESSPEOPLE: PARTNERS

As with suppliers, safeguard partners' private information and ensure that they safeguard yours. See suppliers.

Business Worksheet for Privacy

IMPACT ANALYSIS ID	BEFORE PLAN	PERCENT IMPROVEMENT	NEW VALUE

Quality Management worksheet completed for this element? (check box) ☐

Employees

Write a privacy policy and establish an ongoing educational program so that your employees fully understand it.

_____
_____
_____

Let your employees know the types of technologies, such as e-monitoring, that you may be using. Be up-front.

_____
_____
_____

Write policies and procedures, and train, so that your employees respect the privacy of other people (e.g., customers).

_____
_____
_____

Assign the task of tracking privacy laws and regulations. Incorporate them into policies and procedures.

_____
_____
_____

Customers

Inform your customers about the technology you implement to protect their privacy.

_____
_____

Publish your organization's privacy policy on your public Web site and keep it up-to-date.

_____
_____
_____

Worksheet 3.24   Business Worksheet for Privacy.

For privacy violations involving customers, escalate to the incident response team.

_____

_____

_____

Owners

Specifically address high-impact privacy concerns in your security plan.

_____

_____

Address specific high-risk areas, such as the customer and employee perception of your organization's privacy protection technology, policies, and procedures.

_____

_____

Specifically address the privacy of financial or similar high-impact private information.

_____

_____

_____

Suppliers and Partners

Write contractual privacy policies and procedures for private information held or exchanged with suppliers and partners.

_____

_____

Work with suppliers and partners to agree on compatible technology facilitating privacy between organizations.

_____

_____

_____

Information

Look at privacy from the perspective of information. Identify private information needs for specific groups of people.

_____

_____

_____

Infrastructure

Change your perspective to infrastructure. Look at Web servers, customer data bases, human resource applications, and so forth.

_____

_____

_____

Worksheet 3.24   Business Worksheet for Privacy. *(continued)*

BUSINESS: INFORMATION

Define all high-impact information for which privacy is relevant.
Start by grouping information related to businesspeople (employees, customers, and so forth), then by organizational subcategories such as employees-human resources, employees-accounting, and so forth, and finally by suppliers and partners.

BUSINESS: INFRASTRUCTURE

Take two views.   The traditional view on privacy is from the perspective of infrastructure. Planners look at Web sites, customer databases, accounting servers, human resources databases, and the like, then iterate the privacy requirements for each. When this approach is taken in parallel with an information view of privacy, a more complete and better plan results.

Selling Security

Use Worksheet 3.25 here.

EXECUTIVES

Sell the importance of privacy to executive staff.   Fortunately, that's less difficult to do now, thanks to the widespread media coverage of privacy violations by individuals and organizations. To make the point clear to your executives, simply compile recent data, freely available on the Internet, relating to the corporate/organization impact of privacy violation. Design a three-column table that shows, in column 1, the event in the news; in column 2, a similar scenario that could happen inside your organization today unless the privacy safeguards you suggest are put into place; and in column 3, your impact analysis assessment for the privacy element and expected costs (keep in mind that executives will understand all of this in terms of risk and cost).

MIDDLE MANAGEMENT

Highlight the workflow impact and benefits of privacy management.
If, for example, time will be saved due to increased trust of automated systems, thus curbing or eliminating processes performed manually today, point that out. If your privacy implementation will have the effect of increasing the trust of staff in the organization, then make that point. You get the idea.

Selling Security Worksheet for Privacy

IMPACT ANALYSIS ID	BEFORE PLAN	PERCENT IMPROVEMENT	NEW VALUE

Executive

Provide specific examples of the risk of public embarrassment to the organization in a clean, easy-to-follow format.

_____

_____

_____

Address potential violations of privacy laws, now or in the future, should the organization not follow privacy regulations.

_____

_____

_____

Show the potential reduced privacy-related impact on the organization and the costs and savings from reducing it.

_____

_____

_____

Middle Management

Show any business process impact associated with privacy policies, procedures, and technology.

_____

_____

_____

Give examples of the challenge of privacy violations to managers. Show how your plan makes it easier for managers.

_____

_____

_____

Make management aware of the need for employee privacy policy and procedure awareness training.

_____

_____

_____

Worksheet 3.25   Selling Security Worksheet for Privacy. *(continues)*

Show how employee and customer trust can be better managed through privacy awareness, policies, and procedures.

_____
_____
_____

Staff

Tell staff if you use, or plan to use, technologies such as e-monitoring, and explain what it means to their daily tasks.

_____
_____

Make privacy policies and procedures openly available through training, email reminders, and other awareness programs.

_____
_____

Address their sensitivities straight-on. Nobody likes to feel as if they are being monitored without their knowledge. If you are monitoring, say so.

_____
_____

Explain the benefits of your privacy approach, and show how it better protects them as well as customers and others.

_____
_____
_____

Worksheet 3.25   Selling Security Worksheet for Privacy. *(continued)*

STAFF

Sell staff on the technical safeguards you are putting into place to provide a superior implementation for corporate policies and procedures. Staff members care about privacy; it is an intuitive concept, especially in countries such as the United States where freedom of the individual is a particularly large part of the culture. Staff are especially concerned with how technology may be used to invade their daily lives, from email to Web browsing to their work habits. This topic relates heavily to policies and procedures. As it relates to technology, remind staff that their privacy is as important as the privacy of the organization, its customers, owners, partners, and suppliers. Point out any related technology plans in these areas and their privacy benefits.

Conclusions

If, prior to reading this chapter, you had any doubt that security planning is an intense and rigorous process, I'm confident that going through these worksheets has convinced you. Fortunately, experience has shown that rigorously planning around the 28 security elements eventually becomes second nature. These elements together embody the very essence of secure distributed computing in the real world and, as such, increasingly interrelate with one another and produce a security plan that works.

Now that we've covered the fundamental security elements, it's time to move on to the worksheets for our remaining 9 core elements, plus the 13 wrap-up elements.

Using the Security Plan Worksheets: The Remaining Core and Wrap-up Elements

With the fundamental worksheets under our belt, it's time to delve deeper into the security planning process by focusing on the remaining core and wrap-up elements. In this chapter you continue to learn how to complete the worksheets that will serve as your guide throughout the security planning process. As with the previous chapter, keep in mind that the worksheets contain an important starter set of questions and pointers. By addressing these conscientiously, you will come away with a comprehensive security plan. Here, too, as with the worksheets for the fundamental security elements, many of the questions demand more than a simple yes or no or a one- or two-sentence response. You may, in fact, need to develop a detailed technical plan of some kind or write related policies and procedures.

TIP As in Chapter 3, I recommend that you start the worksheet process by writing notes in your worksheets, to include, for example, thoughts on what's needed, next steps to meet those needs, who you might ask to complete part of the worksheet, or how you might assign responsibilities at your next security team meeting. The goal is to make the worksheets into a central repository, providing links to any related plans, policies, and procedures. And don't forget, you can customize these worksheets to include more questions and pointers related to your particular needs. Electronic copies of the worksheets included in this book are available from the Web site maintained by the author at www.criticalsecurity.com or from the publisher's Web site at www.wiley.com/compbooks/greenberg.

Organization of the Worksheets

Chapter 3 covered the 6 fundamental security elements from the 15 core elements; this chapter covers the remaining 9 core elements, plus the 13 wrap-up elements, to complete our discussion of the 28 security elements.

As for the six fundamental core security elements, for each of the remaining nine core elements, five worksheets are provided, directly correlating with our security template. And, remember, the first worksheet, Quality Management, is somewhat different from the other four. It is "generic," applying equally to all security elements, and it can be modified to meet your needs. You might even find it useful to develop several different customized Quality Management worksheets, depending on the needs of your organization; but in all cases, you will want to complete at least one Quality Management worksheet for every security element. To help you fill out the Quality Management worksheets, refer back to Chapter 3, Table 3.1, where column 2, Security Plan, details how to address each item in column 1.

As in Chapter 3, each of the other four worksheets is preceded, first, by a Summary and, second, by a special figure called Key Relationships. The summary provides a simple recapitulation of the important issues to keep in mind as we examine the particular security element. The Key Relationships figure summarizes the top four security elements tied to the one currently undergoing study. Following the summary and the Key Relationships figure is a series of guidelines, categorized to correspond to the template, outlined as follows:

Quality Management

Security Stack

- Physical
- Network
- Application
- Operating system

Life-Cycle Management

- Technology selection
- Implementation
- Operations
- Incident response

Business

- Businesspeople
  - Employees
  - Customers

- - Owners
  - Suppliers
  - Partners
- Information
- Infrastructure

Selling Security

- Executive
- Middle Management
- Staff

Let's get started.

Addressing, Protocol Space, Routing Plan, Filtering, and Disablement

Summary

This is a large and important area of security, but we tend to make it more difficult than it needs to be simply because we enable more than we should. By enabling less, we have to do and manage less, and we give the hacker fewer methods by which to attack us. But something about human nature drives us to want to "get our money's worth," and vendors respond to this tendency and enable everything in their products by default; needless to say, doing this also reduces the number of support calls they have to answer because everything works "out of the box." As I've noted several times in this book, when we opt for "default enablement" we make things that much easier for hackers. With that cautionary note in mind, review these summary guidelines:

Remember, addressing is everything.   When it comes to network-based hacking, addressing is everything. How you plan addressing, what information you expose about it, and how it adapts all determine the fate of your security plan to a significant extent.

Fill the necessary skill sets.   Security staff must have a solid understanding of static and dynamic IP network addressing, spoofing, routing, tunneling, virtual IP addressing, the notion of protocols and protocol numbers, and how all of this relates to routing. They must understand filtering and all aspects of network address translation (NAT). In sum, they must have the disablement mind-set, as discussed in Chapter 2.

Inform intrusion-detection and vulnerability analysis (IDS/VA) systems as to what belongs and what does not.   This closely relates to your IDS and vulnerability analysis plan because IDS and vulnerability analysis

systems can't operate efficiently and effectively unless you disable
things. Simply put, there's too much to detect, monitor, and analyze
unless you make some up-front decisions about setting limits.

Avoid vulnerabilities introduced when interconnecting networks.   The
easiest way to avoid such vulnerabilities is by having a well-designed
address, protocol space, routing, filtering, and disablement plan. A
prime network segment for interconnection vulnerabilities, as noted previously, is on the administration and management LAN where all systems meet. It is here that we frequently break all our security measures
and provide one convenient place for hackers to get into everything.
Sometimes we violate our own rules, right beneath our eyes.

Security Stack

Use Worksheet 4.1 here.

PHYSICAL

Pull the plug.   There's nothing like pulling the cable to prevent a hacker
from getting access to your machine over the network. Physical disablement is the ultimate security mechanism. Unfortunately, this also prevents us from getting our work done—but not always. Identify systems
that are so critical that they are best kept entirely isolated from anything
but their own dedicated network. In Chapter 3, I gave an excellent
example of a system that can and should be physically isolated from the
network: an organization's smart card initialization and key recovery
system.

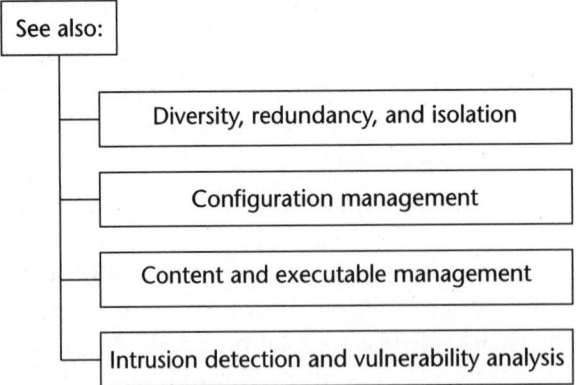

Figure 4.1   Addressing, protocol space, routing plan, filtering, and disablement.

Arrange your physical space.   Consider the physical arrangement of your systems, be they wiring or data centers: Don't make it easy to connect systems that shouldn't be connected. Remember the conference room example in Chapter 1, where a major corporation had an internal network connection in public conference rooms. Think about how you can physically locate network components to avoid accidental interconnection. For example, maybe you shouldn't allow in the same room a jack in the wall or wireless LAN connection with an unfirewalled connection to the public Internet and another connection to your internal network. Even though your administrators may not connect the two, someone else might do so without thinking about the implications.

NETWORK

Define how addresses are assigned dynamically (for example, WINS, DHCP).   How secure are your WINS and DHCP servers? Are you assigning dynamic addresses to sensitive devices, such as servers, that are better assigned static addresses? Static addresses allow you to monitor and log traffic to and from a device far more effectively because the address is known throughout time. From the perspective of your IDS/VA systems, static IP addresses help them as well by giving them a known IP address to focus on. Specific address filters can be developed for static IP addresses.

Describe performance and diversity, redundancy, and isolation (DRI) handling.   Include schemes for firewall load sharing, failover, and any network caching mechanisms. Determine if any of your performance- and scalablity-related designs affect this security element. Because redundant and replicated devices typically must appear to the rest of the network as the same device from an addressing perspective, we often need to plan our addressing approach to include the concept of virtual IP addresses, addresses that, as their name implies, allow multiple network devices on the same segment to share the same address.

Document your subnetting architecture.   Document your routing plan, and show how it minimizes traffic on any high-impact subnet segment to only that required (that is, maximum disablement). Define a routing plan in terms of (1) routes available on a given network and (2) those shared between network segments, sometimes referred to as *injected* or *advertised* routes. The key to security through subnetting and disablement is to share only those routes that you absolutely must. Each route you share represents a bridge over which a hacker can travel. If you minimize shared routes, you make it harder for them to get where they want to go.

Security Stack Worksheet for Addressing, Protocol Space, Routing Plan, Filtering, and Disablement

IMPACT ANALYSIS ID	BEFORE PLAN	PERCENT IMPROVEMENT	NEW VALUE

Quality Management worksheet completed for this element/template? (check box) ☐

Physical

Identify opportunities to physically isolate high-impact physical components. This is the ultimate in disablement.

_____
_____
_____

Examine the physical arrangement of systems, and define a plan to prevent unintended interconnection.

_____
_____
_____
_____

Network

Write a full addressing plan including dynamic/static, translation, protocol numbers, subnetting, disablement, anti-spoofing, and all filters.

_____
_____
_____

Develop your routing plan and show how it minimizes traffic over any high-impact segment to only that which is required.

_____
_____
_____

Based on your addressing and routing plan, develop a tight set of assumptions for your IDS/VA around what is allowable over any network segment.

_____
_____
_____

Define how you use any tunneling protocols, and consider their risks as well.

_____
_____
_____

Describe mechanisms put into place to protect systems delivering dynamic addresses.

_____
_____
_____

List systems assigned static IP addresses, and explain why.

_____
_____
_____
_____

Worksheet 4.1 Security Stack Worksheet for Addressing, Protocol Space, Routing Plan, Filtering, and Disablement.

Describe the use of one-way and two-way NAT and security objectives for each.

_____
_____
_____

List all address and protocol filters used to achieve your plan per network segment.

_____
_____
_____

Application

Write a policy stating that disallowed protocols should be disabled within the application and operating system.

_____
_____
_____

List unneeded applications that implement unapproved protocols. Uninstall these applications from desktop and server computers.

_____
_____
_____

Assess how applications may be affected by your addressing and filtering architecture.

_____
_____
_____

Purely from a network routing standpoint, ensure that, to the extent that is practical, applications are reachable only by those that need to access them. This may involve the use of source IP address filtering, for example.

_____
_____
_____

Operating System

Write a plan to disable/uninstall disallowed protocols and services that use them within the operating system.

_____
_____
_____

Implement tools at the operating system level that enhance address logging. Specify the tools you use—why and how.

_____
_____
_____

Write a plan for implementing address and protocol number filtering specifically within the operating system.

_____
_____
_____

Heavily restrict administrator access to high-impact servers through source address filtering and routing.

_____
_____
_____

Worksheet 4.1   Security Stack Worksheet for Addressing, Protocol Space, Routing Plan, Filtering, and Disablement. _(continued)_

Define exactly which protocols (protocol numbers) are allowed on each network segment.   The best way to understand this is by way of example. If, say, you have no need for telnet on a given network segment, then your routers and firewalls should work together to filter out any packets destined for the telnet port (TCP port 23). It's important to note that it's not the best way to filter by explicitly disabling telnet (or any other protocol) by configuring something to the effect of "deny everything on port 23." That's too much work, simply because there are too many other protocols beyond telnet that you'll want to filter. Instead, first *deny all* packets for *all ports*. Then, *enable* only those ports on a given network segment that you need. For example, if you have a network segment dedicated to http and https (http with SSL) Web traffic only, then you can configure a filter stating to the effect, "Deny everything except for TCP ports 80 (http) and 443 (https)." In this way, port 23, and the thousands of other ports and protocols that you want nothing to do with, are all inherently disabled with little or no work on your part.

Define the precise disablement assumptions that your IDS and vulnerability analysis systems can make; establish alarm events should they be violated.   Following our previous example, we can configure our IDS to issue an alarm if, for some reason, the telnet protocol does somehow appear on the Web network segment, a segment otherwise intended to carry only http and https packets.Why do we configure such an IDS alarm after we have already filtered out telnet? Simply because if those filters or the devices implementing them fail in some unexpected way or are compromised, we want to detect that. The compromise could be as simple as a hacker who has physically entered your building and attached his or her laptop to your network. Whatever the cause, we want the IDS system to detect such things—that's why we have it.

Describe how network address spoof protection is implemented on each segment and within the overall network.   Hackers try to pretend they are a trusted network device by inserting one of your trusted network addresses into their data packets. For example, suppose you have a trusted address in your network, which we'll call "A," and this address should be used only by network devices located safely *behind* your firewall (within your internal network). A hacker intent on spoofing will effectively state "I am A" when sending packets to your firewall. This is called *address spoofing*. Anti-spoof technology can be implemented in your firewall in an effort to prevent a hacker from pulling this off. Your firewall, when so configured, carefully associates the physical network interface from which packets are received with the addresses expected from that interface. For example, if a hacker presents an internal (behind the firewall) packet addressed as "A" but does so while sending the packet through the open Internet physical network interface *in front* of your firewall, *not* from behind it, the firewall will refuse the packet.

Describe which tunneling protocols are overtly implemented (as in SSL/TLS, IPSec, SSH, SOCKS).   As discussed in Chapter 3, these protocols allow for encrypted tunnels to be established between two network devices. Protocols such as IPSec allow, through the security association feature, the ability to effectively break the encryption at your firewall so that you can see what's being transmitted in and out of your organization. Protocols such as SSL/TLS are designed to be implemented end-to-end between a client and server and, as such, are often punched right through firewalls, meaning that their encrypted tunnels go straight through the firewall. In such a configuration, it's impossible to inspect what's inside the tunnel because it goes through the firewall fully encrypted. There are alternatives to this approach, such as implementing an SSL proxy server, as discussed in Chapter 3; however, those approaches have their own individual pros and cons. The tunneling you allow in your network influences the security element we are now focusing on, simply because, if you do punch tunnels straight through your firewall, it's difficult for you to know what, if anything, is being carried inside of them; therefore, it becomes more difficult to disable, filter, and manage content (as discussed later under the Content and Executable Management security element).

Clearly, there is no simple solution to all of this. I suggest that you perform a paper vulnerability analysis to determine how your infrastructure can be defeated via encrypted tunneling. Remember that, although these tunneling protocols operate over only one TCP or UDP port, a hacker's malicious software that has infected an employee's laptop, for example, can use a tunneling protocol to move anything the hacker would like in and out of your organization. Many people make the mistake of assuming that a protocol such as SSL can carry only Web traffic and that, if a hacker leverages such a protocol, all he or she can do is send Web information back and forth. This is not correct. A hacker's malicious software can send anything the hacker wants through a tunnel; if that tunnel is encrypted, you'll have no idea what is being sent. About the only telltale sign you may have is that, for the case of SSL, you'll see large increases of SSL traffic in your network utilization reports (the importance of studying such reports is discussed in the IDS/VA security element later in this chapter), which may tip you off to the fact that a hacker may be moving large amounts of information, such as intellectual property, through your firewall. Develop a plan to help detect and prevent these attacks.

Address how your plan may affect other security elements.   To understand this guideline, consider how addressing may affect another security element, in this case, authentication. Recall from Chapter 3 the discussion about the Kerberos protocol in regard to authentication. Kerberos, to reiterate, is used by Windows 2000 and beyond, as well as by many implementations of UNIX and Linux, and it employs a sophisticated mechanism to manage authentication credentials. It does not simply send your username and password in the clear, as so many other mechanisms do. Instead, Kerberos manages the authentication process by producing something called a *ticket*. A Kerberos ticket is essentially a new, temporary version of your username and password. Tickets last short periods of time and are tied, through various mechanisms, to you and your workstation in order to prevent hackers from just sniffing one of them and replaying it whenever they want to impersonate you. (By the way, it's this reliance on time that makes Kerberos so sensitive to hacked time, another reason for the Secure Time security element discussed later in this chapter.) One of the things a Kerberos ticket contains is the IP address of the computer from which you are authenticating.

For example, that might be the address of your desktop computer at work. Now let's consider the problem as it relates to addressing. If someone installs network address translation (NAT) between your desktop computer and your organization's Kerberos servers, then your address, from the perspective of the Kerberos server, will be *different* from the address in the ticket, simply because your address has been changed (translated) by the NAT server that stands between your desktop computer and the Kerberos server. It's these types of subtle details that need to be considered in your planning process. Obviously, this book can't present all of them because, as you would expect, there are many such nuances. The book can point you in the right direction, though; hence, this guideline.

APPLICATION

List, assess, disable, uninstall, design.   This means the following:

- *List* all protocols approved for use within the organization.
- *Disable* all those not approved for use within applications, if possible. Filter on these protocol numbers, as well as on desktop computers, servers, and within the network itself.
- *Assess* how your applications may be affected by your plan. For example, some applications may behave strangely depending on your NAT configuration.
- *Uninstall* applications that implement unapproved protocols.

- *Design* your plan so that applications are reachable only by those who need them. This can be achieved through a combination of route planning and filtering.

OPERATING SYSTEM

Disable, implement, uninstall, restrict, recompile. This means the following:

- *Disable or uninstall* unneeded operating system services and associated protocols.
- *Implement* tools such as tcpwrapper (UNIX/Linux) to improve address logging and control.
- *Disable* routing protocols within the operating system if not needed. Use static addressing in servers if possible.
- *Restrict* access to preconfigured address ranges for specific servers by installing address filters if possible. Heavily restrict administrator access to the machine, allowing only it through designated administrative protocol ports and to and from specific static IP addresses.
- *Uninstall* services tied to protocols that are to be disabled and *recompile* the kernel for compiled operating systems such as UNIX/Linux-based kernels.

Life-Cycle Management

Use Worksheet 4.2 here.

TECHNOLOGY SELECTION

Make use of tools. Router vendors offer tools to help you manage your address space, filtering, and routing plan. Also check out the tools and standards available from vendors to assist in specifying and documenting firewall rules. Identify operating system-based tools that may assist in your addressing, protocol space, routing plan, filtering, and disablement plan. These include tools for locking down systems, configuring operating system kernels, and building configuration files in an automated, easier-to-use fashion.

Identify the extensibility of your firewall platform. You can do this by identifying the open programmatic interfaces available to third parties for expanding functionality.

Consider how other technologies relate to this security element. This applies when you select technologies for diversity, redundancy, and isolation (DRI); performance; and scalability-related architectures such as firewall redundancy and load sharing.

Life-Cycle Management Worksheet for Addressing, Protocol Space, Routing Plan, Filtering, and Disablement

IMPACT ANALYSIS ID	BEFORE PLAN	PERCENT IMPROVEMENT	NEW VALUE

Quality Management worksheet completed for this element/template? (check box) ☐

Technology Selection

Select firewall, proxy, cache, load sharing, and application server technology to meet your overall plan.

_____

_____

_____

Identify tools that specifically help you manage and lock down your address and filtering plans.

_____

_____

_____

Carefully assess the manageability, performance, and scalability of filtering technology. These are the key drivers.

_____

_____

_____

Implementation

A comprehensive addressing and filtering plan is tedious. Identify policies, procedures, and tools that make it practical.

_____

_____

_____

Write a plan to implement backup filters.

_____

_____

_____

Carefully configure your IDS/VA to rely on assumptions driven from your plan. Tell your IDS/VA what does/does not belong.

_____

_____

_____

Worksheet 4.2 Life-Cycle Management Worksheet for Addressing, Protocol Space, Routing Plan, Filtering, and Disablement.

Operations

Establish training so that the operations group understands why you have such a comprehensive addressing plan.

_____

_____

_____

Develop strict policies and procedures so that the plan is not undermined, things are not "poked through" meaning that, for example, an operations staff member can't simply open up a series of TCP or UDP ports on the firewall and disable router filters without following a procedure of review and approval.

_____

_____

_____

Write an escalation procedure so that changes to your plan can be requested quickly by end users, such as a request to support a particular new application requiring a protocol you have previously disabled (this is also related to the Content and Executable Management security element).

_____

_____

_____

Incident Response

Provide the incident team with full and immediate access to all aspects of your plan.

_____

_____

_____

Provide tools and information so that the team can immediately know if something is present that shouldn't be.

_____

_____

_____

Give the team authority to quickly further restrict your plan (e.g., filters, addresses) in order to respond to an incident.

_____

_____

_____

Worksheet 4.2 Life-Cycle Management Worksheet for Addressing, Protocol Space, Routing Plan, Filtering, and Disablement. *(continued)*

IMPLEMENTATION

Implement backup filters.   To help safeguard against an error or compromise in one area of the network, implement backup filters. For example, just because you may have filtered FTP at the firewall doesn't mean you shouldn't disable it where it isn't allowed within the architecture, to include router-level filters (or simply the inverse: only allowing what you approve of, which may exclude FTP).

Document.   Documentation is the rule of thumb for any tedious task. Documentation for this security element includes all addressing, routing, protocol space, filtering, and disablement plans, policies, and procedures. The documentation should be configuration-managed (see the Configuration Management security element, next).

OPERATIONS

Prevent breakage by clearly defining policies and procedures.   Operations groups require very well-defined policies and procedures so that they do not enable something they shouldn't. The classic scenario occurs when someone reports to the operations group that something doesn't work due to some aspect of this security element's implementation, such as protocol filtering.

Isolate problems.   If an application is "broken" because, for example, a filter is blocking one of its TCP ports or because it doesn't work with NAT, then the operations staff should be prepared to identify the cause quickly. This requires that they really understand the security plan and how it works. The ability to identify this kind of problem quickly will help calm people down and save endless wasted hours of troubleshooting a problem that doesn't exist. The operations staff then punches a hole the size of a truck straight through the firewall. I've seen this happen many times, and in several cases, the firewall was rendered entirely ineffective as a result, and Internet traffic flowed directly into the organization without any control or safeguards due to the hole.

Train to understand motivations.   Train operations staff to understand the motivation of this security element, especially as it relates to backup filtering and protection within the architecture.

INCIDENT RESPONSE

Give the incident response team full and immediate access to all logs, tools, plans, and documentation relating to this security element.   The team should be able to identify if anything is out of place quickly, be it an address, protocol, or route. To do this, the team needs quick and easy access to logs, intrusion-detection system events, addressing plans, routing plans, filtering plans, protocol plans (as in which protocols are allowed on which segment), a clear idea of what has been disabled, and access to actual system configurations as needed, such as access to router and firewall configuration files (for more on this last item, see the Configuration Management security element discussed later in this chapter).

Business

Use Worksheet 4.3 here.

BUSINESSPEOPLE: EMPLOYEES

Help employees to understand and anticipate any potential effect from the plan. Let them request changes. Employees rarely understand the need for disablement, and they regard it as an inconvenience. To increase their comfort level, your plan needs to do several things well:

- Enable what they truly need as seamlessly as possible.
- Explain why disablement improves security.
- Instruct them how to anticipate any problems they may have.
- Provide a rapid and well-known resolution path (to include operations and staff) where they can request changes to your plan to meet organizational needs and where their requests will be processed intelligently and quickly.

BUSINESSPEOPLE: CUSTOMERS

Be prepared to address customer dissatisfaction. Enable customers to interact with you in some way should your plan disable an activity they formally enjoyed. For example, you might disable a type of online chat capability, which some customers may object to if, for example, they became accustomed to using chat to communicate with your customer support department.

BUSINESSPEOPLE: OWNERS

Clear up confusion. Owners may resist the cost of implementing this security element versus the convenience of just letting everything run free. See Security Selling, later in this chapter, for more on this.

BUSINESSPEOPLE: SUPPLIERS

Address interoperability with supplier systems. Today, it's possible that your organization has a business-to-business network connection, either through the Internet or directly with your partners and suppliers. You should take care not to break such connections with your plan but, instead, work to accommodate business-to-business commerce to the extent possible.

BUSINESSPEOPLE: PARTNERS

See the previous text for Suppliers.

Business Worksheet for Addressing, Protocol Space, Routing Plan, Filtering, and Disablement

IMPACT ANALYSIS ID	BEFORE PLAN	PERCENT IMPROVEMENT	NEW VALUE

Quality Management worksheet completed for this element/template? (check box) ☐

Employees

Educate employees on why disablement and restriction exists—for their security and that of the organization.

_____

_____

_____

Prepare your operations group for escalations from employees and others relating to any restrictions.

_____

_____

_____

Help employees anticipate the types of problems brought on by disablement.

_____

_____

_____

Provide employees with a rapid process for requesting any changes in your plan for things they may need to do.

_____

_____

_____

Customers

Identify any areas where your plan may impact your customers and provide a means to satisfy customer needs.

_____

_____

_____

Owners

Owners will want to understand why having less (disablement) costs more (money). See the Security Sell worksheet.

_____

_____

_____

Worksheet 4.3 Business Worksheet for Addressing, Protocol Space, Routing Plan, Filtering, and Disablement.

Suppliers and Partners

Determine if your plan impedes interoperability with suppliers and partners. Address this as part of your plan.

_____
_____
_____

Information

Consider how information is distributed in your organization. Explain how this may interfere with your plan to secure it.

_____
_____
_____

Infrastructure

Describe how you have placed infrastructure components onto their own preplanned, highly disabled network segments.

_____
_____

Describe your infrastructure "funneling" disablement architecture.

_____
_____
_____

Worksheet 4.3 Business Worksheet for Addressing, Protocol Space, Routing Plan, Filtering, and Disablement. *(continued)*

BUSINESS: INFORMATION

Don't put all information on every network segment.   If all your information, leveraged by every protocol, is located on the same network segment, it's impossible to implement a full filtering and disablement strategy. As discussed in Chapter 2, you need to partition information and infrastructure in the most granular manner possible to maximize your ability to filter and disable on that segment. Doing this requires you to assign information and infrastructure to particular network segments.

BUSINESS: INFRASTRUCTURE

Make your infrastructure design like a funnel.   This means that you widen the opening as you move closer to the public Internet (or any public network) and narrow it as you get closer to network segments dedicated to specific information and infrastructure components. Place infrastructure components on their own preplanned network segments.

Isolate the most highly exposed components, such as the first firewalls in your organization, from firewalls and filtering mechanisms deeper within your network. Consider the use of a demilitarized zone (DMZ) infrastructure design. A DMZ is an additional "safety zone" that you can place between your private network and the public Internet. One popular example of a DMZ configuration makes use of at least two firewalls. The first firewall connects the public Internet to your DMZ safety zone. Within the safety zone you may have moderate or low-impact devices such as Web servers. On the other side of the DMZ safety zone is another firewall connecting the DMZ safety zone to your more critical, higher-impact private network. The firewall connecting to the Internet is usually more liberal, having fewer filters and disabling less than the firewall connecting the DMZ to your private network. The firewall to your private network is much more restrictive—it would be, by analogy, the narrower side of a funnel.

Selling Security

Use Worksheet 4.4 here.

EXECUTIVES

Leveraging your impact analysis, show how impact is reduced; simulate potential attacks that are addressed with your new plan.   Similar to the Content and Executable Management (CEM) security element, this element is not a particularly easy sell as it introduces cost and some level of inconvenience.

Highlight reduced administration costs, perhaps more organizational choice.   Relative to ease of administration, certain features such as NAT allow the organization to move quickly from one ISP to another with minimal administrative impact because your internal addresses are maintained separately from those of your ISP. Point out features such as this that bring added benefit to offset the perception of inconvenience.

MIDDLE MANAGEMENT

Highlight workflow impact.   Provide procedures for having specific needs met such as opening a particular TCP or UDP port to make an application work or to allow certain previously disallowed content; point out any benefits.

Show reduced impact.   Demonstrate how the organization's risk is reduced by demonstrating an incident that can be caused by poor address, protocol, and disablement policies and procedures.

Selling Security Worksheet for Addressing, Protocol Space, Routing Plan, Filtering, and Disablement

IMPACT ANALYSIS ID	BEFORE PLAN	PERCENT IMPROVEMENT	NEW VALUE

Executive

Opponents to your plan may passionately argue that it means less flexibility, less convenience, and more cost.

_____

_____

_____

Simulate a very comprehensive incident that can occur without your plan. Compare it to leaving the door unlocked.

_____

_____

_____

As driven by your impact analysis, show how risk is reduced. Rerun your simulation "with the door locked."

_____

_____

_____

Counter your opponents' arguments—sure, the front door unlocked means we don't need keys, but is that the point?

_____

_____

_____

Middle Management

Train management on the procedure for rapidly requesting changes such as enablement of a new application.

_____

_____

_____

Walk through, step-by-step, impact reduction, and simulate different threats in relation to business processes.

_____

_____

_____

Worksheet 4.4 Selling Security Worksheet for Addressing, Protocol Space, Routing Plan, Filtering, and Disablement. *(continues)*

Clearly identify any business processes affected and provide a troubleshooting process for managers to follow.

_____
_____
_____

Staff

Highlight how your plan protects them and the entire organization. Use the "locked door" analogy.

_____
_____

Be sure staff completely understand how your plan may impact what they can/cannot do and can/cannot access.

_____
_____
_____

Provide staff members with a troubleshooting process and a way to request changes to your plan's disablement policy.

_____
_____
_____

Worksheet 4.4 Selling Security Worksheet for Addressing, Protocol Space, Routing Plan, Filtering, and Disablement. *(continued)*

STAFF

Point out the day-to-day impact. To that end, educate on policies and procedures, and highlight the benefits. Help the staff to understand that not everything can be connected to the network and be expected simply to work. Explain that aspects of the network are controlled and disabled in order to reduce the risk of a security incident and impact to them and their work. Remind them of your organization's Content and Executable Management (CEM) security element policies and procedures, the element dedicated to controlling what software is installed on their computers and connected to the network.

Configuration Management

Summary

Security thrives on best practices, order, and repeatability. I've seen it over and over again: If you throw your systems together in an ad hoc manner and do not keep track of what you've done and what you're going to do, and if you have no means to return to a known state, your odds of being hacked increase exponentially.

Configuration management is about bringing order and repeatability to your security solution, and a configuration-management architecture is about defining those key components that require configuration management in the first place, along with practical methods for carrying it out.

Configuration management is also for managing system configuration files, binary (executable) software, and scripts used in applications and operating systems. These must also be maintained in a secure configuration-management archive so that we can rebuild systems, re-create suspect scenarios, and then knowledgeably patch them as needed, moving to our next tested and staged configuration. Security documentation, including the security plan and work-sheets, should be also be configuration-managed. The quality management worksheet, detailed in Chapter 3, contains certain information that's expected from a configuration-management system (revision, date, author, owner, and so forth).

Tools for Configuration Management

Tools to configuration-manage system files include management tools pro-vided by vendors, such as a router vendor, or off-the-shelf products, such as a source code control system (SCCS). Historically used by software developers for configuration-managing software development efforts, an SCCS is equally applicable to other forms of configuration management. Another outstanding example of such a tool is the Concurrent Versions System (CVS), available for many platforms; it has an easy-to-use user interface, supports multiple users, and includes a Web interface. Even better, it's available under an open-source license agreement. Other excellent commercially supported configuration-management software also exists.

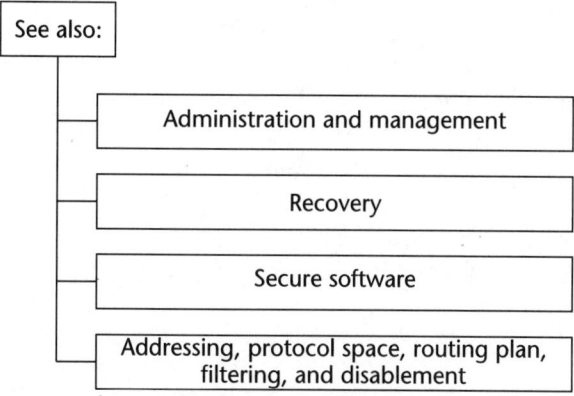

Figure 4.2   Configuration management.

Security Stack

Use Worksheet 4.5 here.

PHYSICAL

Configuration-manage system files relating to all building access control and surveillance systems.   Manage documentation relating to core facilities, including power and all physical network transmission facilities—local, wireless, and wide area network systems. Documentation should track the current state and past configurations of core facilities.

NETWORK

Identify core network components and associated configuration-management requirements.   Router, switch, firewall, proxy server, and network configuration servers (e.g., WINS, DHCP) all require complex configurations, and their executables are regularly updated. Track all this. Too many organizations don't, causing a serious stumbling block to security. For example, an administrator makes whatever changes are needed, maybe keeps a copy on his or her hard drive, then moves on, leaving no history of the previous network device configuration. Imagine how this would impede incident response.

Institute rollback and recovery.   For binary executables, it's important to maintain previously installed versions so that you can choose to roll back to a known configuration should a problem arise, especially if you need to re-create a configuration as part of incident response analysis based on something that might have happened in the past.

APPLICATION

Be prepared to track, re-create, patch, and rebuild.   Like network components, applications also leverage complex configurations, and their binaries are constantly being patched and entirely updated. You need to track these changes and be able to re-create configurations in a manner as just described for network components. The need for application configuration management applies to both server-based applications and desktop applications. Any software you develop in-house has to be carefully configuration-managed so that you can know exactly what vulnerabilities may have existed in any particular deployed revision of your software.

Security Stack Worksheet for
Configuration Management (CM)

IMPACT ANALYSIS ID	BEFORE PLAN	PERCENT IMPROVEMENT	NEW VALUE

Quality Management worksheet completed for this element/template? (check box) ☐

Physical

Develop CM policies and procedures for building access control systems, for example, the files used to manage the company's badging system.

_____

_____

_____

Write a CM plan for all documentation relating to core facilities including building/room power and physical network wiring.

_____

_____

_____

Network

Define how you will implement CM for network-related binary executable (e.g., routers) and configuration files.

_____

_____

_____

Write CM policies and procedures requiring administrators to use the CM system, not bypass it.

_____

_____

_____

Design your CM system to realistically accommodate troubleshooting requirements.

_____

_____

_____

Write a test plan to validate your ability to re-create past configurations using your CM system in response to an incident.

_____

_____

_____

Worksheet 4.5   Security Stack Worksheet for Configuration Management (CM). *(continues)*

Application

Similar to the network, write a CM plan for application binary executables and related system files including configurations.

_____

_____

_____

As with the network, write and implement a test plan to validate your ability to re-create past configurations.

_____

_____

_____

If you develop applications yourself, write a CM plan for your software development source code.

_____

_____

_____

Operating System

Implement a CM plan to precisely track the status of patches, operating system kernel revisions, and system files.

_____

_____

_____

Do not confuse a tape backup (or some other backup) with CM. Establish complete CM functions instead.

_____

_____

_____

Worksheet 4.5   Security Stack Worksheet for Configuration Management (CM). *(continued)*

OPERATING SYSTEM

Track the precise status of patches, kernel builds, and system files as you make changes.   The way operating system configurations are configured, compiled, and installed is core to your security plan. Some administrators aren't used to tracking at this level of precision. Many simply make changes on the fly, usually remember to save them locally, and maybe back up the whole system at some point remotely; from there, they often forget about it.

Don't confuse tape backups with configuration management.   Tape backups are not what configuration management is all about. You have to be able to go to a central configuration-management server and pull off, quickly and easily, the precise information you need about a past configuration. Using tape backups for this process is inconvenient and typically impractical. Another approach is to save whole images out to network drives. This still does not bring into play the rigor of "check-in/check-out" that a configuration-management system offers, nor does it offer nearly as convenient reporting or analysis of changes made.

Life-Cycle Management

Use Worksheet 4.6 here.

TECHNOLOGY SELECTION

Choose between single and mixed-vendor configuration-management software. Often, configuration-management tools are vendor- and product-specific, as, for example, a tool for managing configuration files for routers. You can pull together a perfectly reasonable configuration-management architecture by using individual point solutions; however, if you have a mixed-vendor environment, sometimes this becomes more difficult, as in a scenario where you have routers from different vendors. There is no single "holy grail" approach for threading together your configuration-management plan from individual components. Some organizations have had success standardizing on a single tool originally designed for managing large software development efforts—for example, CVS, as mentioned earlier. Many software products are available today for this, some free and some commercially available. Many configuration-management systems such as CVS offer advanced collaborative capabilities, allowing multiple administrators to configuration-manage systems across your organization together. These systems can be used for all types of files—text configuration, binaries, documentation—pretty much anything.

IMPLEMENTATION

Make it practical and easy to use. When implementing a configuration-management system, it has to be practical for those who will use it. In my experience, the single biggest mistake made in configuration-management architectures is to implement a system that does not allow operators and administrators to do the one thing that they do all the time and rely on: make the "hot fix," a quick change in a system during the troubleshooting process in real time, often made straight to the memory of the device. While it's true that our testing and staging systems are in place for experimentation, often administrators must test a change on a live system. Therefore, administrators have to be able to take configurations they have finally settled on in a given live, potentially hot-fixed device, such as a router, and then check that new configuration in to the configuration-management system.

Life-Cycle Management Worksheet for Configuration Management (CM)

IMPACT ANALYSIS ID	BEFORE PLAN	PERCENT IMPROVEMENT	NEW VALUE

Quality Management worksheet completed for this element/template? (check box) ☐

Technology Selection

Identify vendor-neutral and vendor-specific CM solutions. Address the pros/cons of each.

_____

_____

_____

If your CM system automatically downloads files to components (e.g., routers), assess security of download process.

_____

_____

_____

Assess the overall security of your CM software using the security planning approach provided in this book. For example, assess its authentication and encryption mechanisms, addressing, and so forth.

_____

_____

_____

Evaluate CM technology ease of use. Assess CM system scalability, performance, and multiuser capabilities.

_____

_____

_____

Assess technology in relation to how easily a CM diversity, redundancy, and isolation plan can be introduced and how well CM servers can be protected.

_____

_____

_____

Implementation

Plan so that troubleshooting and hot fixes can be accommodated while CM integrity as a whole is maintained.

_____

_____

_____

Worksheet 4.6   Life-Cycle Management Worksheet for Configuration Management (CM).

When deploying CM servers, you need a solid security implementation plan. You don't want CM systems compromised.

_____

_____

_____

Operations

Write a CM training plan for operations staff. Help them understand its importance.

_____

_____

_____

Write CM policies and procedures for operations staff. They need to be practical and easy-to-follow to minimize resistance.

_____

_____

_____

Incident Response

The incident response team should have a procedure to request test and re-creation of past system configurations using CM.

_____

_____

_____

Worksheet 4.6   Life-Cycle Management Worksheet for Configuration Management (CM). *(continued)*

OPERATIONS

Make sure people use it.   The most difficult aspect of configuration management is making sure people use it. Operations groups are notorious for bypassing configuration-management systems. If the system is implemented so that it's practical within the context of their day-to-day tasks, and if appropriate policies and procedures are in place, then they will use it.

INCIDENT RESPONSE

Be able to re-create something on the drop of a dime.   Incident response demands the ability to re-create system configurations from any point in the past in order to assess vulnerabilities and possible hacker activities at that point in time.

Business

Use Worksheet 4.7 here.

BUSINESSPEOPLE: EMPLOYEES

Avoid a rebellion.   Employees rebel against configuration management in many ways because it often slows things down and adds complexity. People want "quick fixes" and an easy experience when trying to get something done. Maintaining order and method when someone just wants to get something "finished" or "working" is a classic human struggle. To the degree your configuration-management system is easy to use and transparent, it will have greater success.

BUSINESSPEOPLE: CUSTOMERS

Educate customers about overhead.   Customers want it now, fast, and easy. They will, however, object if you appear to be "out of control" with regard to maintaining order in your product or service delivery. The feeling of lack of control is often the result of the absence of configuration management. Therefore, it's important to educate customers that any overhead caused by configuration management is part of providing them a solid, reliable, high-quality experience.

BUSINESSPEOPLE: OWNERS

Stress the importance of predictability and the avoidance of catastrophic loss.   Owners have a vested interest in maintaining predictable performance of their business. Absence of a solid configuration-management plan puts them at great risk in this regard. For example, companies with poor configuration management may suffer outages, in my experience, two to four times longer than those that do it well, not to mention significantly higher levels of stress, general chaos, and wasted resources.

BUSINESSPEOPLE: SUPPLIERS

Evaluate suppliers of infrastructure components on the quality of the configuration-management tools they provide.   Those with which you electronically interact should keep systems to known revisions, to facilitate interoperability and to make you aware of any vulnerabilities that may arise as a result of your interconnection with them.

Business Worksheet for Configuration Management (CM)

IMPACT ANALYSIS ID	BEFORE PLAN	PERCENT IMPROVEMENT	NEW VALUE

Quality Management worksheet completed for this element/template? (check box) ☐

Employees

Prepare for administrator rebellion when you introduce CM. Make the system as easy to use and transparent as possible.

_____

_____

_____

Customers

To the degree that CM introduces a "rigor" that impacts customer response time, customer needs should be addressed.

_____

_____

Help customers who are affected by CM to understand its importance.

_____

_____

Explain why you may make noncritical changes only at specified times. Careful CM procedures sometimes require this.

_____

_____

Owners

List owner expectations in terms of predictability in the incident recovery process. CM facilitates predictable recovery.

_____

_____

Suppliers and Partners

Work to identify high-impact suppliers/partners with whom you rely on configuration management. For example, if you are engaged in a business-to-business network, there may be a need for all businesses to configuration-manage security-related information.

Worksheet 4.7 Business Worksheet for Configuration Management (CM). *(continues)*

Drive suppliers/partners to implement needed CM relating to your products/services or search for those that do.

Information

Identify high-impact information elements crucial to your organization's operation that demand underlying CM support.

Infrastructure

Your strategy is largely and simply driven by the CM needs of high-impact infrastructure components. List them.

Worksheet 4.7   Business Worksheet for Configuration Management (CM). *(continued)*

BUSINESSPEOPLE: PARTNERS

Facilitate interoperability and knowledge of potential vulnerabilities arising out of connections with partners.   Configuration-management coordination with partners is only an issue if you are engaged in any effort with them that requires interoperability of systems, such as in a business-to-business network of some kind. In such a case, revision management is important to them.

BUSINESS: INFORMATION

Determine each high-impact configuration file, executable, script, operating system file, system file, and database that, based on your impact analysis, would most benefit from configuration management.   Examples of ideal information elements to manage include router configuration files, operating system configuration files, router software releases, locked-down Linux kernel configurations, and application configuration files. Look at information elements associated with each layer of your security stack; this may be a helpful way to organize your search for high-impact configuration-management items.

BUSINESS: INFRASTRUCTURE

Identify configuration-management needs by listing each core infrastructure component and relating it to your impact analysis.   Those components servicing high-impact areas should be your first priority for configuration management. The logical choices are typically routers, firewalls, proxy servers, and application servers supporting high-impact activities.

Selling Security

Use Worksheet 4.8 here.

EXECUTIVES

Simulate an attack or outage of system components on a high-impact system by showing what would happen if the organization lost track of system configuration files, binaries, and so forth.   Show how the company can quickly land in a state of chaos, not knowing what has happened nor knowing exactly how to restore systems to their former state. Do this in conjunction with a presentation of configuration-management options and costs as part of your impact analysis. This should help make a tough sell easier. Note: If you can't easily perform this simulation, you might not yet fully grasp the value of configuration management. If you can, you'll do a much better job at selling this to executive management.

Meet opponents head-on.   Opponents to configuration management will argue that it's inefficient, unnecessary, and thus a low priority. In some cases, those who argue against it enjoy the kind of control they are able to maintain and don't like giving it up. One scenario you can simulate is the case where one employee leaves or has an unfortunate accident: Without configuration management, the organization has a more difficult time knowing where its configurations currently are or are going. If an outage or incident occurs while the organization tries to catch up, it can result in a catastrophic event for the organization. Demonstrate how a methodical and well-organized group performs more efficiently when there is order and repeatability.

MIDDLE MANAGEMENT

Emphasize short-term loss, long-term gain.   Middle management may rebel against configuration management because it can add time to their schedules up front. Though it saves time in the long run, quantifying this is difficult; if your middle management is not particularly methodical, they may have difficulty with this argument. Middle managers need to understand, realistically, the impact of ongoing configuration management on their activities. Show how it will work as part of their existing workflow processes, and work with them to introduce it in a gentle but effective manner. That is, you don't need to configuration-manage everything instantly. You can phase it in.

STAFF

Leverage the strengths of individuals.   Employees who must work with the configuration-management plan are split between two camps: the disorganized and the organized, the shoot-from-the-hip and the methodical. Staff members tend to be even more vocal about and resistive to these mechanisms when they don't have a methodical bent. Being forced to follow a process such as configuration management can cause morale problems. The solution is to leverage the strengths of individuals. If some of your staff members are, for example, extremely talented troubleshooters, then perhaps you can focus them there and let someone more methodical support them by taking over some part of the configuration-management responsibility. The art of selling configuration management requires dealing with the range of personalities and strengths and weaknesses within your organization and managing people accordingly. If you go about it in this way, the selling effort will be easier, resistance will be lowered, and your security plan will be greatly improved.

Content and Executable Management (CEM)

Summary

Content and Executable Management (CEM) is the practice of controlling executable programs and network-based content within your organization in accordance with your organization's policies and procedures. It also means controlling which applications staff members are approved to use in the organization and install on their computers. CEM includes technology, policies, and procedures for Web page filtering (so-called acceptable browsing), control and filtering of executable content and email attachments delivered over the network, and control and filtering of any file formats containing something that may automatically execute, such as a word processor file (e.g., Microsoft Word) with macro programming capability. Technology used to perform CEM includes firewalls, proxy servers, application servers, desktop virus and content scanners, desktop configuration-management tools, network-based virus scanning, code signing, and digital signatures.

Selling Security Worksheet for Configuration Management (CM)

IMPACT ANALYSIS ID	BEFORE PLAN	PERCENT IMPROVEMENT	NEW VALUE

Executive

Demonstrate, by example, how inconsistent and poor recovery from a hacker attack severely threatens the organization.

_____
_____
_____

Don't try to sell this as something good simply because order and organization are good. They may not "get" your point. Demonstrate business value.

_____
_____
_____

Show how solid CM means smoother and more predictable recovery from a range of high-impact attacks and failures.

_____
_____
_____

Be prepared to defend against CM opponents who accuse it of being unnecessary overhead. These are nonplanners.

_____
_____
_____

Middle Management

Walk through a very specific realistic scenario that shows how a lack of CM causes confusion.

_____
_____
_____

Present the overhead and workflow restrictions CM may impose. Work with management to address them together.

_____
_____
_____

Worksheet 4.8 Selling Security Worksheet for Configuration Management (CM). *(continues)*

Develop a phased CM implementation plan if needed to accommodate any CM workflow impact.

_____

_____

_____

Staff

When selling CM to affected staff members, be specifically prepared to pitch it to the less organized people.

_____

_____

Talented staff members may have considerable control. CM can reduce control of an individual. Address this in the sell.

_____

_____

_____

Specifically address the range of staff personalities affected by CM when selling it. Sell CM as a necessary compromise.

_____

_____

_____

While some technical staff may be cynical, work to show scenarios wherein a lack of CM has, or will, severely impact you.

_____

_____

_____

Worksheet 4.8   Selling Security Worksheet for Configuration Management (CM). *(continued)*

The flow of content in your organization includes floppy disks and laptops used at home and loaded with unauthorized content, either manually or from the open Internet. These same laptops, brought back into your organization and potentially infected with network-borne viruses, represent significant threats to your security. Because this is so difficult to control, aside from policies and procedures, we need to implement an overall security architecture that is robust to counteract these potential threats from within. If content is not managed, and, for example, a network-borne virus is brought in on a laptop that records and acts on commonly transmitted passwords in the clear, your security will be at risk in a major way. In my experience, people make two very popular, but dangerously incorrect, assumptions about their vulnerability to these kinds of attacks:

- Desktop- and network-based virus scanners will always detect network-borne viruses such as these. Why worry about them?

- Even if a network-borne virus does make its way onto a computer and onto our internal network, it won't matter because our firewall is locked so tight, the worst that virus can do is surf the Web. So why worry?

Let's address these one at a time. Relative to the first assumption, it's absolutely impossible for anti-virus software to keep up with every single virus on the loose. It is inherently an unscalable problem simply because virus scanners rely on known signatures (typically a hash, the same technology described in Chapter 1) to detect viruses. In fact, I can write one now, email it to you, and be quite confident your virus scanner won't catch it. But I'm not your concern; your concern is a hacker targeting you. Because all a hacker needs to do is to slightly modify a readily available virus in order to get past your scanners, he or she doesn't even need to put that much effort into the attack. Virus scanning is still absolutely invaluable, of course, but it cannot be your only defense.

Relative to the second assumption, recall the previous discussion about encryption, addressing, and tunneling, specifically, the point that a hacker can tunnel his or her way through just about anything. Let's suppose, for argument's sake, that you have your firewall locked so tight that you let Web browsers through it only on port 80. Further suppose that you have implemented a proxy server so that all Web browsers must first go through your proxy server to get to the Internet. In such a case, it still doesn't matter because a hacker can get through, simply because a network-borne virus that controls a machine connected to your network (such as a laptop) can look just like a Web browser to your proxy server. The virus can then surf to the hacker's Web site and begin posting interesting information learned by sniffing your LAN. And this is just one approach. Another would be for the virus to work its way through your infrastructure in some other way to compromise it.

While it's true that additional measures could be taken to help prevent any of this from happening (hence this book), generally speaking, today's distributed computing architectures are, themselves, no match for the ingenuity of a hacker. Therefore, you must put solid policies and procedures into place to stop potentially dangerous content, such as a network-borne virus, before it makes it onto your network. It's not just a technology problem. (Note that, in Chapter 6, which looks into the future of hacking and security, I comment about the nonrobust, inherently nonsecure nature of our current technology.)

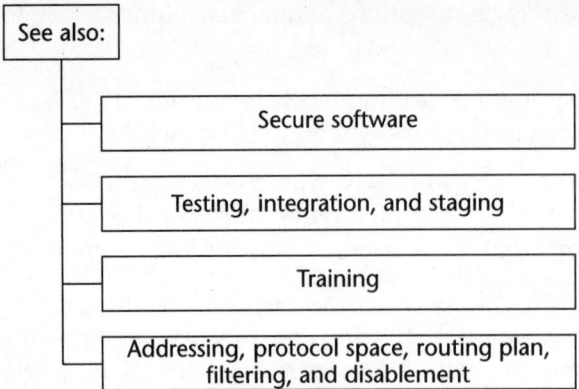

Figure 4.3   Content and executable management.

Security Stack

Use Worksheet 4.9 here.

PHYSICAL

Manage what comes through the doors.   Start by physically managing what comes in and goes out the doors of your organization in the form of laptops or any devices with storage capability and network access. Implement strong policies and procedures for their use. Develop a robust security plan that can withstand compromises to your content-management plan.

NETWORK

Understand interrelationships.   Most organizations today understand that their firewalls, proxy servers, desktop and server mail scanners, and application servers are used to control the flow of content between the organization's internal networks and the Internet. The implementation around all of this is frequently done poorly. Part of the reason is that the art of controlling content is complex and requires a combined knowledge of how the network delivers content and the risk of the content itself.

Draw up sufficient planning and documentation for these systems. Your documentation should address the fundamentals of how protocols transport content and how they can be worked around to defeat what you are trying to do, such as the act of using http (port 80) to send content that would otherwise have been disabled (content-managed) had it been sent on its standard port (e.g., unauthorized executable content that routinely operates in its own protocol space but can instead be tunneled through http).

APPLICATION

Stage and test executable content.   When it comes to controlling network-based content, the network and the application are essentially one topic; thus, application content executable management continues from the previous Network discussion, but with a new dimension: the importance of staging and testing as it relates to executable management. Today, some readily downloadable applications on the Internet give every indication of being infected with some kind of network-borne virus (e.g., malicious software, as in a worm or a Trojan horse). One seemingly innocuous application disabled the intrusion-detection software on my desktop computer and marked it for deletion on reboot. In addition to ensuring that people don't bring these kinds of programs in from home, you need to make sure that the organization itself isn't allowing the download and use of these untested, unstaged applications, This means implementing control via technical means (proxies, firewalls, filtering) and instituting policies and procedures.

Test software with a realistic but isolated network and desktop environment.   Note everything that changes on the machine (such as changes to operating system files) before and after the installation. Subtle changes can be dangerous. Look for changes made by the application that simply make no sense. Especially keep an eye out for changes to any operating system files: This is something you don't want. Unfortunately, a virus may not show you everything it can do to your machine right after installation and a bit of testing. Changes, and their damaging effects, may not occur until some later time, catching you off guard. This is just one more reason why desktop intrusion-detection software can be so valuable. Simply testing software and noting nothing unusual after installation and testing isn't enough assurance, though it is far better than none at all. But a desktop intrusion-detection program can, if you're lucky, effectively disarm a network-borne virus by both detecting unusual behavior and alerting you while keeping the desktop locked tight.

Enable digital code signing.   Code-signing technologies, including Microsoft ActiveX and signed Java files, allow you to verify the source of software and determine if it has been tampered with. Consider how you might put code signing to work in your security plan. For example, if your organization must allow ActiveX objects to executive within your browsers, perhaps you should require that such objects be digitally signed by a trusted source using Microsoft Authenticode.

Security Stack Worksheet for Content and Executable Management

IMPACT ANALYSIS ID	BEFORE PLAN	PERCENT IMPROVEMENT	NEW VALUE

Quality Management worksheet completed for this element/template? (check box) ☐

Physical

Write policies and procedures for the secure handling of physical media, and include discussion of the risks.

_____

_____

_____

Employees can become carriers of viruses, trojan horses, and worms. They do this by bringing their infected laptops from home and connecting them to the corporate network. Make them aware of this risk. Put policies in place to manage what employees put on their laptops, and install desktop virus scanners and intrusion-detection software.

_____

_____

Warn staff that their laptops can become infected with network-borne viruses from software loaded at home. Tell them that a virus scanner can't catch everything, and train them on your content policies and procedures.

_____

_____

_____

Network

Develop a comprehensive integrated plan coordinating your desktop and server-based firewall, proxy server, virus scanner, IDS/VA, and application server systems to meet your CEM objectives. That is, think about how these systems work together to implement your plan.

_____

_____

Carefully document your CEM plan. Define how the systems are administered to achieve your total CEM goals.

_____

_____

_____

Worksheet 4.9 Security Stack Worksheet for Content and Executable Management.

In your documentation, address what protocols may transmit restricted content, which is usually many more than we think.

_____

_____

_____

Application

Develop strict policies and procedures for what software can and cannot be installed on any network-attached computer (see earlier physical-layer discussion; the same applies for stationary desktop computers maintained within corporate offices).

_____

_____

_____

Establish a rapid software approval process. Formally test and investigate software from less identifiable sources as needed.

_____

_____

_____

If you choose to enforce code signing, train employees to understand software-generated messages issued when installing signed code or when an unsigned code installation attempt is made, such as over the Web.

_____

_____

_____

Operating System

Identify all opportunities to disable the ability to execute restricted content at the operating system level.

_____

_____

_____

Worksheet 4.9 Security Stack Worksheet for Content and Executable Management. _(continued)_

OPERATING SYSTEM

Disable support at the operating-system level. This is one of the most effective ways to control content. For example, if you do not want to allow your organization to support execution of a certain file type (such as a certain scripting language or form of Web content), disable any kind of automatic execution of that type, or autorecognition of it, within the operating system.

Life-Cycle Management

Use Worksheet 4.10 here.

TECHNOLOGY SELECTION

Choose a well-rounded solution.   Select content-management technologies, such as firewalls and proxy servers, with an eye toward manageability, performance, and scalability.

Test.   Test the technologies to make sure you understand exactly how to achieve the kind of content filtering you are after.

Integrate with intrusion detection and vulnerability analysis.
Intrusion-detection and vulnerability analysis systems can be effective at spotting violations to your content-management policies and procedures.

IMPLEMENTATION

Break only what you intended to break.   With content management, we may actually want to break one form of content, not a whole range of it. In implementation, the most common problem with content management is that many more things break than we expected. Security engineers routinely struggle with this. The problem is that, with the current state of the technology, coordinating content management among firewalls, proxy servers, routers, virus scanners, IDS/VA, and the general Internet is a complex task. Filtering based on addressing, protocol port assignments, content origin, content signatures, and the like combines to produce an array of content-management approaches.

OPERATIONS

Stress the importance of adhering to content-management policies and procedures.   Operations groups are often pressured to violate an organization's content-management policies. They field calls from irate users who can't understand why their important new application can't run (because some aspect of its operation is disabled by the content-management infrastructure), and they want it fixed. The operations folks often "fix it" by undoing the content-management architecture that has been put into place. The managers get what they want, but new doors have been opened for the hacker.

Life-Cycle Management Worksheet for Content and Executable Management

IMPACT ANALYSIS ID	BEFORE PLAN	PERCENT IMPROVEMENT	NEW VALUE

Quality Management worksheet completed for this element/template? (check box) ☐

Technology Selection

Assess the performance and scalability of the content filtering capabilities offered by firewall, virus scanner, desktop intrusion detection, and proxy server products.

_____

_____

_____

If your organization digitally signs software (code signing), choose a highly secured digital token (e.g., smart card) to store your key.

_____

_____

_____

Assess the support, manageability, and scalability of network-based virus scanners.

_____

_____

_____

Your firewall, proxy, application server, IDS/VA components, and virus scanner technology should be managed, over time, to work together to support your CEM plan. Define this in a CEM policy.

_____

_____

_____

Implementation

Write policies and procedures to guide the configuration and operation of all CEM-related components.

_____

_____

_____

Write a CEM test plan to confirm that you have not "broken" a valid application or denied acceptable content.

_____

_____

_____

Worksheet 4.10 Life-Cycle Management Worksheet for Content and Executable Management. *(continues)*

Maintain a policy clearly defining what content is allowable. Make this policy available and known to all affected people.

_____
_____
_____

Operations

Train staff on the content management policy. Train them to recognize and troubleshoot problems typically caused by CEM, such as an application not working or a Web site presented improperly in a Web browser.

_____
_____
_____

If your organization digitally signs software, establish highly secure key-handling policies and procedures.

_____
_____
_____

Develop policies and procedures preventing operations staff from violating CEM in response to user (customer, employee) pressure.

_____
_____
_____

Develop a well-understood process wherein affected people can rapidly request changes to the organizations allowable content policy.

_____
_____
_____

Incident Response

Give the incident response team a mechanism for instant access to all CEM-related documentation.

_____
_____
_____

Be prepared to quickly confirm, by examining logs and intrusion analysis systems, the flow of content at any point in time.

_____
_____
_____

Build a mechanism for the incident team to quickly modify content policy such as filtering new dangerous content.

_____
_____
_____

Worksheet 4.10 Life-Cycle Management Worksheet for Content and Executable Management. _(continued)_

INCIDENT RESPONSE

Know the flow of content: what, when, and where. The incident response team needs solid knowledge of content that has flowed through the organization, or resided in it, at any given point in time. To achieve this, implement a solid content-management architecture and validate it with sufficient logging such that, if unexpected content exists somewhere in the organization, it can be spotted. Ideally, such content shouldn't flow because, between our CEM architecture and our filtering/routing plan architecture, these things, if reaching into the network, shouldn't get too far. In reality, holes develop despite our best efforts and, in the end, we rely on logging and the status of processes running in servers and desktops to know what may have transpired or is transpiring.

Business

Use Worksheet 4.11 here.

BUSINESSPEOPLE: EMPLOYEES

Train employees to understand what they can and can't do, and why; most important, provide them with a rapid, efficient process to request any needed changes to CEM. For employees, CEM is simply one big inconvenience, but it's a necessary one. You can make it easier for them by training them properly and working with them. For example, if users have a new application they need to enable, have in place a streamlined but complete test and staging process, with rapid turnaround, to quickly assess the implication of allowing that new content. Then communicate the results with employees in terms they understand. Another example of a controversial and difficult-to-balance aspect of CEM is deciding which email attachments to filter with your firewall/mail scanner. Employees can get quite irritated when, for example, they are unable to share basic information with colleagues due to something being stripped at the firewall. If this is a necessary evil in your organization, your CEM plan must anticipate these scenarios and provide processes for working through these issues.

BUSINESSPEOPLE: CUSTOMERS

Define and deal with areas of inconvenience. The way you manage content affects customers only to the extent that they are inconvenienced. Define any such potential areas as part of your plan, along with the means for addressing them. As an example of such an inconvenience, I recall troubleshooting a problem with a very large network equipment provider. During the troubleshooting process it became clear that it would be helpful if I could email a copy of a system file to the technical support representative for her to look at. As you might have guessed, the representative informed me that, due to corporate policies, she was unable to accept email attachments. To work around this problem, we needed some other type of mechanism, something as simple as a fax machine. Organizations interacting directly with customers need to anticipate very basic customer inconveniences such as this and work to meet customer needs in some other way.

BUSINESSPEOPLE: OWNERS

Prepare for debates and decision processes when you begin to manage content aggressively.   Owners expect high-impact security risks to be addressed and, therefore, understand the need for CEM. Even nontechnical people can, today, relate to a malicious program that eats their hard drive or invades their network. What they won't understand, however, is if their decision to fund your particular plan affects company operations in some visible way. You need to relate the risk of uncontrolled content to the company's bottom line. The best way to do this is to simulate an attack on your organization and its business, an attack made possible by unmanaged content.

BUSINESSPEOPLE: SUPPLIERS

Assess any business-to-business activities that may be affected by your CEM plan.   For any business-to-business transactions you conduct with suppliers or partners, it's possible that your CEM plan could get in the way. The example provided in the customers' guideline is potentially equally applicable to a partner or supplier relationship—that is, you may need to exchange something with them that the CEM plan may otherwise disable. What you need to do is keep your CEM plan out of the way of business as much as possible and, instead, anticipate any incompatibilities and inconveniences up front and find a way to securely work around them to everyone's satisfaction.

BUSINESSPEOPLE: PARTNERS

See the previous text on Suppliers.

Business Worksheet for Content and Executable Management

IMPACT ANALYSIS ID	BEFORE PLAN	PERCENT IMPROVEMENT	NEW VALUE

Quality Management worksheet completed for this element/template? (check box) ☐

Employees

Develop a training plan explaining the motivation for CEM—how it affects them and how to ask for content policy changes.

_____

_____

_____

Customers

Identify if customers are affected by your CEM plan—for example, if they cannot send certain email attachments to you.

_____

_____

_____

If customers are affected, work to develop a process to meet their needs and your content management requirements.

_____

_____

_____

Owners

Develop a plan to isolate high-impact systems onto their own network segments, and implement tight CEM on those segments.

_____

_____

_____

Anticipate and prepare for any impact your CEM plan may have on sensitive business operations before you implement.

_____

_____

_____

Worksheet 4.11 Business Worksheet for Content and Executable Management. *(continues)*

Suppliers and Partners

Coordinate your CEM plan so that you do not interfere with partner/supplier information exchange or commerce.

_____
_____
_____

Information

Correlate disallowed content with the executables that make use of them. Work to manage both together in your plan.

_____
_____
_____

Infrastructure

Identify all new infrastructure and infrastructure enhancements needed to achieve your CEM plan.

_____
_____
_____

Write a test plan to carefully measure and manage the performance impact of CEM on users.

_____
_____
_____

Worksheet 4.11   Business Worksheet for Content and Executable Management. *(continued)*

BUSINESS: INFORMATION

Define the relationship between executables and information.   Consider the degree to which the executables you manage are required by particular information used in your business. That is, if you disable the executable used to read a certain type of information, you render that information unusable within the organization. Therefore, as you look at your list of key information elements used in your organization, track the executables used to access them and map this into your CEM plan. An excellent example of why it's a good idea to do this is the case of macros embedded in a Microsoft Word document. These macros have, historically, been used by hackers to spread some particularly malicious viruses. Microsoft has worked to control macro execution in later versions of its software but, nonetheless, macros continue to be dangerous if fully enabled. Before you decide to, for example, disallow such macros in your organization, you would be well advised to find out who in your organization may be relying on them for business. If someone is, then you have to deal with both issues: the security of the macros and your colleague's business needs. Such is the life of a security planner: business, life-cycle management, and technology.

BUSINESS: INFRASTRUCTURE

Recognize the considerable infrastructure investment for any real-time management at boundaries with the Internet.   This investment is required because you are inserting a decision process, or an execution environment, directly into the client/server interaction. Performance becomes a consideration, as does your diversity, redundancy, and isolation (DRI) architecture as it relates to CEM. The components you use for CEM must also typically be diverse and redundant, and you must prevent them from being isolated. They are a core part of the infrastructure and everyday path of information.

Selling Security

Use Worksheet 4.12 here.

EXECUTIVES

Be able to answer this question: Why pay for inconvenience?   Without education, executives will see CEM as an inconvenience that costs money. Following your impact analysis, demonstrate the impact of malicious content on the organization's most sensitive assets. Show them how investing in CEM lowers their potential impact. Keep things simple; communicate in terms of impact, cost, then lowered impact.

Show related benefits.   Your CEM systems plan can, in the end, reduce your organization's administrative burden by reducing the number of problems with software compatibility and administration. This is the case because interactions and problems arising between applications can be limited, simply because the entire allowable set of applications resident in your organization is reduced to only those that have been approved. This is an example of a nonsecurity-related benefit that CEM can bring, one that can save the company money.

Selling Security Worksheet for Content and Executable Management

IMPACT ANALYSIS ID	BEFORE PLAN	PERCENT IMPROVEMENT	NEW VALUE

Executive

Provide a real demonstration of how malicious or inappropriate unmanaged content can impact the organization.

_____

_____

_____

Show how your CEM plan reduces impact. Rerun your demonstration showing the positive effect of your CEM plan.

_____

_____

_____

Provide examples of how CEM can reduce cost and streamline operations through simplified software administration.

_____

_____

_____

Middle Management

Identify very specific business processes that are better protected with CEM in place.

_____

_____

_____

Walk through, step-by-step, the benefits, and simulate different content threats in relation to business processes.

_____

_____

_____

Clearly identify any business processes affected by CEM, and provide a troubleshooting process for managers to follow.

_____

_____

_____

Worksheet 4.12 Selling Security Worksheet for Content and Executable Management.

Staff

Highlight how improved CEM protects them and the entire organization. Demonstrate dangerous content.

_____

_____

_____

Be sure staff completely understands how CEM relates to what content they can and cannot access, visit on the Web, or install. Be specific.

_____

_____

_____

Provide staff members with a CEM troubleshooting process and a way to request changes to CEM policy.

_____

_____

_____

Worksheet 4.12   Selling Security Worksheet for Content and Executable Management. *(continued)*

MIDDLE MANAGEMENT

Be prepared to explain how CEM will impact daily workflow processes. For example, CEM may require content to be reformatted or transmitted in some way differently from how it is done today. If approval processes are required to request new content to be allowed within the organization, then middle management will want to fully understand these processes, and they will want to see them streamlined and fast.

Institute clear and simple policies and procedures.   Managers will want to see clear and simple documentation for CEM policies and guidelines, which they can pass on to staff because they will be the first to spin their wheels when something they want to do, or use, is limited by the CEM architecture.

Explain the benefits on their terms.   Sell them on the benefits of any automated software administration capabilities made available by CEM. Help them understand the reduced potential impact on the business processes they manage by providing a process-specific example of how schedules, deliverables, and customers can be affected by disruption from poorly managed content.

STAFF

Be prepared to answer this question: What can I do, what can't I do?
Staff will specifically want to know what they can and cannot do. Document the answers to these questions clearly in CEM policies and procedures. Educate them as to why they can't, for example, install any software they want, download anything they want, email anything they want, or visit any Web site they'd like to. Detail the risks against which you are trying to protect them and the organization.

Point out the risk to their daily routine.   Provide staff with specific examples of how uncontained content can directly, negatively, affect their lives. A good example is showing them the danger of installing an application not authorized by the organization's CEM policies.

Directory Services

Summary

As it relates to security, a directory service can act as a centralized tool for managing your organization's access control, authentication integration, and secure attribute needs. That said, be aware that if you implement a directory service as part of your security architecture, it needs to be heavily protected and must offer high levels of reliability and safe, high-performance accessibility.

The interoperability and standards support of your directory service will dictate the extent to which you can make it work maximally with your entire network application framework. And how well information in your directory service is organized—its so-called schema—will affect the flexibility you have in managing user, role, and group access to information and infrastructure. Relative to staff management, directory servers provide an excellent means to disable a user's access with one simple command to the directory service, as opposed to the myriad individual ones required when identities are managed across disparate systems without a directory service.

Security Stack

Use Worksheet 4.13 here.

PHYSICAL

Set up directory servers to be maximally reachable by those applications that make use of them.   Physical network placement and physical server security are all important because of the high-impact nature of your directory service.

Security Stack Worksheet for Directory Services

IMPACT ANALYSIS ID	BEFORE PLAN	PERCENT IMPROVEMENT	NEW VALUE

Quality Management worksheet completed for this element/template? (check box) ☐

Physical

Directory services are typically a very high-impact element. Write a physical security plan for all directory servers.

_____

_____

_____

Develop a strategic building access control plan wherein your directory service is integrated with building access-related identity information.

_____

_____

_____

Write a very focused diversity, redundancy, and isolation plan for the physical location and accessibility of directory service components.

_____

_____

_____

Network

Design your network so that directory services are reachable with especially high performance and high reliability.

_____

_____

_____

Develop your addressing "funnel" plan so that the directory service network segment traffic is minimized to only what is needed—simple traffic that is highly monitorable.

_____

_____

_____

List all directory service protocols used and assess their security—for example, LDAP verses LDAP with SSL (LDAPS). Use LDAPS wherever possible because it offers significantly improved security.

_____

_____

_____

Worksheet 4.13   Security Stack Worksheet for Directory Services.

Develop a plan to heavily focus your IDS/VA systems on your directory servers.

_____

_____

_____

_____

Application

Plan your directory service organization (schema) so that it matches your security and identity management model.

_____

_____

_____

Plan to leverage your directory's "inheritance model" so that you can efficiently manage access control and identity.

_____

_____

_____

For any authentication performed to the directory service, carefully assess the strength of the mechanism used.

_____

_____

_____

Assess how access control mechanisms for your applications can be better integrated into your directory service.

_____

_____

_____

_____

Operating System

Describe the precise relationship between the operating system and your directory server. What functions does your directory server perform on behalf of your operating system?

_____

_____

_____

Develop a plan for your organization around your directory strategy—how important is operating system/directory service independence?

_____

_____

_____

How are authentication and access control implemented in your operating system? Is the directory service now involved, or will it be involved in the future?

_____

_____

_____

Worksheet 4.13   Security Stack Worksheet for Directory Services. *(continued)*

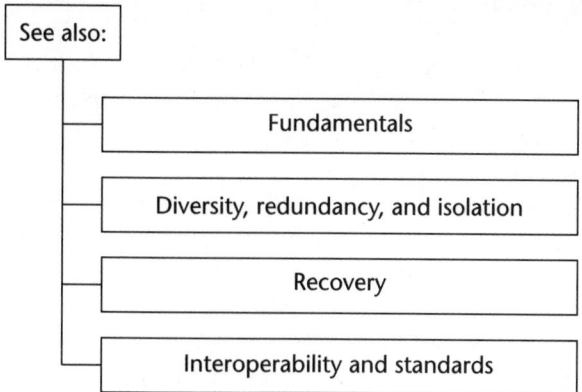

Figure 4.4   Directory services.

In pursuit of single-sign-on throughout the entire security stack, determine whether your organization's physical access control systems (e.g., badging, smartcards) support a directory service interface.   If so, you are one step closer to integrating building access control with access control to your network, application, and operating systems.

NETWORK

Restrict network connectivity.   Network connectivity to your directory service should be focused entirely on those protocols and activities related to directory operations. In other words, place directory servers on their own dedicated network segment, narrow the protocols on that segment to directory-related protocols, and heavily focus IDS and vulnerability analysis resources on that segment.

List all directory service protocols and restrict access to them.   List all directory service protocols used (e.g., LDAP) and any secure variants such as LDAPS; use this list as part of your plan. List any other related protocols that are needed for managing and administering your directory servers. Carefully restrict who, what, and when can make use of those via address filtering.

Define device addresses and restrict admin rights.   Define IP addresses and ranges of only those devices authorized to access and administer the directory service. Restrict directory service administrative rights to a predefined set of static IP addresses.

APPLICATION

Don't go overboard on schemas. Directory services are used to organize people and resources, including files, printers, and individual application information elements, and to apply security mechanisms to any groupings associated with this organization. For example, if you are a member of the accounting department, then the directory service may, by recognizing you as a member of accounting, bestow a range of rights to you that it wouldn't assign to a member of the human resources group. How you organize people, roles, groups, resources, and information in the directory service is reflected in the *schema* you have chosen. Though a discussion of detailed directory service schema design is beyond the scope of this book, it's an important topic, and someone will have to focus on it under the review and guidance of the security planner. At the same time, don't "make a meal" of your schema; that is, don't become an ultra-planner, as doing so can stop directory service rollout dead in its tracks. I've seen this happen too many times in organizations.

Identify and validate the security of the authentication and access control mechanisms of your directory service. Do this against your fundamental security elements. Assess how well these mechanisms integrate with your high-impact applications.

Define the relationship to PKI. If you implement a PKI, define the precise relationship your directory service has with it. For example, historically, *certificate revocation lists* (CRLs) have been stored in directory servers. CRLs are lists of digital certificates that have been "turned off" (revoked). Certificates are revoked when, for example, an employee leaves the company or there is concern that the certificate and its associated keys have been compromised.

OPERATING SYSTEM

Define the dependence between your operating system and directory service and consider any security pros and cons that may result. Some directory servers are integrated with the operating system, as with Microsoft Windows. Others are integrated only through open standards. Some offer one option or the other, as with Novell's products. There is no right or wrong approach when selecting among these products; it's simply a question of what best meets your organization's needs.

Specify how authentication and access control is integrated with the directory service. This applies to the operating system-level integration for operating system-level resources.

Life Cycle Management

Use Worksheet 4.14 here.

TECHNOLOGY SELECTION

Determine security-based protocols supported for access and administration.   Define how client and directory server authentication (mutual authentication) is performed for one or more protocols supported.

Specify how well the directory server integrates up and down the security stack.   For example, does your directory server support seamless integration with your building access control system, network devices, applications, and operating systems?

Define the range of access control flexibility supported by the directory server.   Describe how this access control model maps into the directory server schema.

Define how the directory server integrates with existing authentication mechanisms.   This applies to the network, application, and operating system environment, such as RADIUS, Kerberos, and IPSec.

Assess the quality and flexibility of administrative interfaces for the directory service.   This includes the standard configuration, as well as the provisioning of new users and resources into the directory service.

Seek components that can be integrated into a streamlined staff management procedure.   This will make it possible to add or delete users to the directory service, after which they are automatically granted, or denied, access to all key systems. This contrasts to the ad hoc manner in which users are added to and deleted from disparate nonintegrated systems today.

Other directory service guidelines are as follows:

- List the open standards-based access protocols supported.
- If you intend to operate in a multivendor environment, determine how truly open the directory server is.
- Identify any encryption features supported by the directory server, both for network encryption when accessing the directory service (such as through the use of LDAPS) and for encryption of information stored within the directory server (that is, encryption of information stored on the server's hard drives).
- Identify any PKI-specific features supported by the directory server.

Life-Cycle Management Worksheet for Directory Services

IMPACT ANALYSIS ID	BEFORE PLAN	PERCENT IMPROVEMENT	NEW VALUE

Quality Management worksheet completed for this element/template? (check box) ☐

Technology Selection

Assess the "openness" of your directory service as it relates to protocols and integration.

_____
_____
_____

Carefully list and scrutinize all secure (and insecure) directory access protocols supported such as LDAP with SSL (*LDAPS*). Define how *mutual* authentication is achieved.

_____
_____
_____

Assess the reliability and security of directory server synchronization and referral network mechanisms.

_____
_____
_____

Look for secure staff management features integrated with the directory service or made available by other vendors.

Implementation

Identify your best engineering resources, or obtain them, to assist you with your directory service implementation.

_____
_____
_____

Implement with a full and complete diversity, redundancy, and isolation architecture. Watch carefully the details such as electrical power.

_____
_____
_____

Fully test directory service failure modes of operation for consistency and security.

_____
_____
_____

Worksheet 4.14   Life-Cycle Management Worksheet for Directory Services. *(continues)*

Fully test your IDS/VA components assigned to monitor the directory servers. Place emphasis on this.

_____
_____
_____

Operations

Carefully define how the operations staff will monitor the operational health and security of your directory servers.

_____
_____
_____

Train operations on the critical nature of the directory service. Be sure they understand your diversity, redundancy, and isolation design and why it's there.

_____
_____
_____

Operations staff cannot become expert in detailed directory service jargon. Provide straightforward administrative interfaces.

_____
_____
_____

Incident Response

Provide full and rapid access to directory service logs relating to authentication and access control/authorizations.

_____
_____
_____

The team needs insight into how server-based applications authenticate to and access the directory, such as a Web server looking up information relating to a user. Don't focus just on end-user access.

_____
_____
_____

The incident team must be able to immediately disable directory access to any user or server if needed to protect information or infrastructure.

_____
_____
_____

Worksheet 4.14   Life-Cycle Management Worksheet for Directory Services. _(continued)_

- Define how directory server synchronization is performed, and describe the robustness and security of this approach. Directory servers need to talk to each other to keep their information up-to-date. The process, wherein directory servers update one another, is called a *synchronization process* or, in the case of some directory server architectures, a *referral process*. Whatever the architecture, if directory servers talk to one another, assess the security of that network connection.

- Carefully architect the intrusion-detection and vulnerability analysis approach for directory servers.

IMPLEMENTATION

Make your directory service implementation your cleanest.   As mentioned earlier, because of the sensitive high-impact nature of the directory service, it should be given especially close attention during implementation. Put your best engineers and administration staff on the directory server implementation. Pay special attention to electrical power diversity, redundancy, and isolation; to network diversity, redundancy, and isolation; to routing, addressing, filtering, intrusion detection, and vulnerability analysis. Never forget that though a directory service offers the best opportunity for improved security and management, it also holds the keys to the kingdom from the hacker point of view, should it be compromised.

OPERATIONS

Give operations staff the right tools.   Be sure effective management and monitoring tools are available to the operations staff, so that they can maintain a solid understanding of the health of the organization's directory servers. Streamline and simplify interfaces for securely administering the directory service, to include adding and deleting entries. Don't expect your operations staff to become expert in the language of directory service schemas. Provide them with straightforward, well-secured administrative interfaces.

Write mission-critical policies and procedures.   Operations staff must be given policies and procedures that reflect the fact that compromise of the organization's directory server can stop business altogether, depending on the diversity, redundancy, and isolation design.

INCIDENT RESPONSE

Grant the incident response team full and rapid access to directory service logs, especially as they relate to authentication to the directory service.   The team should have insight into direct user access (e.g., a staff member), administrator access, and application access to the directory service (e.g., a Web server validating the authentication credentials of a user). If you are implementing a PKI in conjunction with your directory service, incorporate the directory service as part of your PKI incident response process.

Business

Use Worksheet 4.15 here.

BUSINESSPEOPLE: EMPLOYEES

Maximize uptime; emphasize convenience.   Employees may never know a directory service exists—unless it becomes inaccessible. In this regard, managing maximum uptime is key to employee satisfaction with a directory service. A directory service paves the way for single sign-on, enabling an employee to log in once to gain access to all authorized applications, networks, and resources. Therefore, directory servers can represent convenience. Administrators can more easily manage an individual, group of individuals, and resources with a directory service.

BUSINESSPEOPLE: CUSTOMERS

Simplify their lives.   Instead of having to maintain multiple login credentials (identities), the directory service greatly simplifies the customer experience by enabling them to maintain a single identity for all transactions.

BUSINESSPEOPLE: OWNERS

Give them the good news.   Explain that directory servers offer the opportunity to improve security, streamline workflow, and thus improve efficiency, reduce the number of usernames and passwords people need to remember, and reduce administrative costs.

Business Worksheet for Directory Services

IMPACT ANALYSIS ID	BEFORE PLAN	PERCENT IMPROVEMENT	NEW VALUE

Quality Management worksheet completed for this element/template? (check box) ☐

Employees

Develop a single sign-on plan for your employees based on your directory service.

_____
_____
_____

To keep employees pleased with application performance in general, focus on directory performance and uptime.

_____
_____
_____

Customers

If applicable to your organization, build a single sign-on plan for customers using your directory service.

_____
_____
_____

Owners

Identify every opportunity to bring value to owners with a comprehensive directory service implementation so that you can justify its expense.

_____
_____
_____

Suppliers and Partners

Determine opportunities to use interoperable directory interfaces to streamline business-to-business commerce.

_____
_____
_____

Worksheet 4.15   Business Worksheet for Directory Services.

Information

Identify high-impact information that can benefit from enhanced directory authentication, access control, and attribute management.

_____

_____

_____

Infrastructure

Specify all high-impact infrastructure components that will integrate with the directory. Assess security of integration.

_____

_____

_____

Worksheet 4.15   Business Worksheet for Directory Services. *(continued)*

BUSINESSPEOPLE: SUPPLIERS

Itemize the benefits of directory servers.   Directory servers that support open multivendor interfaces can give a tremendous boost to the ability of your organization to engage in business-to-business commerce with suppliers and partners. They can provide a common access interface, a means of interoperability, a formalized store of information, standardized authentication, and standardized access control mechanisms, all making business-to-business commerce much more of a reality. The costs, time, and resources involved in achieving business-to-business commerce can be greatly reduced.

BUSINESSPEOPLE: PARTNERS

See the previous text on Suppliers.

BUSINESS: INFORMATION

Identify all high-impact information affected.   Detail information for which authentication, access control, and any additional management are provided by the directory service.

BUSINESS: INFRASTRUCTURE

Identify all high-impact infrastructure components that are to integrate with the directory service.   This includes routers, dial-up servers, operating system resources, file servers, applications, firewalls, proxy servers, and resources such as printers.

Selling Security

Use Worksheet 4.16 here.

EXECUTIVES

Recognize the expense.   Historically, one of the biggest problems with widespread use of directory servers in a medium or large organization has been expense. Vendors of directory service technology expected companies to pay license fees on the basis of the number of information entries stored in the directory service. Some of these fees were exorbitant. Increasingly, this is changing, and vendors are waking up to the fact that organizations don't want to architect their directory services around an inflexible fee structure. Still, no matter how you cut it, the technology is typically not cheap, especially as you introduce large multivendor installations and factor in the cost of any additional software required within your applications, network, and operating system infrastructure to optimally integrate with the directory servers you've chosen.

Contrast expense with benefits.   You do get what you pay for: The benefits of directory servers, if carefully implemented, can improve security, increase workplace efficiency through technologies like single sign-on, reduce administration costs, and greatly simplify and facilitate business-to-business commerce.

Point out reduced impact, coupled with reduced overall cost and improved organizational performance.   Provide concrete examples of how this can be achieved. The best way to do this is via a demonstration based on existing applications and business processes. Show how a system can be compromised today and how the risk of that is reduced with a directory server; then show improvements, such as a demonstration of a user logging in once instead of seven times, for each of the seven applications he or she works with every day.

Selling Security Worksheet for Directory Services

IMPACT ANALYSIS ID	BEFORE PLAN	PERCENT IMPROVEMENT	NEW VALUE

Executive

Provide examples of streamlined workflow, such as single sign-on, that may ultimately be achieved with the directory.

_____
_____
_____

Demonstrate how expensive it is to maintain individual authentication and access control records for each application without the directory service.

_____
_____
_____

Show how, over time, staff management procedures will be greatly simplified and secured through a unified directory.

_____
_____
_____

Quantify reduced impact to the organization from poorly managed authentication and access control, both by users and administrators.

_____
_____
_____

Middle Management

Demonstrate how much easier it will be to add new employees and delete ones no longer with the company.

_____
_____

Walk through, step-by-step, the benefits of a single sign-on architecture. Present it as something you may begin to achieve now or may simply move closer to.

_____
_____
_____

Worksheet 4.16   Selling Security Worksheet for Directory Services. _(continues)_

Show how, by simplifying authentication and access control, organizational impact is reduced.

_____

_____

_____

Staff

Staff members will appreciate the single sign-on idea. Tell them all about it.

_____

_____

_____

Provide examples of how they can be rapidly and efficiently granted access to systems. Perhaps today it's a slow process.

_____

_____

_____

Tell them how streamlining authentication and access control management help protect them and the organization.

_____

_____

_____

Worksheet 4.16   Selling Security Worksheet for Directory Services. *(continued)*

MIDDLE MANAGEMENT

Show how potential hacker impact will be reduced for specific middle management business processes.   Next, show how these and other processes may be streamlined going forward. Then point out how the time to add a new user or delete a user will be greatly reduced. Show how this may simplify, for example, bringing a new employee onboard.

STAFF

Highlight advantages.   Staff members will greatly appreciate single sign-on, if you plan to reduce the number of authentication credentials (e.g., usernames and passwords) they must manage. This aspect alone will win you support. Staff also can relate to reduced time for gaining access to systems they need or shorter time to bring new employees onboard.

Diversity, Redundancy, and Isolation (DRI)

Summary

Diversity, redundancy, and isolation (DRI) is a very important, common, three-part thread running through all high-impact distributed computing

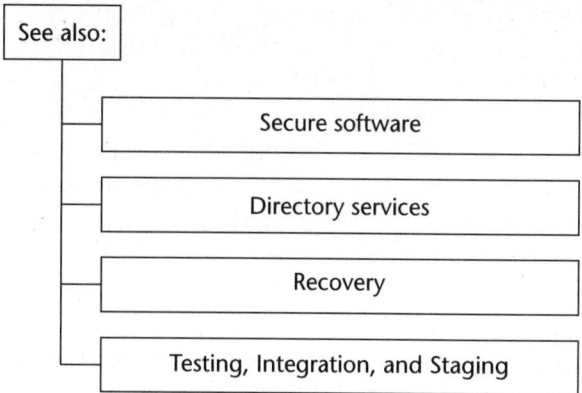

Figure 4.5   Diversity, redundancy, and isolation.

components. These components require special attention to ensure that they are backed up, physically diverse to protect against failure in a single location, and sufficiently isolated either logically or physically to minimize or eliminate single points of failure. These worksheets contain reminders and methods for identifying elements specifically requiring diversity, redundancy, and isolation and addressing those needs. (Note: diversity, redundancy, and isolation are also individually called out in other element worksheets.)

DRI: An Example

Examples always help when trying to communicate the value of diversity, redundancy, and isolation. This example may also provide a few helpful tips on physical security for buildings.

Once upon a time, I was challenged to prove how poorly most home and small building burglar alarm systems were designed and installed. I was presented with a system installed by a leading security alarm company. Knowing that many of these alarm installers look for the simplest, not the most secure, way to install their systems, I walked through the publicly accessible areas of the building trying to assess where the alarm system components were installed. With the alarm activated, I was asked to defeat this system without sounding the alarm or having it called in to the police monitoring center. I first went outside to the back of the building, where I found the building's telephone network interface box. (It's over these telephone lines, leading into this box, that the alarm system calls a monitoring station should the alarm go off.) On the outside of the network interface box were many wires, some of which were put there by the installers as a backup mechanism—security companies tell customers these are "tamper-proof wires," and that if a burglar cuts them when trying to cut the phone lines, the alarm will go off and everyone will be safe. What the installers don't tell the customer is that, certainly—if a burglar were dumb enough to cut this tamper-proof wire—the alarm would go off; but burglars rarely are this dumb, and instead simply reach inside the telephone network interface box and unplug the phone lines, and the alarm does not go off. Although the alarm system is indeed perfectly capable of sounding an alarm if the telephone lines are pulled from the network interface box, this feature is disabled because the installer and the monitoring station are in business together, and they hate getting false alarms every time the phone company has a problem and temporarily turns off phone service to a business.

Getting back to the story: I returned to the front of the building where I saw the keypad for the alarm through the glass lobby doors (by the receptionist's desk). The keypad is used to enable and disable the alarm system. Though this assumption was not required to defeat this alarm system, I guessed that in the closet behind the keypad I would find the "brain" of the alarm system (I know installers look for the easiest install: They put the keypad on one side of the wall and, in the closet behind it, they put the brain). Near it was the siren, just a short cable-run from the alarm system's brain. (If you're wondering who decides this is a good way to install alarm systems, the answer is that many alarm installers don't actually think about security. They're not security people; they are installers, and the faster they install, the faster they are on their way to the next customer.) In this case, the alarm to the building was enabled, but with a 30-second delay. Most alarms of this type are configured this way so that the person with the alarm code can disable the alarm as soon as he or she walks into the building for the first time every morning. With the alarm enabled, I went behind the building and disconnected the telephone lines at the network interface box. I then walked into the building and, immediately, heard warning beeps coming from the alarm system, telling me that I had only 30 seconds to disable the alarm with its secret code. Unfazed, I walked past the keypad and smashed the siren with a hammer. To complete the job, I walked behind the keypad and was not surprised to find the brain for the alarm system. Crash went the hammer, and down to the floor went the brain—the entire cabinet and all of its contents. Note that I didn't need to do this because, by isolating the alarm system from the rest of the world by disconnecting the phone lines and destroying the siren, the alarm brain itself posed no additional threat. Needless to say, my client made immediate plans to get a new, and far better designed, alarm system installed.

When you think through this example, you will find several places where redundancy and diversity should have been provided. You see how easily the alarm system was isolated. If, instead, the alarm system had been installed with a relatively inexpensive wireless cellular backup (a physically diverse communication path), my job would have been much more difficult because the alarm system might have managed to send off an alarm code before I was able to destroy its components inside the building. This, in conjunction with several other diversity, redundancy, and isolation changes to the alarm system installation, would have made it much more secure. A few additional details relating to this example are provided in the physical security element, a wrap-up element discussed in more detail toward the end of this chapter.

Security Stack

Use Worksheet 4.17 here.

PHYSICAL

Look for single points of failure. If, for example, your building access control system, physical burglar alarm system, camera surveillance, or telephone network fails, what happens to security? How about a fire at your data center? When you fail over to your backup systems, how is security handled; is it significantly degraded in anyway?

NETWORK

Look for other single points of failure in the network. Key network components typically relating to security, and particularly benefiting from DRI, include high-impact firewalls, proxy servers, routers, IP connectivity, and physical network transmission facilities (circuits). If any one of these components is compromised by a hacker, which business processes are brought to a halt? How can DRI be used to keep the business process working in the event of such a failure?

Introduce physical diversity. Redundancy without physical diversity is limiting. Regularly I see organizations order redundant network circuits along the same physical network path. What's the point? If that path goes down, the entire network goes down. As discussed in Chapter 2, the solution is to introduce physical diversity—network paths along separate paths. This concept can be extended to protect you against certain denial-of-service attacks. If you, for example, choose a physically and logically diverse Internet connection, it may be possible to recover from certain DoS attacks through use of an alternate Internet service provider. This means obtaining your Internet connections from *different* Internet services providers (ISPs); however, this does *not* mean any two different ISPs.

If you don't choose the two ISPs carefully, your additional Internet connection may not be of help to you if you come under attack. Specifically, you should obtain services from two ISPs that use *physically diverse* facilities (that is, they don't both ride along the same physical network) and that have *complementary Internet peering relationships*. (Peering is how ISPs exchange Internet traffic with one another.) Your ISP should be able to provide you with a list of its peering relationships. ISPs interconnect at *network access points* to peer and exchange traffic. Each of your two ISPs should have its own independent peering arrangements and not, for example, rely solely on one or the other's peering—which is surprisingly common. If you are under a DoS attack, these independent peering arrangements may be what save you. The DoS attack may be more easily controlled through one set of peering arranges and not another; you may be able, for example, to filter out certain attack packets along one route and then send good traffic along another route through the complementary peering arrangements. All of this adds up to true diversity. As you can see, there's a lot more to it than simply ordering a backup Internet connection.

Leave spare capacity.   You don't want allow a small group of hackers to overrun your systems by generating DoS attack traffic from just a few computers. If they're going to attack you, make it harder for them to succeed. One way to do this is to be sure you don't routinely run your network up to its highest capacity: Leave sufficient spare bandwidth so that your network doesn't become saturated with just a small increase in traffic.

APPLICATION

Institute DRI at the application layer.   Doing so means the high-impact applications we rely on don't necessarily go down and stop company operations in the event of a single compromise. Achieving this means we avoid single points of failure for applications and the services they rely on. Core services include authentication, directory, and time.

Have a backup strategy for configuration-management servers to enable recovery.   If we are going to the (necessary) trouble of configuration-managing system files, testing versions of software, and documenting systems, then we better have a backup strategy for our configuration-management servers so that, in the event of a successful compromise, we can recover.

Secure time.   Secure time is another excellent example of something generally requiring DRI. Such a requirement is easily missed by many organizations. A hacker should not be able to take down our entire network by knocking out a single authentication server, time service, or directory service, for example. (Secure time is a separate security element and is presented later in this chapter.)

OPERATING SYSTEM

Plan DRI for operating system installations used for any high-impact applications.   Make sure operating systems and related services (file servers, access control, and so forth) are not a single point of failure for a high-impact application. Protect operating system services with DRI wherever they are needed to keep a high-impact application or related service running.

Security Stack Worksheet for DRI

IMPACT ANALYSIS ID	BEFORE PLAN	PERCENT IMPROVEMENT	NEW VALUE

Quality Management worksheet completed for this element/template? (check box) ☐

Physical

Audit the security of existing physical security-related systems, such as building access control, when components fail.

_____
_____
_____

Determine where DRI is needed to reduce impact and develop a plan—for example, backup building access servers.

_____
_____
_____

Network

Clearly differentiate between physical diversity and redundancy. Audit your network to see the truth on what you have.

_____
_____
_____

Reconfigure your network so that you achieve both diversity and redundancy simultaneously where you can.

_____
_____
_____

Assess increased risk from denial-of-service attacks while the network is operating in a degraded state.

_____
_____
_____

Search for and remedy any high-impact network components or services relied on by the network that can be isolated.

_____
_____
_____

Worksheet 4.17   Security Stack Worksheet for DRI. *(continues)*

Application

Build a DRI plan for high-impact applications.

_____

_____

_____

Specifically address core services including authentication, directory services, and time in your DRI plan.

_____

_____

_____

Establish a DRI plan for high-impact intrusion detection and vulnerability analysis systems.

_____

_____

_____

Operating System

Identify specific high-impact operating system installations that warrant DRI.

_____

_____

_____

Identify high-impact distributed services used or provided by the operating system and develop a DRI plan for them.

_____

_____

_____

Worksheet 4.17   Security Stack Worksheet for DRI. *(continued)*

Life-Cycle Management

Use Worksheet 4.18 here.

TECHNOLOGY SELECTION

Remember that diversity is all relative.   For example, physical diversity may mean two physical machines in the same room or, for better diversity, two machines in separate rooms; it may mean separate buildings in the same or disparate locations. The greater the diversity, typically the higher the cost to implement, especially when considering performance and scalability needs.

Compile a list of high-impact infrastructure elements that would benefit from DRI; select technology and implementations that allow you to implement DRI.   Review other security elements for important tips with regard to high-impact DRI infrastructure.

Life-Cycle Worksheet for DRI

IMPACT ANALYSIS ID	BEFORE PLAN	PERCENT IMPROVEMENT	NEW VALUE

Quality Management worksheet completed for this element/template? (check box) ☐

Technology Selection

Build a model of what DRI means for each of the high-impact core security stack elements.

_____

_____

_____

Consider the value of vendor diversity as it relates to protection against the same security vulnerability or failure scenario.

_____

_____

_____

Implementation

Write a formal DRI test plan and test it by inducing real failures. Do this on a schedule basis. This is crucial to success.

_____

_____

_____

Write strict policies and procedures requiring regularly scheduled DRI testing. Perform testing in off-hours.

_____

_____

_____

Regularly look for DRI violations—for example, two diverse components accidentally linked by a single common failure thread.

_____

_____

_____

Worksheet 4.18   Life-Cycle Worksheet for DRI. *(continues)*

Operations

Architect operations group interfaces, policies, and procedures to avoid violations of the DRI plan.

_____
_____
_____

Carefully train operations staff to understand what you are trying to achieve with your DRI.

_____
_____
_____

Incident Response

The incident team needs a thorough advance knowledge, with documentation, of the DRI plan.

_____
_____
_____

Work to ensure that the team does not erroneously presume a system is protected with a DRI plan when it is not.

_____
_____
_____

Worksheet 4.18   Life-Cycle Worksheet for DRI. *(continued)*

IMPLEMENTATION

Test regularly.   By far the most common mistake made in DRI implementation and operations is the propensity of companies to *not test* their DRI systems. You must do this regularly and take it seriously. The best way to test DRI is to routinely, during nonbusiness hours, force a controlled failure in a high-impact infrastructure component and to directly observe the infrastructure's diversity, redundancy, and isolation plan kick in. Document when these tests will occur, the results of the tests, and any corrective actions needed. This testing can be viewed as an audit or drill from the perspective of the quality management worksheets; therefore, record your test results there.

OPERATIONS

To the extent possible, design operator interfaces to prevent staff from taking down the wrong systems at the same time.   Operators routinely disregard DRI plans and, for example, plug two systems into the same backup power supply, where the DRI plan called for separate ones.

Close monitoring of DRI implementations and associated training are very important because we lose its benefits quite easily with the simplest of implementation errors.

INCIDENT RESPONSE

Verify that the incident response team has a solid understanding of which components are truly DRI before an attack occurs.   Too often, incident response teams discover, at the time of a compromise, that components weren't truly DRI. You need to know this up front, and you need to document it and make this documentation available to the DRI team.

Business

Use Worksheet 4.19 here.

BUSINESSPEOPLE: EMPLOYEES

Understand expectations with regard to DRI.   When a system becomes inoperable for any reason for a substantial period of time, employees want to know why there was no redundant system. The lack of DRI is, in particular, more evident to employees when their daily routine is disrupted. The decision to implement DRI for information and infrastructure used by employees is driven by your impact and related cost analysis.

BUSINESSPEOPLE: CUSTOMERS

Understand their expectations and requirements.   Your impact analysis and associated customer expectations will help drive your DRI plan. Noncritical recoverable systems are of lower impact than those that take your customers completely down. Think about ISPs that still, today, treat email as an optional, noncritical service. The phone company, by analogy, learned long ago of the criticality of the telephone. Understand system-critical components, and implement DRI so that you are prepared to act immediately, on the order of hours, not days, should you be hacked.

BUSINESSPEOPLE: OWNERS

Drive specific DRI requirements by your impact analysis.   Owners have a similar view as customers, in that, for the systems they rely on to understand the business and its basic operation, they expect someone to have implemented a plan such that diversity, redundancy, and isolation have been considered. If something fundamental goes down unexpectedly and doesn't come back up in a timely manner, owners regard it as losing money (as do customers, for that matter; employees lose time).

Business Worksheet for DRI

IMPACT ANALYSIS ID	BEFORE PLAN	PERCENT IMPROVEMENT	NEW VALUE

Quality Management worksheet completed for this element/template? (check box) ☐

Employees

Develop a mechanism to educate employees so that they understand generally that you do plan for DRI.

_____

_____

_____

Customers

Clearly identify how you address customer DRI expectations and needs within your impact analysis.

_____

_____

_____

Customer mission-critical DRI needs should be addressed by your DRI plan and associated impact analysis.

_____

_____

_____

Owners

Owners (e.g., stockholders) are similar to customers relative to DRI. Educate them on what you are doing at a high level.

_____

_____

_____

List owner-sensitive, high-impact DRI expectations, and factor them into your impact analysis and DRI plan.

_____

_____

_____

Worksheet 4.19   Business Worksheet for DRI.

Suppliers and Partners

List your DRI requirements, as driven by your impact analysis, for your suppliers and partners.

_____

_____

_____

Information

Drive DRI information requirements—for example, what information needs redundancy, diversity of access, or isolation protection.

_____

_____

_____

Infrastructure

DRI is heavily focused on infrastructure. Review it again, and look carefully for any high-impact DRI infrastructure holes.

_____

_____

_____

Worksheet 4.19   Business Worksheet for DRI. *(continued)*

BUSINESSPEOPLE: SUPPLIERS

Drive the DRI requirements for key suppliers.   Drive them to the service levels you need to maintain your organizational risk in line with your impact analysis. Set DRI expectations, especially as they relate to contingency plans, should their infrastructure be hacked.

BUSINESSPEOPLE: PARTNERS

Coordinate with partners.   It is particularly important that you coordinate with partners you rely on for a high-impact component, so that DRI is implemented inline as required.

BUSINESS: INFORMATION

Look at your DRI requirements strictly from the perspective of information.   Identify high-impact information elements, and then determine how the DRI infrastructure is implemented to protect them.

BUSINESS: INFRASTRUCTURE

Address any infrastructure responsible for servicing high-impact items.   As previously discussed, search for single points of failure that disrupt business processes, and develop a DRI plan to remove them.

Selling Security

Use Worksheet 4.20 here.

EXECUTIVES

Stick to your priorities.   Using examples from your impact analysis, simulate for the executive staff the effect of an inadequate DRI plan. Show them, if at all possible with real computers and real applications, the catastrophic effect on company operations should key high-impact systems be compromised without a DRI plan in place. Because DRI can quickly become costly, stick to the priorities dictated by your impact analysis and carefully lay out impact reduction; in the face of increased cost relating to DRI, stress the importance of protecting the organization overall.

MIDDLE MANAGEMENT

Illustrate workflow processes that would be halted in response to a successful attack on a component not adequately DRI-protected.   Point out the reduced risk to their schedules and product/delivery efforts brought about by a solid DRI plan.

STAFF

Provide specific examples of what would happen to the daily routine if an inadequately DRI-architected solution were compromised.   To the extent DRI is transparent to staff members, they simply don't care about it. But, if their buy-in is required as part of the DRI justification, then be prepared to defend the plan with examples.

Security Selling Worksheet for DRI

IMPACT ANALYSIS ID	BEFORE PLAN	PERCENT IMPROVEMENT	NEW VALUE

Executive

Simulate the business effect of an inadequate DRI plan on real systems, one that they understand.

_____
_____
_____

Be realistic with your DRI planning because we know it can be costly. Show how you have worked to save money.

_____
_____
_____

Relate each of your decisions and recommendations to your impact analysis as always. Show reduced impact from the plan.

_____
_____
_____

Give examples of customer and owner expectations in relation to system uptime, and show how they are met.

_____
_____
_____

Middle Management

Show how the business processes they manage (provide specific examples) could be halted without your DRI plan.

_____
_____
_____

Point out the reduced risks to their schedules, and show key infrastructure or information that becomes unavailable.

_____
_____
_____

Staff

Describe your plan in terms staff members understand—for example, the time they waste when a system they rely on goes down.

_____
_____
_____

Worksheet 4.20   Selling Security Worksheet for DRI.

Intrusion Detection and Vulnerability Analysis (IDS/VA)

Summary

Increasingly, intrusion-detection and vulnerability analysis components are being viewed as mandatory, just as firewalls are today. With the complexity of today's technology, it seems unimaginable not to do something to keep a close eye on your infrastructure with a well-designed intrusion-detection system and vulnerability analysis (IDS/VA) system. Furthermore, IDS/VA products are evolving and improving rapidly and include open-source software and commercial options. And as the products evolve, so does the terminology. Vendors often speak about host-based IDS/VA and network-based IDS/VA, though the terms *host* and *network* are routinely misused by us all. In this book the focus is simply on what IDS/VA means at each layer of the security stack. And here we evaluate your IDS/VA architecture and products in terms of what is done, and not done, at different layers of the security stack.

> **NOTE** Refer back to Chapter 3, Table 3.1, which defined in regard to the Quality Management worksheets a regular management-level reporting and metric process. This process allows us to track overall security quality, especially as it relates to intrusions, both real and false.

Keep in mind that IDS/VA is not just about technology; it's also about how we *respond* to it. Specifically, we need to decide what our policies and procedures will dictate that we do when an IDS/VA system reports a security concern of one kind or another. The number of security concerns reported by our IDS/VA is very much a function of how we have designed and implemented it and how good our overall security plan is. Some installations constantly ring false alarms, which, as you can imagine, causes problems. Conversely, others are too insensitive to malicious activity or dangerous configurations. Once we have an event of some kind to respond to, we need to define an escalation procedure within our organization that, usually, is tied to the impact of the component registering the concern. For example, if we suspect an intrusion in our company's accounting systems and we view that as a high-impact component, perhaps immediate escalation to senior management makes sense.

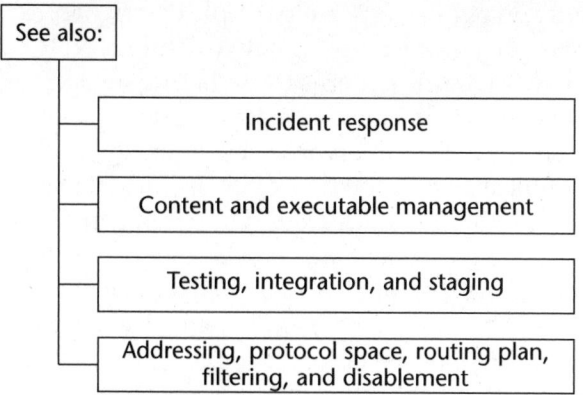

Figure 4.6   Intrusion detection and vulnerability analysis.

Security Stack

Use Worksheet 4.21 here.

PHYSICAL

Detect physical intruders, and assess on an ongoing basis any vulnerabilities in your physical security.   This is the purpose of IDS/VA at the physical layer. Elements of physical security include burglar alarms; building/badge access control; logs relating to physical access, safes, locks on doors and windows; if necessary, securing vent or ceiling access into the room; and video surveillance, alarms, and alarm monitoring. Review the DRI security element already discussed, and take note of the information provided relative to physical security.

NETWORK

Be alert to attacks based on network activity signatures.   Network-based IDS components look for these. They may do this by "sniffing" promiscuously over network connections, as well as by probing network-related equipment and network-related functions on clients and servers to gather network statistics and review logs. An example of a signature might be an unusual increase in a specific type of network traffic. Note that you should analyze network traffic patterns by gathering statistics regularly. If you see an unusual change in network traffic, such as a large amount of traffic to and from a site that otherwise is traditionally relatively quiet, this might be indicative of some type of intrusion at that site, such as a virus, a hacker moving information around or stealing information, or some type of denial-of-service (DoS) attack. IDS components that combine an application/operating system (host) and network view of things process what some call *compound signatures*. These look at events occurring at both the network and host levels and combine them in their assessment of whether an intrusion has occurred or is in the works.

Focus your IDS/VA architecture. This is driven by your impact analysis. If your company's accounting systems have the highest impact, protect them first; if intellectual property is first and foremost, start there. Some security people believe that IDS/VA is not necessary behind their firewalls, for example, believing it should be implemented only on systems closest to the Internet. Others have the opposite view. In my opinion, the solution is balance. You need IDS/VA in both places, tightly driven by your security plan and impact analysis.

Closely couple IDS/VA component configuration planning with your addressing, filtering, routing, content, and executable management strategies. Your IDS/VA systems are effective only if you indicate what should and should not be present on the network. You do this by configuring them with information about what to filter, which addresses, content, and executables should be present, and which protocols should be present on a given monitored network segment.

Consider how tightly integrated (or not) your IDS/VA software is with the precise network devices you are using in your network. For example, is it capable of reading the logs for your particular network routers? It's very important that your IDS/VA oversee activity on your firewall; therefore, architect for compatibility with your firewall.

Consider scalability and performance when it comes to doing anything over the network. Can your IDS components keep up, and scale, with your network? For example, if you're implementing a redundant firewall configuration with considerable load balancing, you need an IDS that can accommodate that type of complex configuration. Load sharing in particular can wreak some havoc on your IDS simply because, if it routes certain packets to and from the same IP address but over two different network links, the IDS somehow must be able to correlate an attack whose signature may effectively be spread over multiple load-shared links.

Define what "real time" means to your organization.   Decide just how real time you want your systems to be in regard to notifying you of a problem. Do you want to be paged, for example, when it appears there may be a problem? Many engineers today are burned out on IDS/VA systems simply because their pagers never stop—it's one alert after another. This happens typically because the overall security plan has not been optimized, not for itself and not for the IDS/VA system. In one very large bank, the IDS/VA systems alarmed constantly. Though some of the engineers complained that the IDS/VA system was not implemented properly, in fact, it was the security plan that was poorly implemented. For example, they had firewalls in place, but the firewalls filtered almost nothing; and they did very little in the way of putting separate key systems on separate network segments; therefore, network segments all around the bank carried sensitive traffic willy-nilly. There was almost no way to know what belonged, or didn't, on any given network segment simply because too many addresses, too much content, and too many routes were allowed on too many segments. No IDS/VA system in the world was going to make any sense of this at the network level.

Select the administration and management interface of your IDS/VA products to allow for straightforward reporting and configuration of security policies.   The interface might include a "filtering language" that enables administrators to effectively use a scripting language to specify policies. It should include a streamlined reporting and alert capability (such as the capability to page you via your beeper).

APPLICATION

Be aware that both your clients (desktops) and servers (hosts) can benefit from IDS/VA.   Desktop IDS technology is advancing rapidly and is proving highly effective at preventing a range of attacks. While you are deciding which virus detection software you're going to use on desktops in your organization, strongly consider adding a desktop IDS at the same time. Desktop IDS systems tend to work around the simple principle of blocking those applications that have not been overtly authorized as permitted to access the network. In addition, they provide other features, such as blocking certain kinds of file attachments. Other new and creative approaches are evolving. Better host-based IDS products offer at least two basic capabilities: tamper-detection (integrity) of key application-specific files and log analysis. Remember, IDS systems integrity-check (hash) system files and check logs for signatures characteristic of an intrusion. Desktop and server VA systems interrogate application configurations for common vulnerabilities and report them to you.

Security Stack Worksheet for Intrusion Detection and Vulnerability Analysis

IMPACT ANALYSIS ID	BEFORE PLAN	PERCENT IMPROVEMENT	NEW VALUE

Quality Management worksheet completed for this element/template? (check box) ☐

Physical

Identify physical intrusion protection for high-impact systems including video surveillance, alarm systems, locks, safes, cages (locked equipment cages), cabinets, and so forth.

_____
_____
_____

Write test plans to routinely assess the strength of your physical intrusion protection systems.

_____
_____
_____

Network

How have you designed your network security plan to minimize IDS false alarms?

_____
_____
_____

Describe the compound signature capability offered by your IDS system.

_____
_____
_____

Decide how "real time" your IDS/VA system should be. The better your design, the more useful real-time notifications can be.

_____
_____
_____

Assess how tightly integrated your IDS/VA systems are with your network components including the reading of logs.

_____
_____
_____

Worksheet 4.21 Security Stack Worksheet for Intrusion Detection and Vulnerability Analysis.

Application

Develop a plan to implement both server and desktop IDS/VA.

_____

_____

_____

Identify how your IDS detects tampering and signature attacks for your high-impact applications. Is it well-integrated?

_____

_____

_____

Coordinate your vulnerability analysis configuration with your lockdown and configuration management systems. If your vulnerability analysis system reports a problem with your system lockdown configuration, you should modify it and store that updated configuration into the configuration management system.

_____

_____

_____

Operating System

Look for any value-added capabilities within your operating system IDS such as monitoring for buffer exploits.

_____

_____

_____

Coordinate your VA configuration with your lockdown and configuration management procedures.

_____

_____

_____

Lock down your operating system and configure only what's needed to increase security and improve IDS/VA operation.

_____

_____

_____

Worksheet 4.21 Security Stack Worksheet for Intrusion Detection and Vulnerability Analysis. *(continued)*

OPERATING SYSTEM

Investigate operating system-level IDS products that detect tampering and analyze logs and system files for signs of intrusion. Vendors are increasingly adding important features such as the ability to detect buffer exploits by preventing the execution of software from unchecked operating system buffers. (Such exploits are discussed as part of the Secure Software security element, later in this chapter).

Life-Cycle Management

Use Worksheet 4.22 here.

TECHNOLOGY SELECTION

Believe in your IDS/VA products and plan.   IDS/VA systems are worthless to you if you view them as "noise" (because, for example, of too many false alarms) and if you question the quality and relevance of what they are telling you. Your success with this technology is greatly influenced by how well you've planned and implemented your security plan overall. But it also relates to how manageable your IDS/VA implementation is and how much support you need to keep it going.

Test.   Because IDS and VA systems can be intrusive with regard to the systems they protect—meaning they may interact at times "aggressively" with components in your security stack—you need to completely test IDS/VA with the exact components you plan to protect. IDS/VA technology can crash the systems they are tasked to protect. I'll say it again: Test carefully.

Identify important features.   Identify the core features of your IDS system in the areas of policy configuration, tamper detection, network signature detection, host and desktop signature detection, and compound signature detection. Assess how well it is designed to work with the precise vendor equipment you have. Determine what kind of logging expectations the IDS system introduces and the ability of your system components to accommodate that level of logging. Logging can be CPU- and processor-intensive.

Probe for a full range of vulnerabilities.   Determine the range of vulnerabilities assessed by your VA system. Your architecture should test for vulnerabilities at the network, application, and operating system layers. Compare technologies you are considering for how well they detect vulnerabilities at each layer of the security stack.

Protect your IDS/VA components.   Ask your IDS and VA vendors to explain to you how the systems themselves are protected from hacking—that is, what should you do, and what does the architecture do, to prevent a hacker from effectively shutting down your IDS and VA defenses? As discussed in Chapter 2, if a hacker detects an IDS binary such as Tripwire on a server, the first thing the hacker might do is replace that binary with his or her own—obviously one that will cover the hacker's tracks.

Life-Cycle Management Worksheet for Intrusion Detection and Vulnerability Analysis

IMPACT ANALYSIS ID	BEFORE PLAN	PERCENT IMPROVEMENT	NEW VALUE

Quality Management worksheet completed for this element/template? (check box) ☐

Technology Selection

Evaluate how tightly candidate IDS/VA systems integrate with your security stack components.

_____
_____
_____

Write a careful test plan to test IDS/VA products; some may crash your systems.

_____
_____
_____

How easily can you configure them to match your security plan, to minimize false alarms and maximize detection?

_____
_____
_____

Very importantly, how does the system scale so you can monitor many network segments and many hosts?

_____
_____
_____
_____

Implementation

Correct and up-to-date configuration of IDS and VA systems is key to success. Develop policies and procedures for this.

_____
_____
_____

Regularly report and analyze the number of "false alarms" coming from your IDS/VA systems. Work to reduce them. This is part of the quality management worksheet.

_____
_____
_____

Worksheet 4.22 Life-Cycle Management Worksheet for Intrusion Detection and Vulnerability Analysis. *(continues)*

Your IDS/VA systems must be heavily protected; they are high-impact systems. Write a plan to protect IDS/VA systems.

_____

_____

_____

_____

Operations

Provide tools to operations staff to monitor the health of IDS/VA systems.

_____

_____

_____

Train operations staff so that they truly understand what the IDS/VA systems are telling them.

_____

_____

_____

Develop well thought-out policies and procedures guiding the maintenance and administration of IDS/VA systems.

_____

_____

_____

Train operations staff to clearly know when to escalate IDS/VA events as "incidents" to the incident response team.

_____

_____

_____

Incident Response

Develop a long-term plan showing how, over time, your IDS/VA provides increasingly more accurate incident and vulnerability reporting.

_____

_____

_____

Give your incident team full instant access to all available IDS/VA system information.

_____

_____

_____

Your incident response team is the "quality owner" for the IDS/VA. Define how your incident team manages IDS/VA quality.

_____

_____

_____

Worksheet 4.22 Life-Cycle Management Worksheet for Intrusion Detection and Vulnerability Analysis. _(continued)_

IMPLEMENTATION

Carefully configure IDS and VA systems in accordance with your security policies.   That is, *correctly* configure the systems as to what should and shouldn't exist within the network and its servers and clients. Incorrect configuration is a common ailment in these systems. The symptom is constant false alarms or, worse, none at all. These systems are for assurance—you cannot always know overtly if they are doing their job. It's not like a file server that either serves files or not. Therefore, they may appear to be correctly configured but may not be. You need to implement them so that your operations staff can reasonably know if these systems are doing what you intended them to do. Test your configurations during implementation. Simulate intrusions and vulnerabilities, and verify your IDS/VA system responds.

OPERATIONS

Implement an operations interface that provides solid reporting on the correct operation of your IDS/VA architecture.   You need to do this so that the operations staff can assess the health of your IDS/VA system.

Provide a system that doesn't numb the operations staff with false alarms.   As discussed many times, poorly implemented overall security plans and IDS/VA components may sound false alarms frequently. If staff begin to ignore alarms, hackers get exactly what they are after. Train them to understand and recognize when real incidents are reported and to escalate incidents to the incident response team.

INCIDENT RESPONSE

Plan your system so that the IDS/VA infrastructure acts as the nervous system for incident response.   That is, design it to be one of the primary sensors used to signal that a hacker is at work or has already successfully hacked your systems. Also, if flags are raised elsewhere, not from the IDS/VA, the incident response team will still query the systems to see if there is anything in the logs that might help them better understand what may have happened or what is in progress.

Business

Use Worksheet 4.23 here.

BUSINESSPEOPLE: EMPLOYEES

Open a direct avenue of communication.   Employees might be somewhat inconvenienced by the IDS/VA architecture, as the architecture works in conjunction with other aspects of your security plan, such as content management, to limit what they can and cannot do. As with your security architecture as a whole, and in accordance with your IDS/VA policies and procedures, give employees a direct way to make requests for certain capabilities that might otherwise be viewed as an intrusion or vulnerability by your IDS/VA components.

BUSINESSPEOPLE: CUSTOMERS

Determine whether your IDS/VA should be invisible or limiting.   Like certain other parts of your plan, IDS/VA implementations tend to limit what customers can or cannot do. Depending on your type of business, your customers may have no idea you have an IDS/VA architecture. In other cases, such as when you provide a service that may involve customers accessing your systems, your IDS/VA plan may restrict them from doing certain things. If that is the case for your customers, you should develop an alternate strategy.

BUSINESSPEOPLE: OWNERS

Recognize that IDS/VA systems can be invisible and limiting and may require training.   Similar to the argument just made for customers, your IDS/VA implementation may either be completely transparent or may introduce limits. In addition, if you implement desktop IDS/VA, employees may need to be trained to understand how to use the software because these systems often report suspicious activity to the computer user and expect him or her to make a decision.

BUSINESSPEOPLE: SUPPLIERS

Consider IDS/VA for business-to-business networking.   For suppliers, IDS/VA may become more relevant should you have a business-to-business network connection. In such cases, the businesses connected over the network may want to agree on a common IDS/VA implementation for business-to-business network segments.

BUSINESSPEOPLE: PARTNERS

See the previous text on Suppliers.

Business Worksheet for Intrusion Detection and Vulnerability Analysis

IMPACT ANALYSIS ID	BEFORE PLAN	PERCENT IMPROVEMENT	NEW VALUE

Quality Management worksheet completed for this element/template? (check box) ☐

Employees

Your IDS/VA may limit what employees can and cannot do. Help them understand what those things are and why the limit.

_____
_____
_____

If your IDS/VA limits what employees can do, provide a procedure for rapidly requesting IDS/VA policy changes.

_____
_____
_____

Customers

Identify any particular IDS/VA configuration requirements affecting collaboration or information exchange with customers.

_____
_____
_____

Owners

Your IDS/VA is a clear way to protect owners. Focus your plan on high-impact owner-sensitive components.

_____
_____
_____

Suppliers and Partners

Identify any particular IDS/VA configuration requirements affected by business-to-business processing needs.

_____
_____
_____

Worksheet 4.23 Business Worksheet for Intrusion Detection and Vulnerability Analysis. *(continues)*

Information

Assess how your IDS/VA plan protects high-impact information. This may bring you a new and useful perspective.

_____
_____
_____

Infrastructure

List high-impact infrastructure and develop a comprehensive IDS/VA plan for those components first.

_____
_____
_____

Worksheet 4.23   Business Worksheet for Intrusion Detection and Vulnerability Analysis. *(continued)*

BUSINESS: INFORMATION

Evaluate your information from an impact standpoint, and focus your IDS/VA architecture on high-impact elements.   Like everything else in your security plan, where in your security stack you focus IDS/VA is driven by your impact analysis. As you look at where high-impact information is distributed in your network application framework, you will be able to identify the associated infrastructure components that demand focus.

BUSINESS: INFRASTRUCTURE

Identify highest-impact infrastructure components, and protect them first, and best, with your IDS/VA architecture.   This is where we usually start, with infrastructure. Identify components such as routers, servers, and network segments servicing high-impact business processes.

Selling Security

Use Worksheet 4.24 here.

EXECUTIVES

Coordinate affected groups.   The most difficult aspect of selling an IDS/VA solution to an executive, beyond the cost/impact analysis argument we make for every element of our security plan, is managing the subsequent roles, responsibilities, and reactions to systems that, without proper implementation, do little more than issue false alarms. Putting an effective system in place, one that addresses the issues discussed thus far, requires a good deal of work, especially for larger organizations, as it requires considerable coordination across different groups (e.g., networking, IS/IT). Typically, the larger the organization, the less effective the coordination; as a result, IDS/VA and the entire security plan suffers. It's particularly useful with IDS/VA to, first, institute policies and procedures and, second, get buy-in to help make this coordination a reality. Address this up front; otherwise, any fully planned IDS/ VA strategy has a poor chance of success.

Demonstrate an intrusion on a high-impact system, to show how, today, only manual log analysis that occurs days or even weeks later would reveal the intrusion or cause it to be missed entirely.   That is, show the IDS/VA architecture for what it is: the equivalent of an ongoing security review and "burglar alarm" for key systems. Executives do not need to understand how the technology works in terms of signatures, hashes, and so forth; just show them that it detects tampering, for example. Show them the kinds of things a hacker tampers with to get control over the systems he or she hacks at a very high level.

Prepare executive management for any inconveniences that might be introduced by the IDS/VA system.   Do this by showing that you are implementing policies and procedures so that, for example, new applications can be quickly brought online and under IDS/VA management without causing unacceptable delays, cost, and overhead. A consistent theme in security planning is to prepare for the reality that security can restrict things; hence, you need to introduce policies and procedures that enable it to adapt and grow with your organization.

MIDDLE MANAGEMENT

Sell on the value of the IDS/VA and associated security policies and procedures.   This is particularly important if the IDS/VA system will interfere with the daily routines of managers, such as loading software on any network segment whenever a manager decides that's important. Clearly identify where their business processes may be affected and ways that exceptions and new applications can be brought online; at the same time, articulate the reduced potential impact from a successful hack on their schedules and objectives. If desktop IDS/VA systems are deployed, employees may need to be trained.

STAFF

See the previous text on Middle Management.

Selling Security Worksheet for Intrusion Detection and Vulnerability Analysis

IMPACT ANALYSIS ID	BEFORE PLAN	PERCENT IMPROVEMENT	NEW VALUE

Executive

Provide a real demonstration of how an undetected intrusion can greatly impact the organization.

_____

_____

Rerun the demonstration simulating how the proposed IDS/VA system *quickly* detects a vulnerability and an intrusion.

_____

_____

Emphasize that an effective IDS/VA deployment means all network and application owners must coordinate together.

_____

_____

Show how impact is reduced through an increased probability of vulnerability prevention and intrusion detection.

_____

_____

_____

Middle Management

IDS/VA policies may prohibit certain things done today, such as loading software on any computer. Prepare management for this.

_____

_____

Similar to your executive sell, show how an intrusion and vulnerability is not detected today (or detected slowly).

_____

_____

_____

Worksheet 4.24 Selling Security Worksheet for Intrusion Detection and Vulnerability Analysis.

Rerun your simulation showing how the intrusion and vulnerability would be detected quickly with your plan.

_____

_____

_____

Provide a procedure for management to quickly request changes in IDS/VA policy if needed.

_____

_____

_____

Staff

If desktop IDS/VA is implemented, implement any training required to operate and respond to information and inquiries from the software.

_____

_____

_____

Follow the same process as you did for middle management; staff perception of IDS/VA is very similar.

_____

_____

_____

Worksheet 4.24   Selling Security Worksheet for Intrusion Detection and Vulnerability Analysis. *(continued)*

Secure Software

Summary

Simply put, it is difficult to obtain secure software, either software that you develop yourself or that you buy. Note that here "software" is also used to include any scripts such as those installed on a Web server. Moreover, the art and science of writing secure software are in their infancy. Only recently, with growing awareness that insecure software is an open door to hackers, and hence a liability, have organizations begun paying attention to the security of their software. Historically, it has been all about features, not about high-quality security.

In this security element, we will look at secure software both from the perspective of the developer and of an organization acquiring software (that would be every organization).

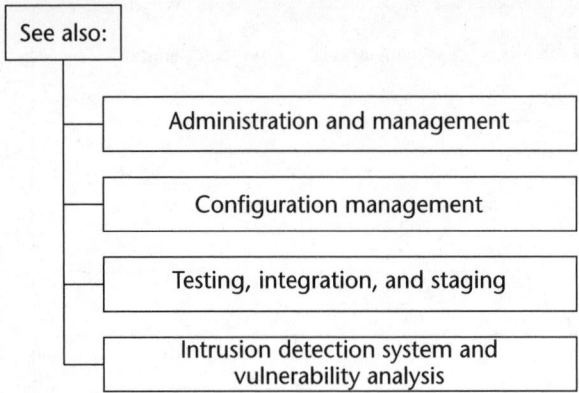

Figure 4.7 Secure software.

Security Stack

Use Worksheet 4.25 here.

PHYSICAL

Describe how your physical software development environment is protected.   Are development servers that house source code (such as your source code control system) located in a protected room, or are they spread across the work area?

NETWORK

Identify any network-based utilities, such as scripts, used to manage network servers and routers.   Describe any embedded trust contained in this software. For example, is a poor trust decision made based on a very weak shared password or an easily spoofed host name? As discussed in Chapter 2, SNMP can cause a variety of security vulnerabilities. Identify how any SNMP-based tools you develop or make use of may fall prey to known SNMP vulnerabilities.

Carefully isolate and protect your software development environment from the rest of the corporate network.   Don't, as one company did, allow free and clear access to the development environment from public areas in your company (e.g., publicly accessible conference rooms).

Security Stack Worksheet for Secure Software

IMPACT ANALYSIS ID	BEFORE PLAN	PERCENT IMPROVEMENT	NEW VALUE

Quality Management worksheet completed for this element/template? (check box) ☐

Physical

Assess how well your software development environment is physically protected. Are CM systems in a protected room?

_____
_____
_____

Network

For your network utilities and the scripts you use, is there dangerous "embedded trust" anywhere?

_____
_____
_____

Be very careful with SNMP. For years it has been a protocol with security issues. Fully examine how you use it.

_____
_____
_____

Develop a plan to isolate, to the extent possible, and protect your software environment from the rest of the network.

_____
_____
_____

Application

Perform a security audit of code and scripts (CGI, Perl, Python), including your own, commercial, and open source/other.

_____
_____
_____

Review logging and traceability of all high-impact software.

_____
_____
_____

Describe how the "fundamentals" are addressed in all software.

_____
_____
_____

Worksheet 4.25   Security Stack Worksheet for Secure Software. *(continues)*

Determine if you use any forms of code obfuscation and, if so, how vulnerable you are as a result.

_____

_____

_____

Assess whether digital code signing (Active-X, JAR) adds value to your software distribution approach.

_____

_____

_____

Review how caches and temporary files are used by your applications.

_____

_____

_____

Review your programming languages and development tools relative to security strengths and weaknesses.

_____

_____

_____

Write a plan to implement source code auditing tools.

_____

_____

_____

Perform an overall analysis and assessment of your software development environment polices and procedures.

_____

_____

_____

Write policies and procedures, train, and put tools into place to reduce the risk from buffer, heap, and stack overflows.

_____

_____

_____

Write policies and procedures, train, and put tools into place to reduce the risk from race conditions.

_____

_____

_____

Specify the steps you take to ensure the quality of cryptographic implementations should you do any.

_____

_____

_____

For network-based applications, plan in advance how your application may securely function in tunnel or proxy.

_____

_____

_____

Worksheet 4.25   Security Stack Worksheet for Secure Software.

Write test procedures to assess the security of your software in the actual environments in which it will be deployed.

_____

_____

_____

Identify what steps you've taken to secure the administration and management interfaces to your application.

_____

_____

_____

Write quality test policies and procedures for security review and testing of software releases and patches/point releases.

_____

_____

_____

Perform a DoS review of your software—where might you be most vulnerable to a DoS attack? How can you protect from it?

_____

_____

_____

Operating System

Try to identify operating system utilities that you might be able to install to help prevent buffer, heap, and stack exploits.

_____

_____

_____

Carefully review operating system configuration differences between test environments and operational ones.

_____

_____

_____

Review the operating system for any security risks relating to temporary files and caching not directly controlled by you.

_____

_____

_____

Assess, manage, and document access control across all system processes, users, and resources.

_____

_____

_____

Define any operating system lockdown assumptions as part of the administration documentation for your application.

_____

_____

_____

Worksheet 4.25   Security Stack Worksheet for Secure Software. *(continued)*

APPLICATION

List all CGI scripts or scripts developed in a scripting language (for example, Perl, Python). Do this for all scripts used, whether developed in-house or acquired.

Cover the fundamentals. In your software plan, describe how the fundamental security elements (authentication, authorization and access control, encryption, integrity (tamper-proofing), nonrepudiation, and privacy) are addressed by your software.

Use code signing. Digital code signing leverages the fundamentals of integrity and nonrepudiation to tamper-proof and prove authorship of software you use and software you distribute. Identify how digital code signing (for example, Authenticode, Java code signing) is used as part of your software release; if it's not, find out why not.

Audit and review. Document your secure design review and source code auditing process. Describe how source code auditing tools, such as the Rough Auditing Tool for Security (RATS), Flawfinder, and ITS4, are used.

Specifically identify how caches and temporary files are maintained by your application. Work to avoid the storage of sensitive information in caches and temporary files; be especially concerned about the contents of these files at any given point should your application crash or be forced to crash. Be certain such caches and files are not available after your program has exited gracefully; address any nongraceful scenarios with some form of cleanup.

Log and trace. Specify the logging and traceability capabilties of your software. Specify software interfaces and logging mechanisms that offer an optimal integration with IDS and vulnerability analysis systems.

Describe any mechanisms you have employed to prevent reverse-engineering of your software. In general, security through obscurity (code obfuscation) is difficult and should be avoided if possible, except when we are trying to prevent people from reverse-engineering our software. Because of the way computer systems are designed today, code obfuscation may be just about the only thing we can do. Making anything more difficult for a hacker is a good idea—merely making it more difficult has value. You may not be relying on code obfuscation for general security, but, at the same time, you may employ it as one means of preventing reverse-engineering of your software.

Carefully choose your programming language and environment, including tools, to address programming language security strengths and weaknesses.   For example, if you decide on the C programming language, then buffer management is a security weakness that requires specific focus.

Consider the pros and cons of open source software.   On the pro side, you get access to heavily scrutinized software typically under very favorable licensing terms. On the con side, too many people integrate this software without adequately testing and understanding it. Do not completely discount the prospect that, at some time, open software you make use of could contain a Trojan horse or backdoor for a hacker.

Be on the lookout for dirty development environments.   Most development environments are far too "dirty." Some developers install their own tools, which have been dug out from some far corner of the Internet, and think nothing of using them. Often, development tools include compiled libraries used during development. You cannot know what kind of backdoor or Trojan horse may be installed on the development machine by these tools or, worse yet, linked into the application they are developing. Distributed software infected with some kind of virus is very common. This particular issue is one of my pet peeves because I regularly encounter software infected in this way. Most of these Trojan horses are network-borne, meaning that, after you install this software, you may notice that your desktop intrusion detection issues a few events or may simply be maliciously disabled. Most developers, I believe, are completely unaware of what they're distributing. If you are serious about security, and if you do any of your own software development, then you need to develop a process, fast and efficient, wherein software developer tools, especially open, shareware, or freeware tools, can be quickly evaluated. Set up a process that works quickly, on the kind of schedule developers need. Set up policies and procedures for how this software will be evaluated, similar to the CEM architectural element, previously discussed. For example, you could assemble a fast review team who looks over the development tool quickly and require that the tool be tested once on a dedicated, and isolated, test system. Such a test can run an integrity check using a tool such as Tripwire before the software is installed, then compare for changed system files by running another integrity check after the software tool is installed. Also look for new TCP and UDP ports that have been opened and "listened to" (for example, via *netstat -a*); you might use a network sniffer to monitor traffic to and from the machine, such as anything tunneled within http.

Protect yourself against overflow exploits—buffer, heap, and stack overflows.   Much has been written about overflow exploits. The threat is real, and it doesn't take a rocket scientist to exploit these should a vulnerability be discovered in your software. Protect yourself by introducing programming approaches, reviewing, auditing, and testing, as discussed in this worksheet.

Win the race against hackers.   So-called race conditions are leveraged by malicious software to "catch" your software while it's "not looking." The hacker may use a race condition to force your application to reveal information midprocess that it shouldn't or allow a change that it shouldn't, simply because the programmer relied too much on a presumed sequence of events that might not, in fact, be relevant in a multitasking environment. You prevent race conditions two ways: first, by implementing software programming standards that encourage software developers to avoid excessive dependence on timing for sensitive operations; second, by testing your software thoroughly, specifically by having your test team look for security vulnerabilities relating to race conditions.

Specify measures to ensure the quality of your cryptographic implementation.   Cryptographic implementations rely on complex mathematical operations that demand that programmers provide sources of randomness (sufficiently random numbers), to carefully "clean up" between operations so as not to leave highly sensitive and secured cryptographic material in memory for any extended period. They rely on secure storage mechanisms of cryptographic material such as storage of a PKI private key.

Manage configurations.   Configuration management, discussed earlier, is core to maintaining a solid, repeatable, manageable software development environment. Introduce a source code revision control system among all of your programmers.

Simulate the target environment with a focus on security.   When testing your software, simulate, as closely as possible, the actual environment in which it will be deployed. Problems with buffer management, processes crashing in an unclean fashion, and other security-related failings may become clear only when the software is run within the kinds of environments you can truly expect, especially in terms of software configuration (e.g., various operating system revisions you intend to support) and performance load.

Consider security administration and management up front.   Administration and management of an application are too often afterthoughts.

For hackers, though, this interface is often their first point of attack. Identify the specific security measures you are taking to protect the administrative and management interface.

OPERATING SYSTEM

Identify where in your plan you might install buffer overflow protection software.   Increasingly, buffer overflow protection software is being made available as a utility that can be installed within the operating system. For example, one such utility claims to identify executable code originating from unchecked (potentially hacked or overflowed) buffers.

Develop your test environment carefully.   Developers typically test their software on a particular operating system configuration; for example, a particular Linux kernel compilation, where they choose to enable or disable certain operating system features or specifically hand-tune buffer, queue, and sockets management parameters within the operating system. The problem with this is that these assumptions often won't hold in the final environment in which the software is deployed. The difference between the final environment and the test environment may produce security holes. Within your test environment, carefully select specific operating system parameters and configurations and communicate specific requirements clearly in software application installation, administration, and management documentation.

Carefully examine operating system activity for security holes introduced by system caching and temporary files.   This is similar to the caching and temporary file problems at the application layer.

Assign and manage access control across all system processes, users, and resources.   Recall this from the discussion in Chapter 3 of the fundamental Access Control security element. A particular application will make use of a number of operating system processes and will introduce a number of its own. The permissions associated with these processes will strongly influence the ultimate security of your entire system. When a hacker compromises a particular operating system process, the hacker assumes all rights assigned to that process. For example, if application developers insist that their applications run with full access to the machine (so-called superuser rights), and if a hacker compromises that process, then the hacker has full control over the machine. Alternatively, if the process has limited permission—only what's absolutely required—then the hacker will, likewise, have limited access to the machine.

Document lockdown assumptions.   If an application is developed with certain operating system lockdown assumptions (see Lockdown in the Wrap-up Security Elements section, at the end of this chapter), then these assumptions must be clearly communicated as requirements in any installation and administration documentation.

Life Cycle Management

Use Worksheet 4.26 here.

TECHNOLOGY SELECTION
Select software development tools that promote secure software.   Carefully choose programming language and related interpreters, compilers, and application server environments so as to minimize exposure due to buffer exploits and the like. When programming languages such as C are chosen, put policies, procedures, and training in place so that programming techniques are used that prevent buffer exploits.

Develop a secure review process for any third-party libraries, objects, and source code used in development.   Examine third-party software for all of the issues raised in this secure software development worksheet.

Choose a configuration-management/source code control system that all developers can agree on and is secure.   Consider any security implementation details/features, such as integration with SSH. Evaluate it using the planning approach provided in this book.

IMPLEMENTATION
Provide security-aware installation, administration, and management documentation with your software.   Include all implementation and configuration guidelines, as discussed earlier in this worksheet, such as operating system configuration requirements. Buck the trend of enabling everything by default and, instead, consider the end user's security needs; disable everything but the core feature set and provide clear documentation on how users can enable features they may need.

OPERATIONS
Consider the needs of the operator during software development.
Make the system easy to maintain and monitor from a security standpoint. Address operator security-related procedures and safeguards as part of your specification.

Life-Cycle Management Worksheet for Secure Software

IMPACT ANALYSIS ID	BEFORE PLAN	PERCENT IMPROVEMENT	NEW VALUE

Quality Management worksheet completed for this element/template? (check box) ☐

Technology Selection

Select your software development tools and language to promote security. Build security into the buying decision.

_____

_____

_____

Develop a security review process for all software and tools you acquire.

_____

_____

_____

Choose a software configuration management system considering your security requirements (e.g., SSH support).

_____

_____

_____

Implementation

Address security with the administration and management documentation you provide with your software.

_____

_____

_____

Where can you "buck the trend" of enabling everything by default and instead provide quality user guidance?

_____

_____

_____

Specify any operating system configuration assumptions or particular concerns relating to security.

_____

_____

_____

Worksheet 4.26   Life-Cycle Management Worksheet for Secure Software. _(continues)_

Operations

Make the security of your application easy to manage and monitor. List examples of simplified operator safeguards.

_____

_____

_____

Incident Response

Assign incident response responsibilities to members of the software development team.

_____

_____

_____

Describe how the team will respond (by analysis, test, and simulation) to reported potential exploits.

_____

_____

_____

Develop quality policies and procedures relating to how software patches are tested for security holes.

_____

_____

_____

Build a streamlined process for hackers to submit vulnerabilities and for following up with them. Involve the incident team.

_____

_____

_____

Worksheet 4.26   Life-Cycle Management Worksheet for Secure Software. *(continued)*

INCIDENT RESPONSE

Organize a specific incident response team to respond to compromises, or potential compromises, that may relate to or involve software developed by the organization.   The team must be ready to quickly investigate buffer overflow concerns or any other concerns relating to the security of their application. They should have a test lab in place in which to simulate scenarios related to compromise concerns. They should have a mechanism that enables them to quickly release software fixes as needed, but they must test those fixes carefully to make sure that new vulnerabilities are not introduced. As discussed in Chapter 1, the ability to communicate with hackers who may have discovered vulnerabilities is an important function of the incident response team.

Business

Use Worksheet 4.27 here.

BUSINESSPEOPLE: EMPLOYEES

Introduce security as a mission for software developers.   Managing software developers (employees) can be a difficult task to begin with. Add the burden of thinking about security during the development, from soup to nuts, and it's understandable why so few bother. Developers are creative free-thinkers who do not like to be bothered with checklists of concerns, caveats, and gotchas. They are typically focused on their particular niche-view of the problem, which often has nothing to do directly with security. Moreover, managers are primarily concerned, historically, with features and schedules, not security. All that said, there's hope. Cross-train developers regarding the security concerns raised here. Require them to introduce security to their documentation and hold regular security review meetings. Reward them for added security measures. Build time into their schedules, where possible, for the introduction of security.

BUSINESSPEOPLE: CUSTOMERS

Address their fears; understand their growing requirements.   The customer view of secure software has evolved in approximately this sequence: In the beginning, security never occurred to them; then they were surprised but complacent; next they moved from complacency to fear; recently, their fear has progressed to a feeling of panic. Their panic is justified. After years of not wanting to pay for security, they are now open to the concept. They are now looking for companies to address their fear and panic. Their wallets are opening up, and their security requirements are becoming increasingly important to them. Finally, their purchasing decisions are, at least, somewhat guided by their security concerns. Whether yours is an internal organizational customer or a commercial one, you must attend to their needs and quiet their fears.

Business Worksheet for Secure Software

IMPACT ANALYSIS ID	BEFORE PLAN	PERCENT IMPROVEMENT	NEW VALUE

Quality Management worksheet completed for this element/template? (check box) ☐

Employees

Introduce security as a fundamental "mission" for software developers.

_____

_____

_____

Cross-train developers, to the next level of detail, on security concerns raised in our worksheets.

_____

_____

_____

Work with developers to make security a regular part of all documentation.

_____

_____

_____

Schedule regular security review meetings.

_____

_____

_____

Build time into schedules for security. Reward developers for thinking about security and for introducing well thought-out security features.

_____

_____

_____

Customers

Work with customers to understand their security requirements and document them.

_____

_____

_____

How are you designing and developing software to better address customer security requirements and expectations?

_____

_____

_____

Worksheet 4.27   Business Worksheet for Secure Software.

Owners

Providers of chronically insecure software will increasingly be held responsible. Communicate this to owners.

_____

_____

Companies that are perceived as providing insecure software, products, or services will be hurt.

_____

_____

_____

Introduce a top-down management philosophy reflecting the importance of public perception relating to product security.

_____

_____

_____

Suppliers and Partners

Develop policies and procedures to hold suppliers and partners responsible for providing insecure products and services.

_____

_____

_____

If you bundle software with a partner and its software is insecure, yours is too. Drive partners to security quality.

_____

_____

_____

Information

Write specific/focused security requirements for all high-impact information of any kind you manage with your software.

_____

_____

_____

Infrastructure

Develop a plan and customer configuration guidance for protecting likely high-impact infrastructure with your software.

_____

_____

_____

Worksheet 4.27   Business Worksheet for Secure Software. _(continued)_

BUSINESSPEOPLE: OWNERS

Assure them that security is addressed in the software development process. Despite the liability disclaimers, both written and implicit, that are delivered with software, distributors of chronically insecure software will increasingly be held accountable. We have already seen dramatic inroads made in various markets, fueled by the perception that one software product is more secure than another. In the past, owners were more concerned with features, price, and schedule (the same priorities as their customers); they are now concerned with security. From the perspective of the owner, if security is not introduced into the software development process, the damage to the business may have no bounds. If your organization sells software to others, introduce security quality and security-related features to the product sales pitch.

BUSINESSPEOPLE: SUPPLIERS

Refuse to accept poor security. Companies that supply you with chronically insecure software need to be either replaced or driven, using the methods described in these guidelines, to produce quality security. (This topic is covered in the Quality Management worksheets.)

BUSINESSPEOPLE: PARTNERS

Introduce requirements for any software development/bundling efforts your organization engages in. If you partner with a company and bundle its software with yours, you become "one" with that company's security strategy. This means that if its software is insecure, the customer will not differentiate between your partner's software and yours.

BUSINESS: INFORMATION

Associate specific security requirements with information elements (a private key, username/password credential of some kind). Information touched by your application in any way (configuration, customer/user information, programming variables) should have a notion of security requirements associated with it. This is not to suggest that you take this to the point of absurdity, as in write a security specification for every variable used by a software developer. Instead, make sure the developers think about what information they place into a variable and how it is managed and made accessible to a hacker. Without the notion of security in the development process, it's difficult to predict the shortcuts people will take. Another example is storing a username/password pair persistently in memory rather than retrieving it, doing whatever check is needed, then immediately wiping it from memory. In each of these examples, there are information elements (a private key, username/password credential of some kind), and there are specific security requirements that should be associated with them.

Selling Security

Use Worksheet 4.28 here.

EXECUTIVES

Simulate a vulnerability, based on risk assessment.   Simulate a vulnerability and parameterize the costs to the organization in terms of public perception, effect on business (different groups reprioritizing, losing time), and, most important, impact on customers. If you supply software to others, simulate a widespread, highly publicized vulnerability; if you supply software to your own organization, show how impact is reduced as you phase in a secure software design and development process. Because secure software design and development may add time to development schedules and cost, your sell will be complicated, but as noted earlier, times are changing and some of the selling difficulties are being solved for you.

MIDDLE MANAGEMENT

Relate the business impact of vulnerabilities discovered in core operational software.   Work to convince them that your objective is to reduce this impact—reduce this risk and overhead. Be as specific as you can about business process workflow impact. Prepare them to accept potentially longer delays in getting the features they are after, assuring them that the reduced impact is well worth it.

BUSINESS: INFRASTRUCTURE

Prioritize vulnerabilities as accurately as possible.   Insecure software is a threat to all infrastructure. While you can argue that a vulnerability in a word processor may be less significant than one in a directory server, when thinking about the myriad deployment and attack scenarios, the conclusion is that it's difficult to predict exactly what will happen. Vulnerabilities can spread like the plague. Nevertheless, the reality is that you often need to prioritize your secure software review for existing deployments. The prioritization would follow the parameters of your impact analysis, as discussed in Chapter 2, and would attempt to estimate the cost of the security review, any rewrites, or new vendors required to meet secure software objectives.

Selling Security Worksheet for Secure Software

IMPACT ANALYSIS ID	BEFORE PLAN	PERCENT IMPROVEMENT	NEW VALUE

Executive

The risk of public perception relating to insecure software you develop or deploy is very high. Demonstrate this.

_____
_____
_____

The impact on customers affected by your security holes can be very high. Provide an example of customer costs.

_____
_____
_____

Show how a streamlined secure software process may improve customer satisfaction and increase market share.

_____
_____
_____

Show how your secure software plan reduces the potential impact on the organization. Show costs including schedule impact.

_____
_____
_____

Middle Management

Highlight how insecure software impacts the workflow process, be it product support, development, or operations.

_____
_____
_____

Show the cumulative costs of responding to security problems, both internally and for the customer. Compare to your planned costs.

_____
_____
_____

Worksheet 4.28   Selling Security Worksheet for Secure Software.

Work with middle management and executives to build a bridge of understanding around schedule impact and benefits.

_____

_____

_____

Staff

Sell staff on security by showing that management cares about it. Show how you add time and resources for security.

_____

_____

_____

Build a security training, awareness, and reward process, as discussed earlier in the Business worksheet.

_____

_____

_____

Worksheet 4.28   Selling Security Worksheet for Secure Software. _(continued)_

STAFF

Use your impact analysis to sell them.   Staff members involved in development have their own view on all of this. Staff impacted by insecure software will understand the risks and can be sold, using your impact analysis translated into day-to-day terms, on the increased costs associated with developing or acquiring securely developed software—fewer features, more time in development.

Secure Time Services

Summary

As discussed in Chapter 2 and throughout the preceding security elements, time has more to do with security than you might first think. It's routinely leveraged up and down the security stack, and sophisticated hackers often attack it first as a means to undermine your security and to better cover their tracks. Intrusion-detection systems may rely on time as well to detect certain attack signatures.

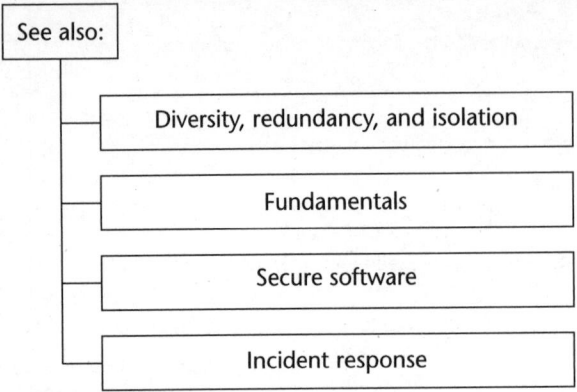

Figure 4.8   Secure time services.

Security Stack

Use Worksheet 4.29 here.

PHYSICAL

Assess time security on systems used for building access control.   These
systems can make use of time as a means for logging movement from
one room to the next, so you need to consider how time is secured on
them, as well as how they are administered. Your incident response team
may need to rely on these logs, and if the recorded time is not reliable,
then their effort will be impeded.

Introduce diversity.   Time servers used throughout the security stack,
where time is centralized and delivered electronically to core system
components, should be physically secured, diverse, and redundant.

NETWORK

Institute a common, consistent, and secure time reference.   Network
components routinely rely on time for system logging, access control,
and authentication. For example, VPNs based on IPSec can use a PKI for
authentication. PKIs are very dependent on secure time because digital
certificates are valid for certain time periods only. Therefore, validating a
digital certificate requires a common, consistent, and secure time reference. Also, authentication protocols, such as Kerberos, implementable at
the network, application, and operating system levels, fail completely or
can otherwise be compromised if your time services are hacked or
brought down.

Security Stack Worksheet for Secure Time

IMPACT ANALYSIS ID	BEFORE PLAN	PERCENT IMPROVEMENT	NEW VALUE

Quality Management worksheet completed for this element/template? (check box) ☐

Physical

Determine how your building access control systems may make use of time.

_____
_____
_____

Identify other physical security-sensitive systems that make use of time.

_____
_____
_____

Assess the reliability and strength of physical time sources.

_____
_____
_____

Develop administrator policies and procedures that place importance on reliability and securely maintaining time sources.

_____
_____
_____

Network

Identify network components that rely on time for security-related services such as logging (e.g., time stamps in logs), access, and authentication.

_____
_____
_____

For all authentication mechanisms used by network components, identify reliance on time.

_____
_____
_____

Develop a plan to maintain time reliably and securely for all security-sensitive network components and related services.

_____
_____
_____

Worksheet 4.29 Security Stack Worksheet for Secure Time. *(continues)*

Application

Perform a complete audit to assess how high-impact applications use time in your organization.

_____

_____

_____

For each application leveraging time, determine the security and reliability of the time source.

_____

_____

_____

Develop a plan to maintain time reliably and securely for all high-impact applications.

_____

_____

_____

Operating System

Determine how time is managed in your operating system. Assess the reliability and security of time sources.

_____

_____

_____

Identify specific operating system functions such as logging and authentication that make use of time.

_____

_____

_____

Develop a plan to ensure the security and reliability of time mechanisms used within your operating system.

_____

_____

_____

Worksheet 4.29   Security Stack Worksheet for Secure Time. *(continued)*

Obtain secure versions of protocols.   Time is distributed across the network using protocols such as the Network Time Protocol (NTP). NTP alone is not a sufficiently secure method of delivering sensitive time. Secure versions of NTP are available, as are other more secure time distribution mechanisms.

APPLICATION

Identify any applications that may benefit from secure time-stamping technology.   Financial applications, for example, make use of time, as in recording the time of a transaction. Nonrepudiation-based applications use time to record the moment an event occurred and was authorized (similar to signing *and* dating a contract). Because some applications rely on time as an important part of their functionality (e.g., an application that manages stock market transactions), their source of time and associated time distribution protocol should be secured.

OPERATING SYSTEM

Monitor how time is set and maintained.   It's of paramount importance that time be set and maintained securely in operating systems because time typically starts there and is propagated outward. The operating system itself also makes use of time for logging, authentication, access control, and housekeeping, such as the last time a file was modified (a favorite item for a hacker to modify). See the preceding text on Network, relating to protocols such as NTP: Typically, protocols such as this one are used to set the time in your operating system.

Life-Cycle Management

Use Worksheet 4.30 here.

TECHNOLOGY SELECTION

Choose technology that derives time consistently.   For example, choose an atomic clock or one that derives time from a satellite signal or uses some other time-derivation technology. Organizations that instead prefer to rely on clocks built into computers today (that is, clocks on the computer's motherboard), must face the fact that such clocks are surprisingly inaccurate.

Make your time source and distribution method diverse and redundant.   Then, if it fails, you will be able to fall back to another reliable time source.

Synchronize time across your stack.   The manner in which time is shared and synchronized up and down the security stack is key. From an incident response standpoint, if you must correlate multiple suspicious events occurring at multiple levels of your security stack (for example, an event recording room access with another showing access to a sensitive application), then you must synchronize time across your stack. Too few organizations think about such things—for example, how many synchronize the time reference on their building access systems with their corporate authentication servers?

Implement secure versions of NTP or other protocol alternatives. If hackers can override your time setting with theirs, then you have given them an easier avenue to hack or disrupt your systems, by, for example, implementing their own hacked version of NTP. As mentioned, many of the time delivery mechanisms used today aren't particularly secure—NTP, for example. Secure versions of NTP (so-called Secure NTP, or stime), as well as other protocol alternatives, should be considered as a secure mechanism. Odds are high that, today, the technology you use to distribute time in your security stack is not sufficiently secure. This is often an overlooked area of high vulnerability.

IMPLEMENTATION

Keep things tight relative to the time protocols allowed between machines when implementing your secure time architecture. A good way to do this is to simply disable access to any time-setting capability for most, if not all, administrators and, instead, set time through your secure distributed time mechanism (through a secure protocol).

OPERATIONS

Educate the operations group about the importance of secure time. The operations groups will tend to assume that time is a noncritical service. If the system starts to have problems, they'll typically downplay the impact of time and focus on other, far less important tasks. Therefore, you need to be sure your operations group understands the importance of secure time; then give them the tools they need to monitor the health and security of your distributed time services.

INCIDENT RESPONSE

Validate the integrity of time. Your incident response team can be severely hampered if your time services are compromised. Time allows the team to re-create events and trace and anticipate the actions of a hacker. Time also provides important evidence should law enforcement become involved because time may be used to track the involvement of one or more individuals. The incident response team needs some form of validation, at the start of their response process, that integrity of the time services has been maintained. If such validation is not provided, the response team may place less importance on time as they piece together events. If, say, time has been tampered with and the team assumes it hasn't, then the hacker essentially "controls" the incident response team and can easily send them into a cat-and-mouse game.

Life Cycle Management Worksheet for Secure Time

IMPACT ANALYSIS ID	BEFORE PLAN	PERCENT IMPROVEMENT	NEW VALUE

Quality Management worksheet completed for this element/template? (check box) ☐

Technology Selection

Select a high-quality time source for your organization.

_____
_____
_____

Develop alternate/backup time sources in the event your primary one is unavailable for any reason.

_____
_____
_____

Select technology that helps you synchronize all security stack components to your common high-quality clock.

_____
_____
_____

Choose technology that allows you to maintain and share time securely. Consider *secure time* sharing protocols wherever available.

_____
_____
_____

Implementation

Develop a plan to implement secure time distribution protocols. Correlate with your addressing and filtering strategies.

_____
_____
_____

Disable administrator interfaces, where possible, to prevent override of centralized time by setting time locally.

_____
_____
_____

Operations

Train operations staff on the importance of time (otherwise, they typically won't "get it").

_____
_____
_____

Worksheet 4.30   Life-Cycle Management Worksheet for Secure Time. *(continues)*

Integrate the checking and verification of correct time into operations staff troubleshooting procedures.

_____

_____

_____

Provide operations staff with the ability to constantly monitor the health of your time sources and time distribution protocols.

_____

_____

_____

Incident Response

Prepare a time source map showing time sources, uses, and distribution mechanisms in advance for use by the team.

_____

_____

_____

Develop a policy and procedure wherein the veracity of time is assessed as part of the response process.

_____

_____

_____

Prepare for incident response scenarios wherein time may not be deemed reliable as part of the response process.

_____

_____

_____

Worksheet 4.30   Life-Cycle Management Worksheet for Secure Time. *(continued)*

Business

Use Worksheet 4.31 here.

BUSINESSPEOPLE: EMPLOYEES

Identify systems that are most affected by a hacked time.   Employees tend to take knowledge of time for granted, yet are highly sensitive to the basic impact of hacked time—that is, the systems they rely on are compromised or become nonoperational.

BUSINESSPEOPLE: CUSTOMERS

Identify all instances where customers expect your organization to maintain a sound time reference.   Customers assume your organization keeps a common time baseline: when they request products or services, when those products/services are delivered, and all of the records in between. From the customer's standpoint, all are assumed to be your responsibility. If your organization is hacked and loses track of, for example, when an order was placed, this can result in a high-impact public perception problem, not to mention a problem of service delivery.

BUSINESSPEOPLE: OWNERS

Meet their expectations.   Owners expect the organization to properly record events relating to its organization's financial health, public perception, and any other time-sensitive activities core to the operation.

BUSINESSPEOPLE: SUPPLIERS

Agree on a secure source of time.   Suppliers you rely on obviously need to maintain a common notion of time; for sensitive transactions, such as financial ones, the agreement between you and your suppliers regarding a secure source of time, and secure time stamping of transactions in general, can be quite important.

PARTNERS

Establish a common secure time baseline.   If you are involved in any high-impact, business-to-business electronic exchange with partners, you must have a common secure time baseline. The issues are similar to those associated with suppliers.

BUSINESS: INFORMATION

Iterate highest-impact information elements that are most sensitive to hacked time.   By now, after reviewing all of the preceding security elements and these guidelines, you will have read many tips on how to spot time-sensitive information.

BUSINESS: INFRASTRUCTURE

Iterate highest-impact infrastructure elements that are most sensitive to hacked time.   As with iterating information that is vulnerable to hacked time, a similar process should be carried out for highest-impact infrastructure components.

Business Worksheet for Secure Time

IMPACT ANALYSIS ID	BEFORE PLAN	PERCENT IMPROVEMENT	NEW VALUE

Quality Management worksheet completed for this element/template? (check box) ☐

Employees

Identify employee work that is most likely undermined by a time source that's hacked.

_____

_____

_____

Customers

Define customer expectations for the way you maintain a sound time reference such as when they place an order.

_____

_____

_____

Owners

Define owner time expectations for recording sensitive events and keeping high-impact systems running.

_____

_____

_____

Suppliers and Partners

For business-to-business transactions, a common baseline of time is important. Define how this is maintained.

_____

_____

_____

Information

Develop a plan for highest-impact information elements that are most reliant on a secure and reliable time source.

_____

_____

_____

Worksheet 4.31   Business Worksheet for Secure Time.

Infrastructure

List high-impact infrastructure components most affected by secure and reliable time.

_____
_____
_____

Define what new infrastructure components may be needed to implement a secure and reliable time architecture.

_____
_____
_____

Worksheet 4.31   Business Worksheet for Secure Time. *(continued)*

Selling Security

Use Worksheet 4.32 here.

EXECUTIVES

Stress high-impact outcomes resulting from time compromise, such as completely stopping business operations.   Assess the reduced impact/risk by deploying your secure time system. Because secure time services can often be deployed transparently, inform executives that your architecture can be implemented in such a way as to not disrupt normal business activities. Or, if deployment will cause disruption, quantify that, and again emphasize the benefits of the overall effort. Provide a high-impact example, such as the recording of an important financial event, and show how, if time were compromised, that event and others could fall out in unexpected and harmful ways.

MIDDLE MANAGEMENT

Provide specific examples of how vulnerability and potential downtime would be reduced as a result of your secure time plan.   Middle management should understand the decreased impact associated with secure time services. Time is something they manage for a living.

STAFF

Itemize the benefits of secure time, in terms of reduced potential impact in day-to-day activities.   If your secure time services are entirely transparent to staff, they won't care what mechanism you are using. You will have to sell staff only if they are asked to sacrifice in any way as part of your secure time plan deployment.

Selling Security Worksheet for Secure Time

IMPACT ANALYSIS ID	BEFORE PLAN	PERCENT IMPROVEMENT	NEW VALUE

Executive

Show impact reduction by securely managing time. Point out the joy a hacker experiences when tampering with time.

_____
_____
_____

Other than how infrastructure components are affected, show how hacked time affects things executives understand such as a tampered time stamp on an important financial transaction.

_____
_____
_____

Middle Management

Show how vulnerability and potential for work disruption are decreased by strengthening the security of time services.

_____
_____
_____

Walk through, step-by-step, how a specific work process can be disrupted or halted when time is hacked.

_____
_____
_____

Staff

Demonstrate a real example of hacked time and the impact for an application that staff members are familiar with.

_____
_____
_____

Let staff members understand the benefit of secure time by highlighting the reduced impact.

_____
_____
_____

Worksheet 4.32   Selling Security Worksheet for Secure Time.

Staff Management

Summary

Staff management addresses the full life-cycle management of your organization's relationships with individuals and organizations. These relationships involve the administration of important fundamentals, including authentication, access control, and privacy.

Security Stack

Use Worksheet 4.33 here.

PHYSICAL

Define badging procedures for all employees, contractors, and visitors. Specify policies and procedures that enable you to maintain security of high-impact systems.

Communicate surveillance policies and procedures. Inform all staff, contractors, and visitors that the company may use video surveillance, record traffic, or perform other tracking activities as needed to secure sensitive corporate assets. (See also Privacy, in Chapter 3.)

Implement well-understood and rapid background checking. This should include any visitor who is granted regular access to your facility, such as contractors and cleaning staff.

Define full life-cycle policies and procedures. This should cover badge issuance, usage management, and disablement/termination.

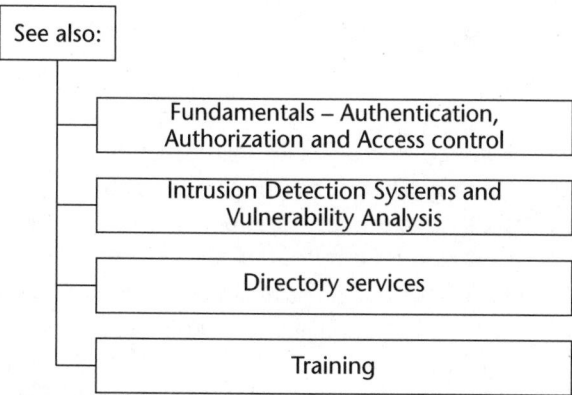

Figure 4.9 Staff management.

NETWORK

Specify policies and procedures for enabling, disabling, and monitoring network authentication and access control.   This is of particular importance if your organization suspects illegal or improper activity, and it should cover all forms of network authentication and access control for individuals, partners, and suppliers. Include internal, dial-up, and business-to-business enablement and disablement of any authentication tokens such as smart cards or SecurID cards.

APPLICATION

Specify policies and procedures for enabling, disabling, and monitoring all forms of application authentication and access control.   As for Network, in the preceding text, this is especially critical if your organization suspects illegal or improper activity; hence, your policies and procedures should cover individuals, partners, and suppliers. Include enablement and disablement of any authentication tokens such as smart cards or SecurID cards.

If called for by your impact analysis, establish an archival mechanism.   Doing so will make it possible to study, in the future, application-level information managed by an employee should the situation call for it— say, if the employee is terminated for violating company policies.

Specify organization policies and procedures regarding confidentiality issues.   These might include requiring employees to turn over all confidential company information to a designated person in the human resources department when they leave the company, who will then destroy all electronic files containing confidential information.

Change system authentication credentials (username/passwords) on termination of any staff members, especially administrative staff members.   This is crucial for all staff members, but more so for administrators who have access to high-impact systems.

OPERATING SYSTEM

As for Network and Application, specify policies and procedures for enabling, disabling, and monitoring all forms of operating system authentication and access control.   Again, this is important to do if the organization suspects illegal or improper activity; hence, your policies and procedures must cover individuals, partners, and suppliers. Address how to enable and disable any authentication tokens such as smart cards.

Security Stack Worksheet for Staff Management

IMPACT ANALYSIS ID	BEFORE PLAN	PERCENT IMPROVEMENT	NEW VALUE

Quality Management worksheet completed for this element/template? (check box) ☐

Physical

Define building access and badging procedures for employees, contractors, and visitors. Define specific high-impact access.

_____

_____

Write policies and procedures for all levels of surveillance, record keeping, and tracking.

_____

_____

Implement well-understood, rapid, and flexible background checking. Include visitors, contractors, and other service personnel granted recurring access.

_____

_____

Address every phase of authentication and access control "lifetime" from issuance, usage management, to disablement/termination.

_____

_____

Network

Specify policies and procedures for access (enable/disable/suspend), usage, and monitoring of all network activity.

_____

_____

Address all forms of network access in your plan including internal, dial-up, and business-to-business.

_____

_____

_____

Worksheet 4.33 Security Stack Worksheet for Staff Management. *(continues)*

Application

Specify policies and procedures for access (enable/disable/suspend) and monitoring of application usage.

_____

_____

_____

For high-impact applications, consider adding the capability to archive more detailed data on staff member actions.

_____

_____

_____

Write specific policies and procedures to remind staff of the terms of your organization's nondisclosure agreement (NDA).

_____

_____

_____

Develop policies and procedures to freeze and archive accounts and change authentication credentials upon termination.

_____

_____

_____

Operating System

Specify policies and procedures for access (enable/disable/suspend) and monitoring of operating system usage.

_____

_____

_____

Similar to the application level, determine what additional archival might be needed for staff in high-impact positions.

_____

_____

_____

Worksheet 4.33 Security Stack Worksheet for Staff Management. *(continued)*

Establish an archival mechanism.   You may find this necessary so that, in the future, you can examine operating system-level information managed by an employee, based on business demand or concerns that suspicious activity has taken place—say, because the employee was terminated for violating company policies.

Life-Cycle Management

Use Worksheet 4.34 here.

TECHNOLOGY SELECTION

Investigate human resource information systems.   For larger organizations, human resource information systems (HRIS) are increasingly becoming a single point of management for certain elements of security stack staff management (for example, an HRIS that's integrated with the company's badging system and directory service). While it's difficult for most organizations to implement all staff management policies and procedures based on a single, integrated HRIS interface, it's worth investigating a practical level of implementation for your organization.

IMPLEMENTATION

Directly address staff access to systems and facilities.   Staff management demands considerable cross-organizational training; consequently, in most organizations, access to systems and facilities is managed in an ad hoc fashion. That is, when an employee joins the company, typically he or she must contact a large, disjointed set of individuals to get user accounts for different systems, badges, and so forth. Similarly, when an employee leaves, often no clean, well-understood process is in place for removing the individual from all the systems for which he or she is enabled. Staff management policy and procedure training is, therefore, a primary concern.

Make the staff management process as seamless as possible.   Most authentication and access control tasks are, today, spread across multiple disjoint systems. Centralizing authentication and access control with a directory services plan, discussed earlier, can provide a significantly more seamless staff management process.

OPERATIONS

Define clear policies and procedures regarding authentication and access control disablement.   This is especially important in regard to terminated administrators and other operations staff.

INCIDENT RESPONSE

Inform the incident response team about terminated employees who had access to high-impact systems.   Especially crucial in this regard are system administrators. Make this information available to the team for the past 12 months.

Life-Cycle Management Worksheet for Staff Management

ANALYSIS IMPACT ID	BEFORE PLAN	PERCENT IMPROVEMENT	NEW VALUE

Quality Management worksheet completed for this element/template? (check box) ☐

Technology Selection

Assess how well your HRIS staff management software integrates with staff management security requirements.

_____

_____

_____

Consider technology that brings you closer, or takes you to, a "one token solution" for the full security stack such as through the use of a smart card.

_____

_____

_____

Select technology to assist you in any advanced archival requirements for high-impact applications and information.

_____

_____

_____

Carefully plan and assess the role of your directory service as part of your staff management architecture.

_____

_____

_____

Implementation

Develop a plan to centralize and strengthen staff management functions. Describe the ad hoc methods used today.

_____

_____

_____

Operations

Define clear policies and procedures for staff management access (enable/disable/suspend) and monitoring.

_____

_____

_____

Worksheet 4.34 Life-Cycle Management Worksheet for Staff Management.

Train operations staff on the importance of careful and secure staff management procedures.

_____

_____

_____

Incident Response

The incident team needs to be regularly notified of terminated employees having access to high impact systems.

_____

_____

The team needs full access to all staff management systems for logs and analysis and to instantly change access rights.

_____

_____

Maintain information on past terminations including an ongoing record of those terminated within the last 12 months.

_____

_____

_____

Worksheet 4.34   Life-Cycle Management Worksheet for Staff Management. _(continued)_

Business

Use Worksheet 4.35 here.

BUSINESSPEOPLE: EMPLOYEES

Implement humane termination policies and procedures.   Staff management policies and procedures are not about alienating terminated employees. Thus, they should be written with a degree of humaneness, with consideration for feelings—that is, don't give the impression you are slamming the door behind an employee who is on the way out. Achieving this has much to do with how you communicate that company policies are "not personal."

Enable new employees seamlessly.   Staff members new to your organization will appreciate a seamless enablement in all of the key security stack elements at one time (e.g., full directory service integration); you'll achieve early buy-in for your security plan with the new employee.

BUSINESSPEOPLE: CUSTOMERS

Let customers know of staff changes that affect them. Staff management is relevant to customers only to the extent that the employee they routinely interact with is now no longer with your organization. In such a case, to avoid customer confusion and to minimize the possibility that former employees may misrepresent themselves to a customer for some malicious purpose, a formal process should be in place to notify customers of a staff change that affects them.

BUSINESSPEOPLE: OWNERS

Just do it. Owners expect you to implement solid staff management policies and procedures. In fact, it's fair to say that they take it for granted and assume you will do so.

BUSINESSPEOPLE: SUPPLIERS

As for customers, explain how your staff management policies and procedures relate to them. Suppliers and partners should be concerned with staff changes only when they are directly affected, meaning when people they routinely interact with are no longer with your organization. In such a case, notify them.

BUSINESSPEOPLE: PARTNERS

See the preceding text on Suppliers.

BUSINESS: INFORMATION

Identify and list high-impact information. You can best determine highest-priority staff management policies and procedures by first identifying high-impact information in your organization and then listing the individuals, partners, and suppliers who have access to that information.

BUSINESS: INFRASTRUCTURE

Prioritize staff management policies and procedures according to the high-impact infrastructure. For example, a firewall administrator is an individual for whom you likely want tight staff management policies and procedures, right away, because of the high-impact nature of that infrastructure component.

Business Worksheet for Staff Management

IMPACT ANALYSIS ID	BEFORE PLAN	PERCENT IMPROVEMENT	NEW VALUE

Quality Management worksheet completed for this element/template? (check box) ☐

Employees

Develop a plan to address employee feelings about staff management, especially feelings of alienation and trust.

_____

_____

_____

Provide full access to all staff policies, especially those that may relate to employee privacy concerns (e.g., monitoring).

_____

_____

_____

Customers

Assess how your staff management procedures protect the security of customers in the event of staff termination.

_____

_____

_____

Owners

Review all owner expectations relating to staff management for high-impact systems.

_____

_____

_____

Suppliers and Partners

Clearly communicate staff management policies and procedures affecting suppliers and partners.

_____

_____

_____

Worksheet 4.35 Business Worksheet for Staff Management. *(continues)*

Information

Identify high-impact information. Correlate it with individuals, partners, and suppliers. Build staff management requirements.

_____

_____

_____

Infrastructure

Prioritize staff management policies and procedures around high-impact infrastructure.

_____

_____

_____

Worksheet 4.35 Business Worksheet for Staff Management. *(continued)*

Selling Security

Use Worksheet 4.36 here.

EXECUTIVES

Explain high-impact risk. Executives inherently understand the need for staff management, but they don't always understand the high-impact risks associated with doing it poorly. Specifically, show the kind of damage a disgruntled employee is capable of doing without fast and efficient staff management capability.

In terms of paying for it, clearly show the efficiencies that a solid staff management system provides. Review the Directory Services security element and the staff management benefits discussed there: That technology provides an excellent mechanism for streamlining staff management.

Leverage your impact analysis. Give examples of benefits and administrative savings. Perhaps simulate the ad hoc manner in which employees are brought onboard and terminated today (along with the risks of that process); this should provide a solid and fluid justification.

Selling Security Worksheet for Staff Management

IMPACT ANALYSIS ID	BEFORE PLAN	PERCENT IMPROVEMENT	NEW VALUE

Executive

Demonstrate several real examples of the impact of poor staff management. Show security and efficiency risks.

_____

_____

_____

Run through the same examples with your staff management plan in place. Highlight reduced impact, increased efficiency.

_____

_____

_____

Show how the organization will save money and reduce impact, over time, with your staff management plan.

_____

_____

_____

Middle Management

Show how new employee introduction and employee termination are all simplified. Give a very specific example.

_____

_____

_____

Walk through, step-by-step, staff management benefits, and simulate different threats in relation to business processes.

_____

_____

_____

Ask and prepare middle management to build employee trust among employees in your staff management policies and procedures.

_____

_____

_____

Worksheet 4.36   Selling Security Worksheet for Staff Management. *(continues)*

Staff

New employees greatly appreciate the benefits of streamlined configuration in all online systems.

_____

_____

_____

Employees will, without extraordinary effort by you, despise you for terminating access hastily. Educate and use common sense.

_____

_____

If employees are terminated, they should fully understand the staff management process. Don't surprise them.

_____

_____

Employees can understand why you must have quick and clean termination policies but only if you educate them and build trust.

_____

_____

_____

Worksheet 4.36   Selling Security Worksheet for Staff Management. *(continued)*

MIDDLE MANAGEMENT

Demonstrate how employee initiation and termination processes will be greatly simplified and made faster and more efficient.   Like executives, middle managers understand the value of staff management. But to achieve buy-in, it helps to provide specific business process examples, if possible. Point out the reduced risk to their schedules by the lowered impact. Show how quickly and efficiently new employees can be brought onboard.

STAFF

Educate and communicate.   On the hiring side, staff members greatly appreciate quality staff management policies and procedures. Conversely, when terminated, they typically object to them because they send a message that the organization does not trust them. This is where education and communication come into play. As mentioned earlier, you need to depersonalize termination procedures as much as possible, explaining to the terminated employee that this is something the organization does across the board to protect itself.

Address terminated employees' perception of the staff management process.   If you don't, you run the risk of instigating exactly the disgruntled response you are trying so hard to protect your organization from. In general, however, how you diffuse a touchy situation (and employee!) has more to do with elements beyond the scope of this book and relate more to people skills, human resource policies on termination and compensation, assisting employees in finding new jobs, employee assistance programs, and so forth.

Wrap-Up Security Element Worksheets

Recall that we will handle the wrap-up security elements differently because, as explained in Chapter 2, these are summary elements that will serve as a final checklist as we complete our security plan, to catch anything we've missed. Therefore, we don't need to go through the entire security template for these elements, as we do for the core elements. Instead, we take a simplified approach, using one summary worksheet per wrap-up security element. The purpose of each security element is also provided in the sections that follow.

Administration and Management

The topic of administration and management is a common thread throughout our worksheets. The goal for this wrap-up element worksheet (Worksheet 4.37) is to identify any holes, anything potentially missed in our earlier security planning process. Identify any vulnerabilities produced by your use of SNMP. Identify all opportunities where SSH can be used but isn't. Be sure that you do not have the trivial file transfer protocol (tftp) enabled because this protocol does not require the use of a password.

Interoperability and Standards

A common theme has been that interoperability and standards are very important but that we should not allow ourselves to become overly driven by them. Remember, in the end, that our mission is to move security and business forward. With that in mind, review your entire security plan and ask yourself, again, where do you get the most benefit from interoperability and standards? Prioritize the importance of interoperability and standards based on their importance to high-impact systems. Where you cannot obtain a high level of interoperability or standardization, define the associated drawbacks and work to minimize their impact. Use Worksheet 4.38.

Administration and Maintenance Worksheet

IMPACT ANALYSIS ID	BEFORE PLAN	PERCENT IMPROVEMENT	NEW VALUE

Quality Management worksheet completed for this element/template? (check box) ☐

Try to identify any areas of administration and maintenance that may have been overlooked in our earlier worksheets.

_____

_____

_____

Worksheet 4.37   Administration and Maintenance Worksheet.

Interoperability and Standards Worksheet

IMPACT ANALYSIS ID	BEFORE PLAN	PERCENT IMPROVEMENT	NEW VALUE

Quality Management worksheet completed for this element/template? (check box) ☐

Where in your security architecture would improved interoperability and standards support garner you the most benefit?

_____

_____

Develop a plan to achieve better interoperability and standards support for these most beneficial areas.

_____

_____

_____

Worksheet 4.38   Administration and Maintenance Worksheet.

Laws and Regulations

Laws and regulations can drive your security plan in many of the areas we've previously studied. Examples include recordkeeping, such as providing proof of events and transactions, the requirement to conform to laws regarding encryption usage and export, certain open standards required by government regulations, public access to information, and so forth. Aspects of your security plan may play a role in supporting these laws and regulations, such as access control, logging, time stamping, archival, privacy, encryption, and interoperability. Use Worksheet 4.39.

Laws and Regulations Worksheet

IMPACT ANALYSIS ID	BEFORE PLAN	PERCENT IMPROVEMENT	NEW VALUE

Quality Management worksheet completed for this element/template (check box) ☐

Identify local, state, national, and multinational laws and regulations governing your organization that may affect your security plan.

_____

_____

_____

Think about how any applicable laws and regulations relate to people, information, and infrastructure.

_____

_____

_____

Worksheet 4.39   Laws and Regulations Worksheet.

Lockdown

Lockdown is an integrated process that takes into account much of what we've covered in the other security worksheets. Nevertheless, there are some consistent lockdown themes that we should review and formalize. The objective of this wrap-up element is to spur you to review your security plan for any lockdown areas that you may have overlooked.

As pointed out many times throughout this book, operating systems and applications—pretty much anything in your security stack—typically come out of the box with too much enabled by default. Therefore, it's safe to say that a general rule of lockdown is to never rely on default settings; rather, you must review all of them. Use Worksheet 4.40.

Here are more examples of best practices relating to lockdown discussed in previous worksheets:

- Review all administrative, management, and maintenance interfaces for security. Assess how you use protocols such as SNMP and http to manage devices; ascertain that these protocols are secured.

- Carefully assign process, file, and directory permissions. Write a careful access control matrix for locked-down systems, and adhere to it.

Lockdown Worksheet

IMPACT ANALYSIS ID	BEFORE PLAN	PERCENT IMPROVEMENT	NEW VALUE

Quality Management worksheet completed for this element/template? (check box) ☐

Implement the "lockdown best practices" for all security stack elements including all network devices, servers, and desktops.

_____

_____

_____

Worksheet 4.40 Lockdown Worksheet.

- Disable and uninstall everything except what you need.
- Carefully configure logging to assist with incident response.
- Use tools to enhance your logging capability where practical and secure.
- Recompile/reconfigure operating systems to their minimally required configuration.

Lost or Stolen Items

Look over your security plan and determine if there are examples of information or infrastructure components that benefit from formalized policies and procedures for lost or stolen items. Loss of credentials (passwords, tokens, smart cards) and laptops are clear examples of components requiring a sound policy and procedure for loss or theft. Others include badges, cell phones, sensitive documents, handheld PDAs, floppy disks, flash cards, and the like. Your policy and procedures for lost and stolen items should involve notification of the lost/stolen event, disabling and resetting of affected systems to minimize compromise, logging for illicit use of lost or stolen components, and archiving of the lost/stolen event in case it's needed for future incident response. Use Worksheet 4.41.

Lost or Stolen Worksheet

IMPACT ANALYSIS ID	BEFORE PLAN	PERCENT IMPROVEMENT	NEW VALUE

Quality Management worksheet completed for this element/template? (check box) ☐

Write policies and procedures for addressing lost or stolen security-related information and infrastructure.

_____

_____

_____

Worksheet 4.41   Lost or Stolen Worksheet.

Managed (Outsourced) Security

If your organization takes advantage of managed, or outsourced, security services, then you should use your security plan to work with them to address your highest-impact systems with a sound security plan. In addition, you should develop your own simplified security plan, using the worksheets in this book, to develop the best, and most effective, working relationship with your managed security service provider, allowing you to set individual and shared responsibilities and expectations.

NOTE The Quality Management worksheet provides particular value for managed security, especially as it relates to performance metrics such as incident response.

Managed security providers can be a big help. It's not possible, though, for them to handle every single aspect of your security, so you need to coordinate with them. Use Worksheet 4.42.

Managed (Outsourced) Security Worksheet

IMPACT ANALYSIS ID	BEFORE PLAN	PERCENT IMPROVEMENT	NEW VALUE

Quality Management worksheet completed for this element/template? (check box) ☐

Divide responsibilities between you and your managed security provider, and set expectations together.

_____
_____
_____

Address the reliability and security of any remote managed security provider access mechanism such as IPSec.

_____
_____
_____

Worksheet 4.42   Managed (Outsourced) Security Worksheet.

Performance

Review your security plan and work to address any areas where your security implementation could affect performance in a non-negligible way, or where something in your infrastructure could severely affect the performance of a component you rely on to, for example, monitor security. Use Worksheet 4.43.

Certain cryptographic operations can be CPU-intensive, such as digital signing. For example, digital signing occurs during the server authentication handshake portion of an SSL/TLS user session. After a user establishes a session, it is cached for 24 hours based on default SSL/TLS parameters. If the user revisits your Web site again within 24 hours, there is no need for another server authentication event. After 24 hours, if the user visits again, another digital signing server authentication event must occur. For performance on Web servers running SSL, this handshake incurs a far greater performance impact than the standard encryption performed over an SSL session. IPSec sessions using PKI for authentication will also be CPU-intensive when any authentication is carried out.

Performance Worksheet

IMPACT ANALYSIS ID	BEFORE PLAN	PERCENT IMPROVEMENT	NEW VALUE

Quality Management worksheet completed for this element/template? (check box) ☐

Identify performance-sensitive components in your security stack (for example, a particular customer service application that must function quickly).

_____

_____

_____

For performance-sensitive components, develop a performance test plan to assess impact of security measures.

_____

_____

_____

Perform your test plan "under load" for CPU-intensive activities including address filters, expanded logging, and cryptographic operations, especially public key operations.

_____

_____

_____

Worksheet 4.43 Performance Worksheet.

Address filtering of all kinds can be very CPU performance-intensive; therefore, you should measure the performance impact of filters on your security stack infrastructure. The simple act of logging information can also be very CPU-intensive. Logging forces a computer process to perform *interrupt processing,* wherein it stops what it's doing (its primary mission, whatever that is), traps a certain amount of information, then writes that information to memory. When you turn on logging in your components, take care to measure the performance impact, especially as it relates to system stability.

Physical Security

When it comes to the most basic of physical security, such as building access control and alarms, there are, of course, excellent resources available to you (for example, alarm companies) to help you meet your needs. That said, you must be aware that many physical security people see themselves as installers, which is not the same as security people; that means they really don't think about methods of compromise. Instead, they look for the easiest way to install your system to do its basic function (sound an alarm if a door is opened, call out over a phone line if there's a problem). Moreover, the money they make is usually determined by how much time it takes to do the installation, not by how resistant to compromise it is. Agreements are often "fixed price" so the sooner they get done, the more money they make. Therefore, they sometimes install your security system the easiest way possible, which may have nothing to do with security or robustness. As a result, usually it's possible to predict where the core components are of most security system installations, either by doing a building walkthrough or by accessing any building flooring plan. These systems can be disabled a variety of ways, and a roadmap for compromising your systems can typically be drawn up after one casual walk through the basic entrances of your building.

Many of these systems, by the way, rely on a callout to a central alarm monitoring system over standard phone lines. Few of them incorporate a (very inexpensive) cellular phone backup system. Whereas cutting your phone lines is is easy to do (even on so-called tamper-detection systems), disabling a cellular backup system and your alarm system's "brain" within a predetermined time frame (usually what an intruder must do) is typically more difficult.

Another physical security concern not addressed thus far relates to handling of paper containing confidential information. Trash cans and wastebaskets still remain useful places for an intruder to learn valuable information about compromising your organization. Don't forget to institute a policy, procedure, and convenient mechanism for shredding sensitive documents.

You also should add policies and procedures relating to the physical handling, protection, and disposal, of bulk media carrying highly sensitive information (for example, tapes, hard drives). Use Worksheet 4.44.

NOTE Though this book does not address the issue of physical phone wiretaps (so-called *bugs*), evidence suggests there is reason for concern. According to one report, a significant percentage of those who performed a bug sweep in their organization reported finding one or more wiretaps.

Physical Security Worksheet

IMPACT ANALYSIS ID	BEFORE PLAN	PERCENT IMPROVEMENT	NEW VALUE

Quality Management worksheet completed for this element/template? (check box) ☐

Write a comprehensive physical security review plan and pay special attention to high-impact infrastructure.

_____

_____

_____

Identify where installers designed your physical security instead of "security people." Think like an attacker.

_____

_____

_____

Walk through your facilities like an attacker. Look for policy and procedure holes. Look for sensitive information left on white boards and desks.

_____

_____

_____

Form a physical security audit team that regularly tests and assesses the quality of your organization's physical security.

_____

_____

_____

Worksheet 4.44　Physical Security Worksheet.

Procurement

Much has been said about procurement and technology selection thus far. Look back over your security plan, and identify any areas you may have missed with regard to procurement of components affecting your security. Use Worksheet 4.45.

Support Interface

Your support interfaces—be they technical support for employees, customer support lines, or simply administrators who pick up the phone and answer questions—are some of the first places an experienced hacker turns to derive important information.

Procurement Worksheet

IMPACT ANALYSIS ID	BEFORE PLAN	PERCENT IMPROVEMENT	NEW VALUE

Quality Management worksheet completed for this element/template? (check box) ☐

Review the Secure Software worksheets. Procure from software vendors who demonstrate a knowledge of secure software. Refer back to your quality management worksheets to track the performance of your software providers.

_____

_____

_____

Emphasize quality of security in your procurement decisions. Factor this more heavily than features. Be less feature-focused.

_____

_____

_____

Develop a security confidence and reliability measure for your vendors.

_____

_____

_____

Worksheet 4.45   Procurement Worksheet.

Because support interfaces typically have an abundance of information valuable to a hacker, and because support staff can often be tricked or intimidated into giving up information they shouldn't, it is imperative that you put solid policies and procedures in place to define (1) how to authenticate people calling in for information, (2) what information may be given out in any form (phone, writing, etc.), and (3) how to handle sensitive information that is released. Use Worksheet 4.46.

Support Interface Worksheet

IMPACT ANALYSIS ID	BEFORE PLAN	PERCENT IMPROVEMENT	NEW VALUE

Quality Management worksheet completed for this element/template? (check box) ☐

Train, train, then train support staff more on dealing with a hacker employing social hacking skills.

_____

_____

Test your support interface's ability to resist social hacking attempts. Regularly call in and pose as a hacker.

_____

_____

_____

As mentioned in other worksheets, develop strict policies and procedures around sensitive information managed by support.

_____

_____

_____

When testing, pose falsely as various characters including an employee, law enforcement representative, user in need, irate customer, and irate executive.

_____

_____

_____

Worksheet 4.46 Support Interface Worksheet.

Testing, Integration, and Staging

The testing and staging of security-related components is a common thread in this book, with three important guidelines to remember (use Worksheet 4.47):

- Carefully choose when you will test, stage, and integrate.
- Define how you will simulate basic aspects of your live environments.
- Define metrics for testing and staging success and failure.

Testing, Integration, and Staging Worksheet

IMPACT ANALYSIS ID	BEFORE PLAN	PERCENT IMPROVEMENT	NEW VALUE

Quality Management worksheet completed for this element/template? (check box) ☐

Write and work to justify a budget for a test, integration, and staging lab. For justification, see the Security Selling worksheets.

_____
_____

Write test/integration/staging plans for high-impact items.

_____
_____

As part of your plan, develop capability and write procedures for simulating realistic "live" environments.

_____
_____

Pay special attention to stability and functionality during testing. Make sure your security solutions do not crash or break things.

_____
_____
_____

Worksheet 4.47 Testing, Integration, and Staging Worksheet.

Training

Security-related training is another thread running through many of the discussions in this book. Guidelines to follow in this regard (use Worksheet 4.48) include the following:

- Define policies for training content: topics to cover, when and how often, the approach(es), prerequisites, instructors and participants.
- Detail how different training elements will be used: classroom training, posters, presentations, physical reminders, emails, physical documents (such as security guidelines), and so forth.
- Specify training techniques—for example, role-playing and simulated drills (such as testing a support interface for vulnerability to a hacker who is attempting to get information).

Training Worksheet

IMPACT ANALYSIS ID	BEFORE PLAN	PERCENT IMPROVEMENT	NEW VALUE

Quality Management worksheet completed for this element/template? (check box) ☐

Build sophistication into your training program. How can you use posters, emails, classes, presentations, physical reminders?

_____

_____

_____

Develop a "new employee security awareness orientation." Train as much as you can up front and refresh it over time.

_____

_____

_____

Managers should be compelled to send employees to security training on an ongoing basis. Make it a priority.

_____

_____

_____

Worksheet 4.48 Training Worksheet.

Recovery

We touched on the topic of recovery in several areas, including its relation to the diversity, redundancy, and isolation (DRI) security element. One of the most important, and often overlooked, areas of recovery, aside from simply testing your recovery mechanism (number one in importance), is defining roles and responsibilities during the recovery process (use Worksheet 4.49). These roles and responsibilities should be assigned to the incident response team under the leadership of the security planning team. Too many organizations are sent into a tailspin when they've been hacked and need to recover. Be prepared: have a team ready to recover; make sure each member of that team has an assigned role and clearly understands his or her responsibilities and capabilities.

Recovery Worksheet

IMPACT ANALYSIS ID	BEFORE PLAN	PERCENT IMPROVEMENT	NEW VALUE

Quality Management worksheet completed for this element/template? (check box) ☐

Regularly simulate hacks and system failures for high-impact information and infrastructure. Write improved recovery procedures. Refer back to your Quality Management worksheet.

_____

_____

_____

Where you rely on backups for high-impact systems, such as tape backups, then routinely test your ability to successfully restore from the backup.

_____

_____

_____

Build a relationship with an external security organization that can provide support if you have difficulty recovering.

_____

_____

_____

Worksheet 4.49   Recovery Worksheet.

Conclusions

These worksheets, completed and customized to your individual needs, provide a comprehensive security plan. Keep in mind, however, that your security plan is a "living document" and, as such, requires ongoing review and maintenance. Your reward for this vigilance will be a repeatable and highly workable security planning process that provides a high level of assurance for those assets that matter most to your organization.

In Chapter 5, I amplify a topic touched on throughout the book: digital certificates and public-key infrastructure (PKI). This often poorly understood technology stands to play an increasingly more important role in security architectures; therefore, understanding PKI technology and its full range of implications is important for strategic security planning.

Strategic Security Planning with PKI

Over the past several years *public key infrastructure* (PKI) technology and digital certificates have received so much media attention that you would think we'd be seeing more adopters by now. One reason for the long adoption cycle is that the impact of PKI is broad and is not easily understood from a business or technical standpoint. This, coupled with a tendency on the part of some to pursue a path of technology overload, as opposed to one focused on usable business solutions, in the standards groups and commercial products, has resulted in a confused marketplace. That said, it's important to recognize that PKI, either in the form of an increasingly important behind-the-scenes toolkit or as an expansive presence in the enterprise, is going to play an increasingly important role in strategic security planning. That's the reason I'm devoting an entire chapter to this important topic. My purpose is to unravel, as much as possible in a few pages, the mysteries of PKI so that you will be better able to factor them into your strategic security plans.

To that end, I also include in this chapter a case study summarizing my own experiences, as well as those of my colleagues, in implementing one of the world's largest PKI-enabled networks called TradeWave, which supports more than $30 billion in online transactions with more than 3,000 users and 500 participating companies.

PKI Primer

The best place to begin is by defining four terms used throughout this chapter: PKI itself, digital certificate, certificate authority, and digital signature. Note also that the glossary of this book provides definitions for additional PKI-related terms.

Public key infrastructure.   PKI provides a comprehensive cryptographic framework, a suite of protocols, security policies, and desktop and server components that strongly and efficiently implement the six fundamental security elements introduced in Chapter 2 and detailed in Chapter 3. In doing so, PKI provides a powerful electronic trust mechanism for individuals and organizations, one so strong that most believe it can effectively replace a handwritten signature in all forms of contracts and agreements. PKI relies on a cryptographic framework based on the existence of two keys, one public and the other private. These two keys are sometimes simply referred to as a *key pair*. The private key is secret; that is, you should not share it with anyone. An excellent place to store a private key is on a smart card. The other key is public, meaning that everyone can know it. A key pair can be assigned to an individual, such as yourself, or on behalf of an organization to devices such as servers and network routers. Your public key needs to be shared with others in order for them to conduct secure transactions with you. Your public key is contained in something called a *digital certificate* (see the text that follows).

Digital certificate.   A digital certificate is an organized collection of data (a data structure) containing your public key and specific attributes that describe you, such as your job title and the organization with which you are affiliated. So that others may trust that the certificate truly contains your public key and nobody else's, the certificate is digitally signed by a *certificate authority* (CA; see the text that follows).

Certificate authority (CA).   A CA is a trusted third party that signs certificates. CAs guarantee that the holders of digital certificates are who they say they are. If you trust a particular CA to guarantee this, then you trust certificates that it has signed. A CA can sign certificates issued for individuals, organizations, and other CAs. To understand the latter case, consider an example. Suppose that you trust a CA named "A." Also suppose that there is another CA named "B." If A signs B's certificate, then because you trust the certificates issued by A, you also trust certificates issued by B because B's certificate has been signed by A. This chain of trust is sometimes referred to as a *trust hierarchy*.

Digital signature.   Your key pair, when combined with a public key cryptographic algorithm such as RSA, exhibits a very important property that PKI leverages over and over again. Sometimes I refer to this property as *key reciprocity*. The idea behind it is that, if one of your two keys is cryptographically (mathematically) applied to some data (using a public-key cryptographic algorithm such as one called RSA), the output is a jumbled collection of bits (1s and 0s) that only someone with the other key can read. If I apply your public key to some data, then only you can read the result because only you have the private key. In doing so, I have encrypted the data so that only you can read it. This process is called *asymmetric encryption*. On the other hand, if you apply your private key to some data, then anyone can read it because everyone can have your public key simply by obtaining your digital certificate. They can validate your certificate with the help of a trusted CA. Furthermore, because you are the only one who has access to your private key, they can know for sure that the result must have been produced by you. This result, something that only you could have produced, is called a *digital signature*. In practice, we first produce a hash of the data (see the Integrity security element introduced in Chapter 2) and then digitally sign the hash rather than the data itself. Remember that a hash uniquely corresponds in a 1:1 fashion to the original data, so signing the hash essentially has the same meaning as signing the original data. We go through the trouble of signing the hash, rather than the original data, because a hash is typically much smaller than the original data from which it was computed and is therefore quicker and easier to sign digitally. A digitally signed hash is also sometimes called a *Message Authentication Code* (MAC).

Now let's delve into how PKI, digital certificates, certificate authorities, and digital signatures work together.

Authentication and Nonrepudiation with Digital Signatures

Leveraging the key reciprocity property just defined, you can authenticate yourself by applying your private key to data and sending it to someone who can read it by applying your public key from your digital certificate. The idea is that because only you have access to the private key, you must be who you say you are. This personal authentication enables you, for example, to apply your private key to a contract, thereby digitally signing it and indicating your agreement to it, just as if you had signed a paper version. Digital signatures provide the important property of nonrepudiation for electronic transactions—that is, the ability to enter into a binding agreement electronically. And finally, if someone would like to send you private (encrypted) information, they need only apply your public key to it. Because only you have the private key associated with that public key, only you can decrypt it.

The X.509 Standard and Certificate Authorities

Digital certificates commonly used in business and within the enterprise conform to the ITU-T Recommendation X.509 standard. X.509 digital certificates are themselves digitally signed by a certificate authority (CA), who is responsible for validating that the public key contained inside the certificate truly belongs to the individual identified within it. For example, a CA might ask you questions and request documentation before issuing you a digital certificate on which others rely.

CAs digitally sign the certificates they issue and incorporate an integrity-checking capability so that someone cannot tamper with a user's certificate. Companies that require digital certificates for their internal use may choose to run their own CA. Those wishing to outsource the operation of a CA or to engage in business-to-business transactions, plus individuals on the Internet, may use a commercial CA. Directory servers are used to store digital certificates and may leverage them for access control.

Making a Business Case for PKI

PKI technology offers a great deal of potential, specifically for fueling the next wave of services and technologies aimed at further advancing the security, virtual private networking (VPN), e-business, and transactional and collaborative capabilities of our networked world. PKI offers a comprehensive suite of services for individual, enterprise, and business-to-business transactions of all kinds. Similar to the dramatic return on investment (ROI) experienced with Web technologies, PKI-based solutions have the potential of yielding significant gains by streamlining business processes and eliminating fraud. At the same time, using PKI is not without challenges, and this chapter explores both the benefits and difficulties inherent in this technology.

Arguably, traditional username/password security is one of the remaining vestiges of the non-Internet economy. While it is adequate for a range of applications in the near term, we need something better for the future. The underlying technology of PKI paves the way for implementation of higher-value, more sensitive transactions between consumers and businesses, among businesses, and within corporations.

NOTE Throughout this chapter, sensitive transactions, those requiring substantial accountability, commitment, and security, are referred to as *assured transactions.*

Classifying PKI

At the highest level, PKI services can be seen as solving three classes of problems:

Automate physical interactions. A PKI can help us electronically automate nearly any assured transaction we perform in person or on paper. One example would be buying a house, which typically involves numerous in-person appointments by the purchaser and the other parties engaged in the transaction, endless paperwork, and integration with a variety of ad hoc electronic systems. A PKI provides sufficient power to potentially automate the entire house-buying process (the financial portion), including the required legal ceremony of signatures and notarization.

Improve existing electronic interactions. A PKI can significantly improve the implementation of existing electronic assured transactions. It can dramatically raise the trust level of participants engaged in electronic commerce with one another.

Institute virtual private networks (VPNs). A VPN combines the public Internet with powerful PKI-enabled security features, allowing corporations and end users to essentially create *secure pipes* through the Internet. Today, corporations create similar pipes with expensive private networks, separate from the public Internet. VPNs leverage PKI technology via the IP Security (IPSec) Internet Key Exchange (IKE) protocol.

Let's consider the benefits of VPNs and these roles in more detail.

Benefits of Virtual Private Networks

Topping the benefits list is the simple fact that the public Internet is considerably less expensive to use than private networks. Also, nearly all corporations have Internet connections. Rather than continuing to maintain their separate private network to interconnect remote corporate sites, companies can use a single Internet connection for all traffic, public and private. This is sometimes referred to as LAN-to-LAN VPN.

In order to enable telecommuters to access private networks and back-office systems, corporations have historically maintained their own expensive banks of modems and phone lines. These same telecommuters required remote dial-up Internet access as well. Instead, why not use the same dial-up Internet connection for both public and private network traffic? By doing so, corporations save money and management overhead by removing expensive private modem banks. In addition, the company saves on telecommuter long-distance charges because most Internet service providers (ISPs) have modems in every city, whereas corporations usually maintain private modem banks only at their headquarter's data center. Already, today, many corporations are doing this; unfortunately, they are doing it with relatively weak security. PKI paves the way for use of a stronger authentication credential (a digital certificate) that can be shared up and down the security stack.

The high cost, fragmentation, and nonstandardization of private networks has traditionally been one of the biggest obstacles to business-to-business (B2B) electronic commerce. When businesses can quickly and securely construct VPN connections over the Internet at very low cost, the VPNs provide a key enabling technology for corporations to conduct e-business over the Internet. Companies in complementary industries, such as automobile manufacturers and suppliers or members of the banking industry, can create what are called *community of interest (COI) VPN networks*. COI VPNs can greatly enhance efficiency in areas such as supply chain management.

Corporations with high-speed access to today's Internet backbones may see performance increases over their existing private networks. Consider, for example, the tens of gigabits/second long-haul Internet backbones being offered by top-tier ISPs. Companies deploying VPNs over these networks may see great performance improvements compared to, for example, their considerably lower-speed private line or frame relay networks built around lower-speed network links.

PKI Services

Assured transactions require, and PKI technology provides, a comprehensive framework for one or more of the following services:

Authentication.   Authentication is achieved through issuance and life-cycle maintenance of a digital certificate and the associated public/private key pair.

Authorization.   Once an individual has been authenticated, the digital certificate, and possibly any attributes within it (such as organizational title), may be used to determine what he or she can and cannot access.

Revocation.   To prevent further use of a digital certificate—for example, in the case of a staff management event such as termination—a digital certificate can be terminated. Terminated certificates are maintained in something called a *certificate revocation list* (CRL).

Nonrepudiation and Integrity.   PKI provides a convenient means of digitally signing information so that a contract, for example, can be signed online. The digital signature provides for nonrepudiation of the contract. PKI also provides the cryptographic tools for enhancing integrity by enabling MAC digital signatures—that is, the "hashing" of sensitive information.

Accounting, archival, notarization, and receipts.   Recordkeeping capability is greatly enhanced because PKI allows for digital signatures and life-cycle management of those certificates.

Ceremony, policy, reliance, liability, and risk management.   Once an individual has been authenticated by an organization such as a CA, that organization can essentially digitally sign that individual's digital certificate. This then lays the foundation for a *ceremony and reliance architecture*. That is, if an organization attests to authenticating you according to some well-known procedures and issues you a digital certificate, that enables another organization, say a mortgage company, to rely on that digital certificate to issue you a home mortgage or engage in other high-value or sensitive transactions with you online.

PKI Business Integration

The uses for PKI technology are endless, and in this section, we'll look at just a few key examples of how PKI can be integrated into a business. Later we'll look at specific industry examples.

Before considering all its possibilities, I must stress an important point: If it is to be successful, PKI technology must become a part of the business processes of the organization. That means that, when exploring how PKI might fit into your organization, in addition to consulting cryptographers and IS department staff, you must involve PKI security planners with thorough knowledge of how the organization functions. Our security planning team (see Chapter 2) has business members on it and, therefore, is ideally suited to providing this knowledge.

Collaboration, Workflow, and Business Processes

Most jobs involve one form of collaboration or another—orders, specifications, records, requests, announcements, memoranda, reports—the list of collaborative workflow elements could go on and on. We often use terms such as *workflow processing*, *document management*, and the like to describe aspects of this collaboration. How does a PKI fit in to this collaboration? Simply, it provides a framework for providing assurance for collaborations occurring within and between businesses.

Consider the electronic processing of a purchase order within a corporation. A PKI not only allows individuals to sign off on the purchase order, just as they do in traditional paper processes, but when coupled with the appropriate PKI-enabled software, it can also allow the business rules of the organization to be securely encoded and enforced. For example, a secure code might stipulate that a departmental manager can sign off on purchase orders only up to $5,000, whereas a divisional manager might be cleared to sign off on orders up to $25,000. (Later we'll talk about the eXtensible Markup Language (XML), which will play an increasingly important role in enabling this type of richer assured transaction support.)

Looking at a much simpler example, a PKI can form the basis for the secure exchange of electronic mail. Today, corporate email is nearly ubiquitous; organizations rely on it for their daily operation, and a great deal of that mail contains sensitive/private information. This email could be secured by leveraging PKI services. Similarly, Web pages that today are routinely protected with myriad username/password combinations can, using PKI, be protected with a single digital certificate. In addition, authorization (access control) to information on Web pages can be tied to the digital certificate.

Inventory and Supplier Management

By leveraging a PKI to manage orders with suppliers as well as inventory levels, companies can save money and create new markets for their products. To demonstrate this aspect of business integration, the case study presented at the end of this chapter details an application for the electrical power industry that relates to this topic of inventory and supplier management. Though the impetus for this application was industry deregulation, it has, at the same time, created a high-dollar-volume online market between suppliers and consumers for a fundamental commodity: electricity.

Invoices are another excellent example of an assured transaction that can benefit from a PKI. Digitally signed invoices can be received, proofs of receipt can be automatically generated, approval functions can be automated, and electronic payment can be made through a sequence of assured transactions.

Software Distribution Methods

PKI technology offers a diverse range of applications. Looking at the organization from the perspective of an information systems (IS) professional, for example, PKI provides a basis for securely distributing screened and trusted software to the desktop by digitally signing it. This capability, referred to as code signing, was introduced in Chapter 2 and discussed within the context of several security elements in Chapter 3, including content and executable management (CEM), secure software, and nonrepudiation.

Single, or Reduced, Sign-On

Keeping the IS manager's hat on for the moment, it has long been argued that users are forced to remember too many usernames and passwords. Because of this, they often circumvent the overall system, thus rendering it less secure. They often paste their passwords to their computer monitors or stick them on bulletin boards or in other, easy-to-access spots in their workspaces, thereby compromising security. Or they make passwords so easy to guess that hackers barely even have to work at doing so. In short, users do a whole host of things that work to undermine overall system security.

Typically, so many passwords are required because each software application used by an employee has been developed by a different company, each of which uses its own *nonstandard* way of implementing security, based on username/password schemes. PKI technology provides hope for reversing this trend by providing a single, standardized mechanism for users to authenticate themselves to all software applications, thereby eventually (it is hoped) making it possible to log on once to all applications; at least in the short run, this process will reduce the required number of logons.

Formalization of Policies and Practices

From the perspective of a company's executive staff, a PKI allows an organization to formalize and standardize the way it manages business process assurance. Today, these processes are implemented through a hybrid collection of *manual paper-based* and electronic records. We typically revert to paper when some very sensitive authorization is required, such as the signing of a high-value purchase. With PKI, we can keep the entire process as an electronic one and thus streamline it.

Legislation

For PKI technology to have as broad an impact as possible on our networked economy, governments will have to get involved, specifically by passing legislation that grants legal status/acceptance to a PKI digital signature—making it as binding as a handwritten one, a signature that can be upheld in court. Efforts are underway throughout the world to achieve this goal. In the United States, the State of Utah adopted the Utah Digital Signature Act on February 27, 1995, making it the first jurisdiction in this country to implement an electronic authentication legal infrastructure using digital signature technology. Many other states have passed, or have initiated, similar legislation.

Another important aspect of legislation relates to international export control laws. Cryptography, which PKI technology leverages, has proven to be an important instrument in national defense and law enforcement efforts, used by governments to eavesdrop on criminals, enemies, or perceived enemies, and, in some countries, anyone who opposes those in power. Export control laws, therefore, influence the availability of PKI technology. Let's say that Canada has no export restrictions on what you need from that nation in the way of PKI technology; however, the country you operate in, or your subsidiaries or remote offices operate in, may have laws preventing the import of the technology from Canada.

Unfortunately, there's no single place you can go to learn in a reliable way about cryptographic import/export laws in all countries and jurisdictions in the world, but your PKI vendor can often provide you with the information you need. In the United States, the responsibility for cryptographic export control has changed hands several times; the most recent group having responsibility for it is the Commerce Department.

PKI in Vertical Industries

PKI professionals I consult with are often surprised when I describe an operational PKI-based business-to-business network that, since 1997, has handled more than $30 billion in assured transactions. This network, which played a fundamental role in the deregulation of the U.S. energy industry, is the focus of the case study you'll find at the end of this chapter. As mentioned briefly earlier, this PKI network is used by the U.S. electric power industry, and the commodity traded over it is electricity. This network has more than 3,000 PKI-enabled users and 400 participating companies. I'll detail that success story shortly, but first I want to introduce the use of PKI technology in other vertical industries.

Financial Services

The financial services profession is not inherently a brick-and-mortar style of business, so PKI technology is well positioned to help financial services organizations put all their capabilities online. In the future, financial institutions will want to provide more than the account balance and bill payment capabilities they provide today. A robust public-key infrastructure offers the potential for these organizations to offer all their services over the Internet, including payment instructions, changes in negotiable financial instruments, and other forms of financial communication. One such new breed of application would be real-time, high-dollar-value loan application, approval, and online funds transfer, all in a matter of minutes for customers, with no handwritten signatures required.

A PKI will work through the establishment of trust hierarchies and bilateral trust (cross-certification) among financial organizations worldwide—in short, forming a chain of trust between financial institutions. Examples of other financial-based PKI-enabled services might include the following:

- High-dollar trade finance/letter of credit
- Corporate purchasing
- Online contracting
- Online procurement solutions
- Electronic content delivery
- Securities trading
- Insurance sales
- Government filings

Health Care

As we're all too well aware, costs associated with patient services are rising rapidly throughout the world, followed concomitantly by increased pressure—by patients, doctors, hospitals, insurance companies, labs, and other related parties—to use the Internet and integrated business processes to reduce these costs. To achieve this, security must be ensured for all parties in all transactions. Former U.S. Surgeon General C. Everett Koop, states the case clearly:

> It is imperative that the healthcare industry lowers costs. One of the prime ways to cut costs is to increase efficiency in how information is exchanged. With a security system that works, the healthcare industry has the opportunity to safely use the Internet's low-cost delivery system. It is essential to provide physicians with the information they need in the secure, inexpensive manner required for a national Health Information Infrastructure (HII).

Legal

Today, the paperwork that passes within and between law firms and with government agencies is overwhelming. The need to assure this paperwork is equally enormous. The ability to digitally sign documents, notarize them, and electronically file them with government agencies with the legal ceremony and the backing of a handwritten signature would have an enormous impact on the daily operations of law firms. Clearly, government legislation, discussed earlier, will determine how quickly this capability will become a reality.

Retail and Manufacturing

Industries such as retail and manufacturing regularly engage in the sale and exchange of goods. In so doing, they potentially benefit greatly from a PKI. This section touches briefly on a few key areas in which PKI can play a role: invoices and receipts and business-to-business trading portals.

Invoices and Receipts

A number of efforts are underway to standardize invoicing and receipt mechanisms, many of which leverage the eXtensible Markup Language (XML) and PKI. These secure XML standards seek to produce global interoperable data formats that allow a comprehensive list of data elements to be exchanged in an assured manner. Digital receipts will increasingly become an important part of assured transaction solutions and will leverage XML.

XML, a specification developed by the World Wide Web Consortium (W3C), is a trimmed-down version of the Standard Generalized Markup Language (SGML). XML was designed specifically for Web documents. Using XML, designers can create customized tags for defining, validating, and interpreting data between applications and organizations. Hence, XML can greatly enhance the way data is exchanged in business-to-business transactions, allowing data formats and their intended purpose (bill totals, inventories, etc.) to be included as part of the transaction and to be encoded in a standardized cross-platform format. Using digital signatures, one party in a transaction can sign the XML form, or the separate parts of it relevant to him or her, and other parties to the transaction (whether people or organizations) can sign the parts relevant to them. Clearly, then, by providing a common semantic structure for data, PKI technology and XML are ideally suited to be implemented together. The ability to assure and digitally sign specific elements of data and manage that data as part of an assured transaction is quite powerful.

Business-to-Business Trading Portals

Business-to-business (B2B) portals allow trading communities to barter goods and services among each other, in many cases of very high value. Surplus B2B online portals allow companies to offload surplus items quickly, such as raw materials for manufacturing, excessive inventory of equipment parts, precious metals, such perishable goods as food, computers, or what have you. PKI technology is increasingly being considered an important component of this growth industry, given the high value of these transactions, the potential for fraud, and the need for ceremony and nonrepudiation should a party to the transaction challenge it.

Government

Governments worldwide have seen the wisdom of implementing PKI, and they represent a very important vertical market segment for those selling PKI products. The security needs of governments are comprehensive, and PKI provides an excellent framework for meeting them. For example, an important U.S. government initiative related to PKI is the General Services Administration (GSA) Access Certificates for Electronic Services (ACES) program. The vision behind the ACES program is to provide a common PKI for granting public and government vendors electronic access to privacy-related U.S. government information and services. ACES has the goal of providing individuals and business entities that are communicating with the government identification, authentication, and nonrepudiation services when accessing, retrieving, and submitting information. Commercial PKI service companies that meet published ACES requirements and have been approved by the GSA will be permitted to issue certificates under the ACES program. More information on the ACES program can be found on GSA's Web site at www.gsa.gov/aces.

Challenges of PKI

As I've mentioned throughout the discussion so far, the benefits of PKI don't come without a price. This section specifically addresses the more prominent challenges to using PKI as part of a security plan.

Business Justification

Perhaps the major challenge to PKI deployment, from a business perspective, is simply being able to cost-justify it in quantitative terms. Selling PKI is not like selling indoor plumbing or electric lighting; its benefits are much more subtle and infinitely more difficult to realize. Computing the return on investment (ROI) for PKI is difficult, except perhaps in the case of VPN deployment, where a straightforward comparison to existing conventional private network costs can be drawn. Quantifying the PKI vision can be analogous to past difficulties of quantifying private networks and the benefits of the connectivity they offered to the organization and, in more recent years, of justifying the costs of Internet connectivity. Because of this difficulty, many organizations become gridlocked when it comes time to make an investment decision.

Furthermore, the costs of a PKI cannot easily be related to money spent on new software, existing software modification, services, operations, and administration. Costs also are counted in the complexity of a company's operations, service offerings, and their time to market. Up front, PKI technology can take longer to implement than simpler solutions; therefore, when making a decision to deploy a PKI, a company may, at the same time, be delaying the deployment of a product or service. Assessing the impact of this on a company's bottom line is important, yet doing so can impede PKI deployment.

In sum, PKI is a strategic investment; as such, computing a meaningful ROI estimate in the general case may be very difficult in all but the simplest scenarios. Though PKI doesn't hold up well when compared to simpler, albeit less secure, solutions for a given problem, it does hold up well against the risks associated with deploying less secure mechanisms for more sensitive, feature-rich, high-value assured transactions. These risks to a company's information assets, which include theft, impersonation, and misuse, coupled with risk to the underlying assured transaction service being offered (such as online purchasing, trading), may help an organization acknowledge and support the benefits of PKI technology.

Scalability

The scalability challenges associated with the broad acceptance of PKI technology are considerable. Just consider the breadth of it: At some time nearly everyone in a company, a collection of companies, a state, a nation, or the world could have one or more digital certificates. Obviously, this raises concerns about the scalability of our systems. Whether PKI technology is confined to company boundaries or extends to states, nations, and continents remains to be seen. Many are predicting that it will eventually grow as the Internet has grown.

Clearly, anything the scale of the Internet represents a challenge. For PKI to scale, the primary challenge is in the coordination of CAs and associated certificate revocation lists (CRLs). CRLs are used to indicate when a certificate is no longer valid. Everyone needs this information quickly when conducting transactions in order to rely on a certificate that has been presented. Furthermore, revocation information needs to be maintained forever (indefinitely) in order to prove that some nonrepudiable transaction, at some time, was digitally signed with an unrevoked certificate. For example, if someone signed a contract in the year 2002, and somebody else, five years later, wanted to verify that the contract had been signed with a certificate that had not been revoked at the time the contract was signed, then five years later that person must have reliable access to any CRL information related to that certificate in order to trust the digital signature on the contract. The management of revoked certificates by CAs for millions of people is, in my view, the primary scalability challenge. Others exist, such as maintaining complex trust relationships between CAs; however, I do not see those as the major challenges.

All that said, and in the face of all these challenges, for a typical company or group of companies, this problem isn't such a problem. CRLs, for example, can easily be kept around indefinitely. Furthermore, even though scalability is a challenge for PKI, it's a surmountable one given state-of-the-art technology and PKI standards.

Interoperability

PKI software and services from different vendors can suffer from interoperability issues, despite the existence of a wide range of PKI-related standards. The primary organizations involved in PKI standards are the Internet Engineering Task Force (IETF) (www.ietf.org/html.charters/pkix-charter.html), RSA's PKCS standards (www.rsasecurity.com/rsalabs/pkcs/), the International Telegraph and Telephone Consultative Committee (CCITT), and several other international organizations. Interoperability issues exist for many reasons, not the least of which is the complexity of the many standards. PKI suffers from standards overkill wherein many of the standards try to accomplish too much. There are too many people trying to do too much at once in the standards committees. Before PKI can run, it has to walk. We need to get the basics right before we try to solve every imaginable feature. Other factors include the vagueness of certain standards, and, as with other technologies, certain vendors may use the lack of interoperability as a weapon against their weaker competitors.

From the perspective of the organization deploying a PKI, the more interoperability, the better. Interoperability allows the assured transaction vision to be more easily realized between different entities deploying different technologies (businesses, users, and government). It helps the organization to select the best software or service provider based on the quality of product offered (customer service, reliability, cost, needed features) rather than out of interoperability concerns.

Emerging Standards

There are several PKI-related standards, many of which are still changing. Continued changes in PKI-related standards and uncontrolled competing standards efforts represent an ongoing challenge to PKI deployment.

Complexity

I've said it before: PKI technology is complex; in addition, in its early stages of implementation, PKI may introduce more complexity for the end user, though eventually it will result in a simplified user experience. To meet this challenge, organizations will have to maintain some amount of in-house PKI expertise, although it's fully possible to outsource certain infrastructure components such as the operation of the CA and the issuance and revocation of certificates. In-house expertise is especially needed to assist with PKI business application integration, as well as to provide end users with day-to-day support, training, and troubleshooting.

Maturity

PKI technology is not new; however, software and services implementing PKI must mature as we expand our PKI deployment. Looking at the array of PKI standards will not help you assess whether PKI is mature enough for your organization. Rather, you must evaluate currently available PKI products and services and assess how they integrate with, and provide value to, your current and future business applications. Performing such an evaluation means working with consultants experienced in the field, as well as searching over the Internet. Because the list of companies providing PKI products and services is constantly changing, it would not be useful to provide such a list of companies here. The book would date itself instantly. Instead, you might visit an Internet search engine, type **PKI products services**, and start from there. I just did that, and the first page returned provided a hit for every current major player.

Physical Security

PKI technology introduces certain components (for example, the private key used by a CA to sign certificates) that, if compromised by a hacker, can undermine the security for all users managed by that component. PKI deployment, when done in-house, raises the bar for a company's physical security operational procedures. Organizations that have relied on a simple locked door to the server room will find, instead, a few special servers (the certificate authorities) in their organization that will require especially stringent physical security.

Security of the CA private key, as noted, in all systems is of the utmost importance. In addition, employees that have digital certificates also need to secure their private keys. Furthermore, they may need to be able to take their private keys with them for working at another job location or at home or for telecommuting. This is called *private key portability*. For this reason, and for security purposes, it may be desirable to store users' private keys on a smart card. Smart cards can be configured so that, once the private key is generated on them, it can never be taken off. Smart cards and their security features were discussed several times in Chapter 4, and additional detail was provided in the discussion of the Encryption security element. The point of all of this is that maintaining the physical portability and security of private keys can be a PKI deployment challenge.

Disaster Planning and Recovery

Earlier I mentioned the benefits of single user logon and a reduced requirement for user credentials. But now I need to make you aware of the drawback
inherent in this advantage: dependence on a single homogenous mechanism
for authentication—the PKI. If it fails or is compromised, and if we haven't
designed the system for reliability, developed an adequate incident response
team, built needed backup systems, and the rest, we may wish we were back
in the legacy days of usernames and passwords. Therefore, PKI deployment
challenges the organization to develop stringent disaster planning, diversity,
redundancy, isolation, and recovery technology, processes, and procedures.

Integration

Integration of a PKI with new and existing (legacy) applications is another significant challenge for the organization. Fortunately, products and standards
are becoming increasingly available to assist with PKI integration; however,
these are still in their infancy. As part of this integration, an important aspect is
user interface design. Specifically, a user, or any entity, should control, at all
times, how its digital identity and digital signature capabilities are used.

Policies, Practices, Reliance, Risk, Liability, and Trust

I've discussed these topics earlier in the chapter. Managing them within a corporation, between businesses, end users, and financial institutions, and with
government is no small task. Today it's done through a series of ad hoc paper,
human, and electronic processes. While benefit can be gained from implementing a PKI without solving all these problems within an electronic framework, because of the core services a PKI can offer, the temptation will exist to
do exactly that. Therefore, a challenge will be to choose exactly which aspects
of these problem sets to manage within the PKI deployment and which portion to leave to existing systems and agreements.

Legislation

As mentioned earlier, government legislation, to include legislation supporting the legal enforcement of digital signatures as well as cryptographic export,
can be challenges to PKI deployment, especially for multinational companies,
where each country may have its own legislative issues. Typically, multinational companies must assign or retain an individual who is responsible for
knowledge of the import/export regulations of the countries in which the
company operates and for apprising the company's PKI planning staff of that
information.

Case Study: A Real-World Business-to-Business PKI Success Story

The remainder of this chapter summarizes the experiences and lessons learned from the deployment of one of the world's largest PKI-enabled networks called TradeWave, which supports more than $30 billion in online transactions with more than 3,000 users and 500 participating companies.

NOTE This study is based on the first-hand implementation and operational experiences of myself and my colleagues.

Background

As a result of U.S. Federal Energy Regulatory Commission (FERC) Order No. 889, electric power transmission providers were required to provide an Internet-accessible Open Access Same-Time Information System (OASIS) for online electric power trading no later than January 3, 1997. (OASIS is a transmission reservation system wherein utilities check for the availability of transmission power.)

Previously, electric utilities operated as monopolies, authorized by the federal and state regulatory authorities to be the sole proprietor of electricity service to consumers who lived within a specific service territory. The FERC order effectively introduced competition into the wholesale market for electricity, and as a result, electric utilities and others could now sell electric power to one another across state lines on a competitive basis. Here's how it works: Electricity marketers check on the price and availability of a utility's power grid and then schedule and reserve transmission capacity for the transfer of wholesale electricity. This allows a company to buy electricity wherever it's cheapest and move it on the lines that lie between the power source and the customer.

The Joint Transmission Services Information Network (JTSIN), a task force representing more than 200 electric utility companies, responded to the FERC mandate by hiring companies to create and maintain the JTSIN OASIS. In defining the OASIS requirements, it was clear to the task force that a strong digital certificate-based security solution was needed so that valid users could be recognized at any server and so that sensitive business agreements between transmission provider and transmission customer companies could be enforced.

Components of the Solution

TradeWave, a developer of software products and services that enable secure business-to-business commerce over the Internet, was chosen to deploy the OASIS digital–certificate-based solution. This included the hardware, software, policies, and expertise to authenticate users and to issue, manage, and maintain their digital certificates. TradeWave provided all the necessary components, including integration and consulting services, client and server security software, outsourced CA services, and customer support services.

The TradeWave digital certificate solution for OASIS includes several key components:

- TradeAgent Client secures the user's Web browser and is required to view information on OASIS Web servers. TradeAgent Client secures information transmission by encrypting and digitally signing messages, providing privacy and authentication.

- TradeAgent Server secures the Web server. Only authenticated TradeAgent Client users can view secured Web pages. TradeAgent Client and Server exchange encrypted and digitally signed messages.

- TradeAccess Control Server works closely with the TradeAgent Server and the underlying Web server to ensure that Web resources are available only to authorized users. The collection of all access control definitions for a resource is called an Access Control List (ACL). After a user is authenticated, ACLs for resources requested by the user are checked for any restrictions to ensure that the individual is authorized to access that resource. ACLs can be based on business agreements between transmission providers (sellers) and transmission customers (buyers).

- TradeAuthority Certificate Authority (CA) is responsible for registering new users, distributing, revoking, and updating certificates, and maintaining audit trails for administrative changes to the system. The CA interfaces with an LDAP-compliant directory server for storage and retrieval of certificates.

When a user makes a request to a TradeWave secured Web site, the request is processed through all of the major system components. The following steps illustrate a user requesting information from a TradeWave secured server:

1. From his or her browser, the user makes a request by clicking on a special TradeWave-secured hyperlink embedded within an OASIS Web page.

2. By integrating with the user's browser, the TradeAgent Client detects that a secure hyperlink was accessed. The TradeAgent Client then contacts the CA in order to obtain certificate information about the secured Web server referenced within the hyperlink.

3. TradeAgent Client and Server authenticate each other.

4. The user request is then secured through public-key encryption and transmitted to the TradeAgent Server. Because the client and server have authenticated each other, the server knows the identity of the client user when it receives the request.

5. TradeAgent Server decrypts the message and sends the request to the Web server.

6. The Web server contacts the TradeAccess Control Server to check the ACL database and approves or denies the request. The server restricts access to information at the document level.

7. The Web server returns the requested resource (e.g., Web page) to the TradeAgent Server.

8. The TradeAgent Server encrypts the resource and returns it to the TradeAgent Client.

9. The TradeAgent Client decrypts the resource and returns it to the Web browser for display to the user.

Roles and Responsibilities

Certificates are only as good as the authentication process for issuing them. Having clearly defined roles and responsibilities and personnel who valued the importance of their roles was critical to the successful deployment of the OASIS digital certificate infrastructure. The key personnel involved included the following:

Security officer.   Sets policies and procedures for handling confidential and sensitive information within the organization. Provides verification of employees within the security officer's organization.

Local registration agent (LRA).   Acts as a contact between a company and the CA and oversees user registrations for the company. The LRA is a trusted individual who works closely with the security officer. The LRA serves as the gatekeeper, verifying the identity of anyone in his or her company registering to use the OASIS TradeWave system. The LRA is also responsible for the certificate life-cycle management, including adding, enabling, and revoking user certificates.

Service administrator.   Responsible for setting up and administering the TradeAgent Server and TradeAccess Control Server.

Network administrator.   Responsible for administering the company's Internet connection and firewall and for ensuring that all machines on the corporate network are secure. The network administrator and service administrator typically communicate regularly to ensure that there is no interruption of service.

TradeWave support staff.   Manage the CA service and assist LRAs in managing the certificate life cycle of the users for whom they are responsible.

Help desk staff.   Assist users in the installation and troubleshooting of software and related Internet connectivity. The staff may contact the LRA if there is a certificate problem or the TradeWave Support CA staff is there is a problem with the CA service.

Challenges and Lessons Learned

The deployment of a digital certificate infrastructure in January 1997 posed many challenges. Computer security, in general, was gaining visibility, but its importance was not well understood by most users. And digital certificates were, and still are, a relatively new technology from the perspective of large-scale deployment. An additional challenge was the fact that this new technology was being deployed to users with a wide range of computer experience.

Educating Users on Internet and Digital Certificate Technologies

Users were accustomed to doing business using traditional power trading methods such as making personal contacts, faxes, and phone calls. With the deployment of OASIS, users were required to get connectivity to the Internet, install the TradeAgent software, get a digital certificate, and perform everything online. This was a major change for users who were not accustomed to doing business on their computers every day.

Educating the users to the point of making them comfortable with the new technologies was key in successfully deploying the TradeWave solution for the OASIS community. Users new to the Internet had to deal with new types of problems: the lack of support from Internet service providers, the Internet's unpredictable connectivity and performance, and the complex issues associated with configuring a corporate firewall. Providing incremental training and support by phone proved to be most beneficial and put the technologies within their grasp. One-on-one phone support allowed the help desk staff to provide as much or as little information as the users wanted on the issues they were working on.

Having the right kind of online documentation was also important. The initial version of the online documentation focused on the system architecture and provided too much information about the technology being used. This overwhelmed some users to the point that they wanted to give up before they even started. After the initial beta rollout, the online documentation was edited to focus on simple step-by-step processes for registration and installation. This change in focus made things easier for users to follow, especially if they needed to consult with another person in their organization to perform a step. The support Web site was also reworked to provide high-level troubleshooting information. In addition, background information on the Web browsers and the Internet was provided if the users needed it. As users became more familiar with the system, they used the Web site as a reference and became comfortable communicating with the support staff via email.

Defining Roles

Certain roles were critical to the successful rollout and implementation of the system. Security officers, LRAs, and service administrators were particularly important because they have an ongoing role after the deployment of the digital certificate infrastructure. For this reason, these roles had to have an ongoing education process to emphasize the importance of the job being performed and of following the right policies and procedures for a secure digital certificate-based application.

Linking Corporate Security with Doing Business Successfully

Having enough trained personnel dedicated to the task of corporate security was important. In cases where personnel were not yet available or were not yet trained, the TradeWave help desk staff assisted the administrators and security specialists with connectivity and security issues. Supplemental information in these areas was added to the support Web site for future reference. These actions helped to ease the frustrations in introducing new Internet and security technologies.

After OASIS was deployed, management began to understand the important link between their corporate security and successfully doing business over the Internet. They started to see that they were losing money whenever employees could not do their daily business because of an Internet security issue. Management investigated what kinds of security improvements needed to be made and took action to make corporate security a priority.

Developing Digital Certificate Policies and Procedures

Even the most advanced security hardware and software cannot protect important corporate data without a clear-cut set of security policies and procedures for the human beings involved. Because digital certificate technology was in its relative infancy at the time this effort was underway, there were no existing policies and procedures to follow. Such policies and procedures would outline the responsibilities of the outsourced CA vendor and the customer.

The management and legal counsel for both JTSIN OASIS and TradeWave documented the security needs of the utility companies and outlined each party's obligations and legal limitations. Because there was no legal background information on digital certificates and electronic commerce, extra time was required to investigate new policies. In addition, different types of policies had to be developed. General corporate policies—those that needed to be integrated into the existing policies of companies—had to be developed. These policies had to clarify the expectations for employee performance, behavior, and accountability when using the TradeWave solution. Also, more specific technical policies were developed. Technical areas addressed included how much security each transaction and data type would need, as well as what level of network access each employee, customer, and partner should have. These technical policies required frequent revisions as changes in technology and the Internet security market took place.

Another challenge was to ensure that these policies were followed by company personnel. In order for these policies to be effective, the TradeWave policies and procedures had to be visible within the companies and become a part of the corporate policies and procedures. For example, a part of a new employee orientation in a company would include information on the process of obtaining a digital certificate and the importance of that certificate in doing business on the Internet.

Coordinating Product Dependencies

TradeWave software works closely with the Netscape and Microsoft browsers and servers. The testing cycles of the TradeAgent Client had to be carefully coordinated because the product was originally supported on Windows 3.1, Windows 95, Windows 98, Windows NT, Sun Solaris, IBM AIX, and HP-UX. Also, Microsoft and Netscape released frequent software updates. Even with careful coordination, trying to test the latest version of these products with the TradeWave software was often problematic. In one case, the TradeAgent Client went through a full testing cycle with the beta version of Microsoft Internet Explorer and then was released to customers. When the commercial version of Explorer was finally released, it had a major change, causing TradeAgent Client software to malfunction. A patch release of the TradeAgent software had to be made available to customers. Coordinating when users would upgrade to the latest browser software and providing easy methods for installing a patch release made it easier for customers to deal with a browser compatibility problem.

OASIS Today

Power companies have traded more than $30 billion in electric power using the TradeWave digital certificate-based solution. JTSIN OASIS has more than 3,000 digital certificate-enabled users and 500 participating companies. Power companies have expanded their use of TradeWave by writing their own applications, leveraging existing TradeWave software and certificates. OASIS is a thriving and extremely successful example of how business-to-business e-commerce can be enhanced and streamlined through the use of digital certificates.

Conclusions

At this point, your view of PKI has been broadened, so that you can see its pros and cons in a clearer light. As you evolve your security plan over time, return to this chapter and consider where and how PKI technology may assist you. The next, and last, chapter includes important reminders and a look forward at future security threats.

Ahead of the Hacker: Best Practices and a View of the Future

My purpose in this concluding chapter is to review the best practices for security planning presented in this book. I hope I've made it clear that the best way to implement any security plan is to treat it as a dynamic, ideally self-adapting shield against the shifting tactics of the hacker. To ensure that you come away with that viewpoint, in this chapter I also invite you to look with me into the future at what we might expect from hackers and how our approach to security planning can be continually applied to protect our information and infrastructure as we face those oncoming challenges.

Practice Makes Perfect—Or at Least More Secure

When we begin to plan how best to protect our systems and organizations from intruders, it helps to think of those who maliciously attack the security of our organizations as entrepreneurs in their own right—though entrepreneurs of havoc and, in extreme cases, evil. As such, they are always looking for opportunities to be more effective and efficient. That means they frequently change their tactics as they seek to perfect their skills. As security planners, we must do the same to deal with these attackers effectively; that is, we must work with greater conviction and stay as fast on our feet as they are.

By using security planning best practices and by understanding their complex interrelationships, we can see further into the future and better anticipate our adversaries' next moves. These best practices, as detailed throughout the book, are summarized for review purposes here:

Sell security; don't force-feed it.   Demonstrate to your organization that security adds value, as opposed to presenting security as a necessary burden. Detail the value of security in terms businesspeople can understand.

Remember that security planning is neither an absolute science nor an ad hoc process.   Security planning is a process that must be constantly managed and optimized; hence, it can never be regarded as "finished." Help people in your organization understand that security planning is an ongoing activity, not something you do until you reach some ultimate solution.

Achieve balance when planning.   Avoid the extreme practices of ultra-planning and nonplanning. A lack of focus is the enemy of security.

Prioritize and focus your information and infrastructure security planning and budgets.   Regularly perform impact analyses.

Create a cross-organizational security planning team with an executive mandate.   Manage the effectiveness of your security plan through a structured quality management process.

Plan security within the context of business, life-cycle management, and technology.   Security planners must understand the plethora of technologies they are protecting, not simply the tools designed to protect them.

Treat security policies, procedures, and training as the backbone of your security plan.   Go back over the previous chapters often, and by taking into account the specific needs of your organization, regularly look for opportunities to introduce needed training materials, policies, and procedures or to improve existing ones.

Profile hackers and plan your interactions with them.   Understand the different types of hackers presented in Chapter 1 and try to anticipate which ones will be most attracted to your organization. Provide clear mechanisms that hackers or those who find security problems with your infrastructure can use to communicate with you should they choose to; for example, institute a very accessible email address on your Web site (for example, security@your_company.com). Finally, train customer service staff so that they know how to deal with hackers who contact them to point out a vulnerability.

Build an incident response plan and team.   Determine your organization's security strength by assessing its response to actual and simulated incidents.

Most important, remember that the security of your organization's distributed computing environment can be planned around these 28 security elements:

1. Authorization and Access Control: Opening and Closing the Gates

2. Authentication: Knowing Who You Are Dealing With

3. Encryption: Keeping Information Away from Prying Eyes

4. Integrity: Hashing It Out

5. Nonrepudiation: Signing on the Dotted Line

6. Privacy: Separating Hype from Reality

7. Addressing, Protocol Space, Routing Plan, Filtering, and Disablement: Closing the Hacker's Route to You

8. Configuration Management: Tracking Changes

9. Content and Executable Management: Controlling the Flow

10. Directory Services: Location Is Everything

11. Diversity, Redundancy, and Isolation: The Triple Threat against Hacking

12. Intrusion Detection Systems and Vulnerability Analysis: Monitoring in Real Time

13. Secure Software: Starting at the Source

14. Secure Time Services: Keeping Your Eye on the Clock

15. Staff Management: Managing Employees and Contractors

16. Administration and Management: Watching over the Enterprise

17. Interoperability and Standards: Working Together

18. Laws and Regulations: Staying Out of Trouble

19. Lockdown: Keeping Things Tight

20. Lost or Stolen Items: When Important Things Disappear

21. Managed (Outsourced) Security: Working with Outside Security Vendors

22. Performance: Security Takes Time

23. Physical Security: Locking Up

24. Procurement: Be Discriminating

25. Support Interface: Protecting Confidential Information

26. Testing, Integration, and Staging: Get It Right before Betting the House on It

27. Training: Achieving Security through Education

28. Recovery: Getting Back on Track

Into the Future: The Top 10 Methods of Attack

Obviously, it's impossible to predict with certainty the future behavior of hackers. That doesn't mean we shouldn't try; by trying, we prepare ourselves as well as we can. To that end, then, to complete this book, I present what I believe to be the top 10 most likely future methods of information and infrastructure hacker attack. I have derived this list based on two primary factors.

First, 10 or 20 years ago, who of us could have imagined the economic, political, and increasingly life-critical importance of our networked infrastructure? Because of its centrality in our society, it has become a prime target for those who would seek to undermine it, for whatever reason. With the growth of terrorism and technology-savvy organized crime, the chances increase daily at an astounding rate that we will become a victim of a hack attack, be an unwilling participant (wherein our own infrastructure is, unbeknownst to us, used to attack others), or be affected by an attack on infrastructure on which we depend heavily.

Add to that the fact that much of our modern distributed computing technologies—namely our operating systems, network routing protocols, and computer architectures—were not designed for the kind of rampant software distribution and fully connected world we now have, not to mention the type of threats we now encounter.

With those thoughts in mind, I make my predictions for the top 10 future hacks.

HACK 1: TARGETED HIGH-IMPACT COMPUTING INFRASTRUCTURE ATTACKS

Description. To date, most attacks have been unfocused; for example, if there's a vulnerability in your Web server, the attacker goes after it. But as hackers become more sophisticated, they will focus on probing deeply into your infrastructure, going to those components that will most likely bring your organization to its knees. These will be the most predictable high-impact components, such as your directory servers, time servers, authentication servers, and dynamic configuration mechanisms such as DHCP servers.

Defending against it. Everything about this particular risk points to the importance of implementing the security planning process presented in this book, from each and every one of our best practices to our security elements.

HACK 2: GREATER NUMBERS OF PHYSICAL IN-PERSON HACKS

Description. Security as a field of study is advancing rapidly. As a result, some hackers will determine that entering your offices physically is the most direct route for achieving their aims. Therefore, expect more hackers to violate your physical space. These physical attackers may even be employees of your organization—operatives, terrorists, or thieves misrepresenting themselves in order to gain easier access.

Defending against it. The security stack component of our planning template includes a persistent look at physical security. By following our security planning best practices and focusing on physical security, your organization will be far more resistant to the increased trend of physical attacks. The staff management and authentication security elements will help you better understand and work to address the danger of those who attempt to misrepresent themselves.

HACK 3: EXPANDED WIRELESS AND HANDHELD ATTACKS

Description. Wireless networking in general, including highly sophisticated wireless handheld devices with links to your desktop, will continue to grow in popularity. Consider, for example, the sophistication of the handheld computers available today, running the Linux operating system. As has often been the case historically with any distributed computing technology, the security of handheld devices and wireless technologies, in general, is lagging behind product availability and deployment. Most wireless networking mechanisms offer little or no strong "over-the-air" security; if they do, people don't enable it due to an overwhelming configuration burden imposed by unsophisticated security mechanisms (for example, hand-configuring shared secret keys/passwords).

Consider a personal example: I own a handheld computer (a PDA, personal digital assistant) that runs Linux. I purchased a wireless Internet service for it, which is hardly sufficiently locked down for Internet access. But it seems nobody is focused on this—certainly not the folks who sold this combination to me. Furthermore, this configuration is anything but "disabled" (per our best practices and security elements), but instead is an open door for hackers. At the same time, this same combination offers thrilling potential as a PDA and ultimately as a great, truly secured device. Nonetheless, as security planners, we must focus on what's here now. I have to be aware that when I connect my wireless modem to this handheld, it becomes a hacker's playground. If I then connect the device to my desktop for synchronization and other purposes, at that point the hacker potentially has an open door to my desktop and then to the rest of the organization to which I connect. Note also that the handheld device may hold several poorly protected passwords also used on my desktop, such as my email password.

Neither is the handheld's desktop synchronization software very secure—it uses no password for FTP with the device. Early versions of this handheld allowed no password-required FTP access over a particular TCP port. Add all of this up, and it spells very serious trouble from a security standpoint.

Returning to the wireless aspect of all of this, wireless LANs (for example, IEEE 802.11), as well as wireless networking in general, require encryption to ensure the privacy and security of your transmissions. As discussed many times in this book, especially when reviewing our security element fundamentals, secret encryption key management is a general problem and is the reason why configuring security for these wireless links can be cumbersome in the first place. We need to continue to evolve our wireless encryption technology. Even if we do achieve this, widespread wireless access, whether such access is securely encrypted or not, provides greater opportunity for hacking poorly secured devices such as handhelds because these devices are now generally reachable over the network.

Defending against it.   Many of our security elements help protect us from the wireless risk; however, we must adapt them to be successful. Specifically, we need to manage the security of handheld devices and their related software, both desktop synchronization software and the software running in the device, with the following elements: content and executable management; addressing, protocol space, routing plan, filtering, and disablement; configuration management; lockdown; and procurement. Handheld devices, if connected to a network, need to be highly filtered, disabled, and locked down. Institute policies and procedures with regard to the transmission of sensitive company electronic mail over wireless handheld devices. Prohibit wireless LANs from anywhere in your organization unless strong encryption is implemented, along with strong authentication of any device connected to the wireless network.

HACK 4: CONTINUED BUFFER EXPLOITS AND SIMILAR ATTACKS ON OUTDATED COMPUTER ARCHITECTURES, OPERATING SYSTEMS, AND PROGRAMMING LANGUAGE DESIGNS

Description.   The fundamental design assumptions in our operating systems, computer CPU architectures, and programming languages did not take into account the widespread connectivity that we have today. The level of network interactivity available to nearly everyone today was not anticipated. Furthermore, attempts at secure programming languages and operating systems have continually failed because the security assumptions on which they were based have not held up to the intensity of our connected world (our secure implementations have continually proven to be anything but, as hole after hole is discovered once put to the acid test of the worldwide security community and the Internet).

The legacy design philosophies we now live with include an emphasis on performance, followed by features, functionality, and multiplatform capability. The CPU architectures do not incorporate security at their core. There is no concept of verifying authenticity and ensuring trust at the computer instruction set level—hence, the many buffer exploits that now exist. Programming languages such as Java, while undoubtedly enhancing security by allowing the user to control what a program is allowed to do (this is the so-called Java sandbox, or permissions-based software architecture), still ride on top of operating systems and CPUs that are continually prone to running untrusted code through one type of buffer exploit or another. Code signing, discussed earlier in this book, does not entirely address the trusted code problem because the holes in our design assumptions can allow malicious software to pass right through just about any lock we put in place, such as one requiring signed code. To address these design problems, we are constantly patching what are, at the core, inappropriate designs for our fully connected world. The ongoing set of new vulnerabilities we see each day is clear evidence of this.

Defending against it.   This risk is particularly difficult to protect against simply because many of the vulnerabilities are introduced by the very best software available. This software is executing in, as just discussed, what amounts to a flawed computing environment. For software you develop yourself, to include simple scripts written by your administrators, you should pay close attention to the secure software security element. The Quality Management worksheets will allow you to spot problem software vendors who don't themselves demonstrate a commitment to the development of secure software. If the vendor-supplied software you use is continually getting hacked and the vendor is issuing patch after patch in response, it's time to consider choosing a product from another vendor. Hold vendors accountable for security, not just performance, features, and price. Reward those software vendors that demonstrate a commitment to security by buying their products.

Beyond all of this, if you adhere to the best practices in this book, you will have a sufficient infrastructure that has been disabled and filtered, as described throughout this book, with high-impact systems monitored, so that, in many cases, many of these exploits will never affect you. You will have shut down most or all of the paths into your critical infrastructure from a software process or machine that has been compromised. For example, let's say your Web server process is compromised, but that you have given that server process minimal privileges or otherwise isolated the Web server from the rest of your network (through filtering, for example).These are the steps a mission-critical security planner takes, the steps our security elements drive us to take. Consequently, vulnerabilities in one of your systems, in this case the Web server, will be less likely to propagate to your other systems simply because you have implemented a thorough security plan.

HACK 5: MORE TROJAN HORSES AND NETWORK-BORNE VIRUSES

Description.   Network-borne viruses will continue to be commonplace, despite the fact that today nearly everyone has anti-virus software installed on his or her desktop. These viruses will continue to make their way undetected into downloadable software and even commercial products. Increasingly, the germs of these viruses will make their way into the software development environments of less-than-security-aware software companies. The viruses will have longer periods of dormancy, during which they will be able to achieve greater levels of desktop and server penetration simply because, by showing no symptoms of infection for longer periods of time, people may not be aware that this virus exists; this lack of awareness will allow more time for the virus to spread. This will increasingly become the era of the patient virus, one not necessarily enacted on some particular date or time, but enacted either via remote activation or some random but important moment chosen by the authors. Extortion attempts and threats may precede activation.

Defending against it.   Your protection will include your implementation of the intrusion-detection and vulnerability analysis system security elements. Then, if these viruses are activated in your network, your intrusion and vulnerability systems have a better chance of spotting them. Desktop intrusion detection software products will increasingly act to protect your organization from these Trojan horses and network-borne viruses. In many cases, desktop intrusion detection and firewall software can act to essentially neutralize this malicious software, even if it is present on the desktop or server, by disabling the mechanisms the malicious software relies on and alerting the user accordingly.

Your adherence to the testing, integration, and staging security element will allow you to spot oddly behaving software up front, though a dormant virus may not show itself during such testing. Solid procurement and content and executable management planning will allow you to stop malicious software more frequently, before it can make its way into your infrastructure.

HACK 6: EXPANDED NETWORK ROUTING ATTACKS

Description.   The security of the routing protocols we use today in the backbone of our public, corporate, and government networks is inadequate. At issue is maintaining the veracity of the routing information exchanged. Network devices rarely authenticate to one another; if they do, they do so very poorly. Relying on routes from a network neighbor that cannot be trusted is a bad idea. Such routes may have been maliciously modified to disrupt overall connectivity or to route sensitive traffic to the hacker's network to extract information needed for follow-on attacks. These types of vulnerabilities have existed for decades and have been quietly leveraged by hackers. As high-impact infrastructure attacks become more prevalent, we will see more of these attacks.

Fortunately, today, the routing standards groups are focusing more heavily on security. The deployment of secure routing protocols, given the widespread installed base of the equipment we have today, could take some time. Furthermore, adequately securing routing protocols and, at the same time, keeping them easy to administer are nontrivial exercises.

The good news is that this future hack may not come to fruition if the standards groups and networking manufacturers coordinate quickly to provide a smooth path for change. Unfortunately, the bigger risk remains: Even if these secure routing features become available, people may not bother investing in their configuration and deployment unless their viability has been proven—ironically, through a devastating hack—and that genuine risks exist. The ISPs are the first, most important candidates for deployment of secure routing protocols.

Defending against it.   As security features become more widely available in the routing protocols you deploy, implement them. Use network providers and ISPs that do the same. Perhaps the most important feature of a secure routing protocol is one that strongly authenticates all routers and maintains the integrity of all routes exchanged, so that hackers cannot tamper with them. Aside from advances in secure routing protocols, your best defense is your adherence to the addressing, protocol space, routing plan, filtering, and disablement security element, as well as the ongoing focus provided by the network layer of your security stack.

HACK 7: TARGETED NETWORK MANAGEMENT SYSTEM ATTACKS

Description.   For years substantial security vulnerabilities have been associated with network management protocols such as SNMP. Many organizations continue to use SNMP, not only as a means for gathering device statistics, but also as a way to configure devices. The security in the original version of SNMP is extremely weak, relying on a simple shared password sent in the clear. The intent was to improve this security in later releases, but politics in the standards committees, coupled with virtually no market demand for security features, considerably slowed their development and availability. Other highly vulnerable management protocols may still be accidentally enabled by administrators, including the trivial file transfer protocol (tftp), a protocol that does not require a password. These vulnerabilities have existed for quite some time, yet only in recent years have we begun to see (in the public eye) high-profile examples of these vulnerabilities being exploited. Hackers are becoming more knowledgeable about deeper-level infrastructure attacks. Because of the expanded range of motivations hackers now have (nationalistic, terror, crime), they will look for more targeted methods for attacking high-impact infrastructures. The network management infrastructure of an organization represents an easily identifiable high-impact target.

Defending against it.   Your network management system LANs need to be carefully monitored (see the "Home on the LAN" sidebar in Chapter 2). Your intrusion-detection and vulnerability analysis systems should be heavily focused on your network management-related systems. In addition, strongly consider disabling the use of SNMP for configuration of devices; enable it only for nonsensitive statistics gathering (for those statistics not clearly useful to a hacker). Use SSH to configure your devices, not straight SNMP or telnet and FTP alone. All of these points have been made repeatedly in this book.

HACK 8: MORE EFFECTIVE SOCIAL ATTACKS

Description.   Hackers will continue to perfect the art of extracting sensitive and valuable information over the phone and in person from customer service representatives and other support staff. Hence, social hacking will continue to be a popular means of getting past increasingly improved electronic security measures and as a way for less technically skilled hackers to get closer to their objective. In addition, attacks on public utilities (see Hack 9) may involve social hacking techniques. Companies will continue to put highly sensitive information at the fingertips of support staff, who continue to be poorly trained and lack well-understood policies and procedures to guide them.

Defending against it.   Focusing on the support interface security element, in conjunction with conducting aggressive training, are the two best practices we can follow to protect against this threat. For social attacks that involve physical access, use tough physical security planning techniques to help defend against this threat.

HACK 9: HACKERS IN THE FORM OF TERRORISTS AND SOLDIERS

Description.   Today, many countries are employing hackers as part of their national defense mechanism and, in some cases, their offense as well. Terrorists are following suit, threatening to practice their brand of evil in the electronic world. These types of hackers will increasingly focus on highly coordinated hacks with the objective of causing panic and loss of life. Even if you do not believe your organization will be a direct target of such an attack, your systems may be unwittingly hijacked and/or you may be excessively dependent on other public systems that are attacked (see Chapter 4, "Diversity, Redundancy, and Isolation," to protect against this) unless you practice solid security planning.

Future trends we can expect from this genre of hacking include attacks on public utilities systems. Water, phone, and electric utilities will be attacked in an attempt to cause systems (such as those that control a dam or power to a region of the country) to fail, as well as to cause widespread panic.

More coordinated attacks are anticipated, too, whereby a network infrastructure, such as a large ISP and a public utility, will be attacked simultaneously, in conjunction with a physical attack (such as a bomb or bioterror scare) in an attempt to disrupt communication and recovery mechanisms and cause widespread panic.

Attacks, too, will be focused on the financial systems that support national and worldwide equity markets and banking, in an attempt to disrupt confidence in the financial markets of a given country and for theft.

Defending against it.   If your organization is a public utility or high-profile financial organization, work to communicate the potential for this threat within your organization as an integrated part of the security-selling process. Incident response planning will help guide your organization to a smoother recovery should you be the victim of such an attack. Together, the full breadth of our security planning best practices serves as the protection against this broad set of threats.

HACK 10: HACKERS WORKING IN ORGANIZED CRIME

Description.   Over the past four years there has been an extraordinary increase in extortion attempts by hackers. Typically, they contact the victim, claiming to have planted something very dangerous within a high-impact system or claiming to have obtained damaging information that they now threaten to release. If you agree to give these hackers what they want, they typically promise to disable their hack, destroy the sensitive information, or tell you how to do so. Some percentage of the time, these people are bluffing; sometimes they're not. Several companies have already lost a considerable amount of money when they guessed wrong on one of these threats.

The point here is, many companies have no formalized incident response process and no experience in negotiating with hackers, thus they typically react poorly to extortion attempts. Thieves are learning that the Internet offers a great deal of extortion potential: It provides the anonymity they need to go undetected, the technology to stage or actually carry out a threat, and sufficiently valuable assets to make a payoff more likely. The trend in extortion attempts will continue, and extortion attempts will become more widely known to the public, whereas today many are kept secret by companies in an attempt to avoid losing face with their customers, investors, and owners.

Defending against it.   If you have loose security, such as poor intrusion-detection technology, policies, and procedures, you are especially vulnerable because you have very few mechanisms to verify whether your systems have been compromised. Understanding the hacker, as discussed in Chapter 1, a sound incident response team and plan, and strong intrusion-detection and vulnerability analysis systems all go a long way to protect you from falling prey to extortion attempts.

In Closing

Ideally, one day we'll redefine distributed computing technology in such a way that it is far more robust than today—better able to defend itself, autonomously, against the hacker threat. But there will always be the human factor. Humans will always make mistakes; our spirits will always be subject to the sins of greed, malice, selfishness, and hatred. Security planning will, therefore, be part of our existence; the process is ours to master forever.

For Further Reading

This list contains books I recommend to those of you interested in more detail related to security planning. I also provide comments as to why I think you'll find each title useful. Though several of these references are old, these can be considered classics on the subject and continue to be outstanding references for the security planner.

Adams, C. and S. Lloyd (1999). *Understanding Public-Key Infrastructure: Concepts, Standards, and Deployment Considerations* (Indianapolis, IN: Macmillan Technical Publishing).

If you have an interest in learning more about PKI at a high level, this book is one place to start.

Cheswick, W.R. and S.M. Bellovin (1994). *Firewalls and Internet Security: Repelling the Wily Hacker* (Reading, MA: Addison-Wesley).

Many of the vulnerabilities these authors wrote about years ago still exist today. The insight they offer into hacking is highly useful. The book remains a classic.

Doraswamy, N. and D. Harkins (1999). *IPSec: The New Security Standard for the Internet, Intranets, and Virtual Private Networks* (Upper Saddle River, NJ, Prentice Hall).

If you are interested in learning more about VPN technology and IPSec, this book is a good reference.

Garfinkel, S. and G. Spafford (2002). *Web Security, Privacy and Commerce* (Sebastopol, CA: O'Reilly).

This book provides an excellent overview of Web security technologies.

Greenberg, E. (1999). *Network Application Frameworks: Design and Architecture* (Reading, MA: Addison-Wesley).

This, my first book, is essentially a treatise on secure distributed computing. Security is covered in detail throughout. Important topics include SSL; Kerberos; PKI; directory services, including LDAP, Active Directory, and Novell NDS; security of protocols and applications contained in the TCP/IP protocol suite; Microsoft object and networking technologies; and many others.

Howes, T., M. Smith, and G. Good (1999). *Understanding and Deploying LDAP Directory Services*. (Indianapolis, IN: Macmillan Technical Publishing).

If you want to learn more about directory services in detail, especially LDAP, this is a very good reference.

Viega, J. and G. McGraw (2002) *Building Secure Software*. (Reading, MA: Addison-Wesley Professional).

This is an excellent book on the topic of building secure software. It provides a very focused view with highly useful detail.

Kaeo, M. (1999). *Designing Network Security* (Indianapolis, IN: Cisco Press Macmillan Technical Publishing).

Though this book was published as part of the Cisco Press series, it is anything but a book dedicated to Cisco topics. It provides a surprisingly broad and balanced view of network security. It will provide you additional detail on topics including VPNs, addressing, firewalls, protocol vulnerabilities, security policies, and many other topics important to the security planner.

Kaufman, C., R. Perlman, and M. Speciner (1995). *Network Security: Private Communication in a Public World* (Englewood Cliffs, NJ: PTR Prentice Hall).

A classic book discussing general network security technologies in detail.

Kopparapu, C. (2002). *Load Balancing Servers, Firewalls, and Caches* (New York: John Wiley & Sons, Inc.).

When planning security, you are bound to run into the performance trade-off between load balancing servers, possibly caching devices, and the firewall. There are few if any books that combine the study of these three important topics. This is a reasonably technical book, not just a high-level overview.

Kosiur, D.R. (1998). *Building and Managing Virtual Private Networks* (New York: John Wiley & Sons, Inc.).

This is still one of the best books written on VPNs, and I highly recommend it if you intend to deploy a VPN.

Lynch, D.C. and M.T. Rose (1993). *Internet System Handbook* (Reading, MA: Addison-Wesley).

Though written in 1993, most of this book remains extremely relevant. It is one of the best networking textbooks ever written, in my opinion. You will find an in-depth discussion of Internet-related network protocols, application protocols, performance, security—you name it. And it serves as a fantastic primer on the origins and evolution of the Internet.

Northcutt, S. (1999). *Network Intrusion Detection: An Analyst's Handbook* (Indianapolis, IN: New Riders).

Provides good insight into the topic of intrusion detection.

Power, R. (2000). *Tangled Web: Tales of Digital Crime from the Shadows of Cyberspace* (Indianapolis, IN: Que).

An entertaining book offering interesting stories and insight into hacker exploits. This is not a technical book, rather more of a behavioral storytelling view of hackers and particularly interesting attacks.

Proctor, P.E. (2001). *Practical Intrusion Detection Handbook* (Upper Saddle River, NJ: Prentice Hall PTR).

A comprehensive, well-written book on intrusion detection.

Scambray, J., S. McClure, and G. Kurtz (2001). *Hacking Exposed: Network Security Secrets & Solutions* (Berkeley, CA: Osborne/McGraw-Hill).

If you want to learn more about buffer exploits and myriad other hacks in more detail, you will enjoy this book.

Schneier, B. (1996). *Applied Cryptography: Protocols, Algorithms, and Source Code in C* (New York: John Wiley & Sons, Inc.).

To learn more about encryption and cryptography in general, at a very technical level, this is the classic book written on the subject.

Schneier, B. (2000). *Secrets and Lies: Digital Security in a Networked World* (New York: John Wiley & Sons, Inc.).

An interesting and entertaining overview of general landscape of security including technologies and strategies.

Stevens, W.R., and G.R. Wright (1994). *TCP/IP Illustrated* (Reading, MA: Addison-Wesley).

This is the number-one classic book for those who want to dive deeper into the inner workings of the TCP/IP protocol and implementations of it. If you have an interest in such detail, this book delivers it with excellence.

Summers, R.C. (1997). *Secure Computing: Threats and Safeguards* (New York: McGraw-Hill).

This is a well-written, underrated, detailed security reference book. It's hard to imagine anything important relating to security that isn't somehow addressed, either directly or indirectly, in this highly comprehensive book. Everything from cryptography, auditing, security policies and procedures, tokens, access control, and the like, is covered.

Glossary

Active Directory   Microsoft directory service technology introduced with the release of Windows 2000. Active Directory allows for resources, including file servers, Web servers, and printers, to be located over the network. Importantly, it is used to manage user accounts and associated access control for resources in the Windows environment.

ActiveX   Standard for object-oriented executables for Windows desktops and servers, sometimes encountered on a Web page. ActiveX is Microsoft's object-oriented standard for management and distribution of executables. The ActiveX standard is based on Microsoft's Object Linking and Embedding (OLE) architecture. ActiveX objects are sometimes embedded within Web pages. Because the objects are capable of attaining full control over the computer (such as erasing a hard drive), security planners should control whether or not they should be allowed to be executed. ActiveX execution can be controlled with code signing.

Application Server   A server program that serves as the "front end" for an organization's complex backend applications. In a Web environment, users will connect to the application server, and that application server will manage complex transactions with the organization's backend servers. From a security standpoint, an application server can be configured to effectively shield the backend systems by not allowing any direct connectivity to them. All users must instead connect to the application server, and only the application server has permission to connect to the backend. Application servers are also called *appservers*.

Asymmetric encryption   Encryption mechanism that relies on two keys (a key pair). The most popular example of asymmetric encryption is public key cryptography.

Attribute   Descriptive information associated with an individual or resource managed by a directory service. The best example of an attribute would be an individual's job title or department. Thus, the directory service might contain an entry for an individual, as well as certain attributes about that individual, such as job title.

Authentication Header (AH)   Used by the IPSec protocol to authenticate and provide integrity for the IP header authentication including IP address. IPSec may be combined with ESP, AH, and IKE by configuration of security associations (SAs). *See also* IPSEC.

Authenticode   Microsoft's code signing standard for objects such as ActiveX.

Basic Authentication (Basic Auth)   HTTP Basic Authentication is a username/password authentication mechanism commonly used by Web servers. If using basic authentication, you should combine it with SSL because basic authentication usernames/password are otherwise easily hacked.

Binary   A term used to describe the file you actually execute on a computer. It contains the version of a software program that is fully processed (compiled) for execution by the computer.

Biometric   Defines "what you are" for the purpose of authentication. A biometric is one of three factors that can be used for authentication. Biometric authentication systems capture and store physiological traits such as those of the finger, hand, face, iris, or retina; or behavioral characteristics, such as voice patterns, signature style, or keystroke dynamics. To gain access to a system, a user provides a new sample, which is then compared with the stored biometric sample.

Boot Protocol (BOOTP)   A protocol used to provide network-based devices with configuration information including IP addresses. DHCP is based on BOOTP. *See also* DHCP.

Buffer   Computer programs store frequently accessed information in buffers. These buffer areas are read by the computer's CPU and manipulated. Through a buffer exploit, hackers force the CPU to execute their own malicious programs by causing a buffer to overflow and fooling the CPU into executing those programs.

Buffer exploit   A computer, such as a Web server, can be forced to run a hacker's computer program by exploiting a buffer management vulnerability within your computer operating system or its applications. Computer programming languages require that programmer's carefully manage memory allocated for buffers. If a computer program is forced to overflow one of its buffers by the hacker, such as by the hacker filling-out a form read by a CGI script with large amounts of unexpected data, then the hacker can "push" onto the computer's central processing unit (CPU) computer instructions for his own malicious program. If the hacker discovers a buffer exploit vulnerability on your Web server for example, and if your Web server software process is given full control (full authorization) to do anything it wants on the computer (sometimes referred to as superuser control), then the hacker can gain full control over the entire computer, not just the Web server program. From the Web server, the hacker may quietly work to further attack your organization or may simply damage your Web environment and be done with it.

Cache   (1) Inside a computer, in order to speed up access to information, computer programs may store information in random access memory (RAM), in something called a cache, rather than constantly fetching it from a slower storage device such as a hard drive. Caches, from a security standpoint, can be dangerous if sensitive security information such as passwords or encryption keys are stored unsecured in a cache, allowing the hacker to gain access to them should they have a virus installed on your machine or if they perform some other exploit. (2)Network caching applies the same concept as computer caching, except the idea is to store (cache) frequently accessed content on a caching server located in front of an organization's Internet connection. This is done to improve performance. For example, if all employees tend to visit a popular Web page over the Internet every morning, then rather than using up Internet bandwidth to fetch one copy of this page for every employee in the organization, a network cache can intercept requests for that popular Web page and deliver it from its own cache. Periodically, the network caching server will visit the popular Web site and refresh its cache. If a network cache ends up holding confidential company information (if, for example, the popular Web site is a company page containing intellectual property), then the network cache could be the target of a hacker.

Certificate   A collection of data (a data structure) containing your *public key* and specific attributes that describe you and any organization with which you are affiliated. So that others may trust that the certificate truly contains your public key and nobody else's, the certificate is digitally signed by a certificate authority (CA). The most popular certificate format is specified in the International Standards Organization (ISO) X.509 standard. These certificates are referred to as X.509 certificates. Certificates can be issued for individuals as well as organizations.

Certificate authority (CA)   A trusted third party (an organization) that signs certificates. If you trust a particular CA, then you trust certificates that it has signed. A CA can sign certificates issued for individuals, organizations, as well as for other CAs. To understand the latter case, consider an example. Suppose you trust a CA named A. Suppose there is another CA named B. If A signs B's certificate, then because you trust the certificates issued by A, you also trust certificates issued by B since B's certificate has been signed by A.

Code obfuscation   The act of trying to make a program difficult and confusing for a hacker to reverse engineer. By reverse engineering your program, a hacker may be able to more easily attack the program.

Code signing   The act of digitally signing a computer program. In order to assure a program has not been tampered with by a hacker and is written by the organization that claims to have written it, the program can be digitally signed. Software development organizations can be issued code signing certificates by a certificate authority (CA). They use these certificates to sign programs. *See also* certificate authority.

Common Gateway Interface (CGI)   An software application programming interface for external scripts and programs that can be run by your Web server. Advanced functions on a Web server, such as a shopping cart, require advanced functionality that can only be accommodated by an external program running on the Web server or on some other backend machine(s). CGI provides a software interface for external programs.

Concurrent Versions System (CVS)   A program used by one or more people for keeping track of changes to files such as those containing program source code. CVS can be used to meet the requirements of the configuration management security element.

CPU-intensive   Programs that make heavy use of the computer's central processing unit (CPU). Programs that perform cryptographic operations, especially those that perform digital signing, are typically more CPU-intensive.

Demilitarized Zone (DMZ)   An additional "safety zone" that you can place between your private network and the public Internet. One popular example of a DMZ configuration makes use of at least two firewalls. The first firewall connects the public Internet to your DMZ safety zone. Within the safety zone you may have moderate or low impact devices such as Web servers. On the other side of the DMZ safety zone is another firewall connecting the DMZ safety zone to your more critical higher impact private network. The firewall connecting to the Internet is usually more liberal, having fewer filters and disabling less than the firewall connecting the DMZ to your private network. The firewall to your private network is much more restrictive.

Denial-of-Service (DoS) attack   A malicious attack on a network and its computers intended to prevent it from operating. A DoS attack typically achieves its goal by forcing one or more devices in your network to process many more requests than it can handle. This usually involves flooding your network with one type of data packet or another.

Digital signature   *See* Public key cryptography.

Directory service   A highly structured distributed database of information potentially used by all network-based devices including desktop computers, servers, and routers. Directory servers may store high impact information such as access control rights for people and other computers in the network. They also can work closely with your authentication service. For example, in the case of current Microsoft products, Active Directory and Kerberos work closely together. Directory servers are ideally suited for information that must be read quickly and that is changed far less frequently. The relationship between data in a directory service, and its overall organization, is described in something called a directory service schema. Most directory service products allow information to be organized in a treelike hierarchical manner. When looked at in the simplest of terms, information further down the tree (the leaves) is organized into containers (think of containers as branches of the tree) and other branches are organized into more branches (more containers, as in one container containing several other containers). Access control rights can be assigned to individual directory service entries as well as to containers. If access is enabled to a particular element or container, this may be translated into permission being allowed, by a user, to some range of computing resources within the organization. By compromising the directory service, hackers can therefore potentially gain access permissions to anything managed by the directory service.

Distributed DoS attack (DDoS) A DoS attack that makes use of many computers to increase the flood of packets sent. Often these other computers have themselves been hacked, and the owners of these computers are unwilling participants in the distributed DoS attack.

Domain Name System (or Service) (DNS) A directory service that maps IP addresses to easier-to-use domain names such as whitehouse.gov. If hackers compromise your DNS, then they can maliciously reroute traffic destined for one Web site to another one by tampering with the mapping between IP address and domain name.

Dynamic Host Configuration Protocol (DHCP) Based on BOOTP, a protocol that uses broadcast packets on a local LAN to provide configuration information for devices. DHCP can be used to provide configuration information including IP address, directory server names, and routing information. By intercepting and then spoofing DHCP packets, hackers can read this configuration information, learn from it, and tamper with it for the purpose of performing an attack. They can, for example, modify the routing in your network so that sensitive information is sent directly to them rather than its intended destination.

E-monitoring The electronic monitoring of workers within an organization, as in the monitoring of Internet browsing patterns and electronic mail.

Encapsulating Security Payload (ESP) Used by the IPSec protocol to provide encryption and data integrity between two IPSec endpoints. ESP also provides authentication, but only authenticates the part of the IP header in an IPSEC ESP tunnel. IPSec may be combined with ESP, AH, and IKE by configuration of security associations (SAs).

Encryption See symmetric encryption and asymmetric encryption.

Executable Any computer file that contains something that a computer will run, such as a script or any software program, is called an executable.

File Transfer Protocol (FTP) TCP/IP-based protocol used for transferring files from one network device to another. Often used by system administrators to maintain and configure devices. For security, should be used in conjunction with SSH. *See also* Internet Protocol and SSH.

Filter   A configuration entry in a computing device such as a router or server preventing designated types of network traffic from entering, leaving it, or passing through it. For example, a router can be configured to filter out the Telnet protocol so that no Telnet requests can pass through it from one network segment to another.

Firewall   A separate hardware device, or software running on a computer, designed to control the flow of network traffic and content through it in order to prevent the risk of being hacked. Firewalls can filter packets based on complex rules. Such rules may be based on fields of a data packet such as source IP address, destination address, and protocol type. Firewalls can help prevent IP spoofing, can interact with applications such as FTP so that they cannot be easily hijacked by a hacker, and can work in conjunction with a proxy server.

Frame relay   Private networking transport technology used to carry data traffic such as IP or other data protocols. Frame relay is a simplified high-speed packet switching technology that does not provide guaranteed delivery of data. Guaranteed delivery of data, if needed, must be provided by another protocol, such as at the TCP protocol.

Hash   A mathematical algorithm used in the field of cryptography, often used for the purpose of assuring the integrity of information. A cryptographically secure hash function produces a unique number based on the data provided to it. The probability of obtaining the identical unique number for two different data inputs is approximately zero.

HTTP   HyperText Transfer Protocol (HTTP). The protocol used to browse the Web. HTTP uses TCP port 80.

HTTPS   HyperText Transfer Protocol (HTTP), when combined with the SSL or TLS protocol, is referred to as HTTPS. HTTPS is built-into all major Web browsers for providing a secure connection between the desktop and a Web server for, for example, making a purchase online. HTTPS uses TCP port 443.

IDS/VA   Acronym used in this book to refer to both an *intrusion detection system* (IDS) and *vulnerability analysis* (VA) system. Intrusion detection and vulnerability analysis often go hand-in-hand in the security planning process. *See also* Intrusion detection system and Vulnerability analysis.

Internet Key Exchange (IKE)   Used by the IPSec network security protocol to negotiate crytographic keys between two IPSec-based network devices. This allows for enhanced authentication such as X.509 digital certificate-based authentication between two IPSec devices. IKE may be combined with ESP, AH, and IKE by configuration of security associations (SAs).

Internet Protocol (IP)   The packet (datagram) specification used on the Internet and in private networks. The current version of IP used on the Internet is version 4 (IPv4). The next version to be deployed is expected to be IP version 6 (IPv6). IP version 5 was skipped; the specification never received widespread adoption.

Internet relay chat (IRC)   An online chat system used to communicate with other users over an IP network using your keyboard and in real time. IRC is often used anonymously by hackers to work together and share information about their exploits.

In the clear   Data that is sent over the network, or stored inside a computer, without any form of encryption. It can, therefore, be read by anyone that gains access to it.

Intrusion detection system (IDS)   Intrusion detection is a real-time analysis of the behavior and interactions of a computing entity to determine whether penetrations have occurred or are likely. An intrusion detection system (IDS)—typically a server running IDS application software—probes servers, workstations, firewalls, and routers, and analyzes them for symptoms of security breaches. The IDS monitors for known attack patterns, determines if important system files have been tampered with (i.e., verifies integrity), analyzes system logs (audit trails), and issues alerts based on violations of security policy.

IP address   IP addresses are 4 bytes (32 bits) in length. Addresses used on the open Internet are unique and assigned by an *address authority*, sometimes referred to as an *address registry*. These registries globally administer the Internet address space. There are five classes of IP addresses: A, B, C, D, and E, which differ in the number of networks, subnetworks, and hosts that they support allow for. For example, you may receive one class B network address that can be subdivided into subnetworks. A class B address takes the form of 255.255.0.0 (called dotted decimal notation). For each network segment in your organization, you will assign one subnet address. To enhance security, manageability, and to conserve increasingly scarce unique Internet addresses, corporate networks are often configured with a feature known as network address translation

(NAT) in conjunction with a private internet address space. The Internet Assigned Numbers Authority (IANA) has reserved three blocks of IP address space for private IP networks, 10.0.0.0, 172.16.0.0, and 192.168.0.0. NAT capability can be configured on the network devices that connect to the Internet, whereby the NAT devices translate between your private IP address space and unique address registry-assigned IP addresses given to your organization. In this way, hackers on the Internet do not directly know the IP address of any device within your organization, since all they see are the external unique IP addresses and not the internal private ones. Also, you can use as many private IP addresses as you'd like and not concern yourself with running out of unique registry-assigned addresses. And finally, with private IP addresses you have the full flexibility to administer addresses within your private network in a way completely independent of address assignments provided by your Internet service provider (ISP).

IP Security (IPSec)   IPSec is a network-level security protocol that has been retrofitted to work with IP version 4 (IPv4), the current version of IP used on the Internet. IPSec is directly integrated into IP version 6 (IPv6), the next version of IP (version 5 was skipped). IPSec may be combined with ESP, AH, and IKE by configuration of security associations (SAs).

Information Systems (IS) group   *See* Information Technology (IT) group.

Internet service provider (ISP)   An organization that sells connectivity to the Internet.

Information Technology (IT) group   The group of people within an organization responsible for maintaining distributed computing technology including desktop computers, servers, and routers.

Java   An object-oriented high-level programming language originally developed by Sun Microsystems, heavily promoted by Netscape, and now adopted by others. Java interpreters, called Java Virtual Machines (VMs) are included with most popular Web browsers and in major operating systems. Java provides for the ability to, up-front, allow or disallow certain permissions to the application, such as accessing the hard drive or not. This ability to confine a Java application to only certain authorized capabilities on a computer differentiates Java, as a programming language and execution environment, from others such as C or C++.

Java archive (JAR)   A file format for combining all of the individual Java components required by a Java program into one compressed file. JAR files can themselves be digitally signed (via code signing), and applications can be made to only use JAR files that are digitally signed by a trusted software developer.

JavaScript   A scripting language, used within Web pages, that allows Web sites to perform more complex functions and to provide greater interaction with the user. Javascript was originally developed by Netscape.

Kerberos   A security protocol used for authentication. It provides the capability for single sign-on, meaning that a user can, for example, enter his or her username and password just once to access five different applications instead of entering it five times, once for each application. Kerberos was adopted by Microsoft beginning with Windows 2000. Different versions of Kerberos are available for other operating systems such as UNIX and Linux. Kerberos was originally developed as part of MIT's Project Athena. The name Kerberos comes from Greek mythology. A three-headed dog named Kerberos stood guard over the gates of Hades. In order to make it past this dog, you had to be particularly truthful and of exceptional moral character. Kerberos employs a sophisticated authentication mechanism whereby usernames and passwords are never transmitted over the network, but only cryptographically related authentication credentials. In this way, a hacker cannot steal a Kerberos username and password simply by sniffing a LAN.

Key   A very long number used by a cryptographic algorithm. *See also* Symmetric encryption, Asymmetric encryption, and Public key cryptography

Key escrow   The act of taking an individual's PKI private key (as in the the private key associated with the public key stored in his or her X.509 digital certificate) and securely storing the key away with a trusted party such as a corporate security officer. The problem with key escrow is that the fundamental characteristic of non-repudiability can be challenged by an individual simply because, with key escrow, it can be proven that someone else had their private key and, therefore, their signature had been forged. If hackers access the stored private key from the key escrow system, they can then forge their signature and impersonate the private key. The advantage of key escrow is that, if an individual loses his or her private key, or there is information that has been encrypted while making use of an individual's public key (such as information on a hard drive), the organization can still recover and gain access to that encrypted information.

Key pair   A public key and the private key associated with it are, together, referred to as a key pair.

Key recovery   The terms *key recovery* and *key escrow* are often used interchangeably. *See* Key escrow.

LDAPS   LDAP, when combined with the SSL protocol, is referred to as LDAPS. LDAPS send all LDAP network exchanges through the SSL protocol, thereby greatly enhancing security. *See* Lightweight Directory Access Protocol.

Lightweight Directory Access Protocol (LDAP)   A multiplatform directory service standard.LDAP defines a standard and associated data formats for exchange directory service commands and responses between LDAP-enabled clients and servers. LDAP also defines an application programming interface (API) allowing software developers to integrate LDAP into their applications. There are also free open-source versions of LDAP available. LDAP can be used by itself or in conjunction with other directory service technology such as that offered by Microsoft (Active Directory) and Novell.

Local area network (LAN)   A shared communications medium, either wired or wireless, on which computers within close proximity to one another can communicate. An Ethernet network is an example of a LAN.

Log   The place where a device such as a desktop computer, server, or router records information relating to a particular event. For example, a log entry may be made if someone successfully authenticates to a server or someone makes a change to a critical system component. Often log files contain the date and time of the event (timestamp). Sometimes hackers will modify log files as well as the system date and time in order to disguise their actions.

Macromedia Flash   Animation technology, enabled through the use of a Web browser plug-in. Application developers write Flash-enabled programs and can embed those on Web pages. As with many applications, Web browsers enabled for Flash have sometimes been vulnerable to a hacker.

Malformed packets   Incorrectly formatted data packets sent by a hacker for the purpose of causing the receiving device to behave in a manner not originally intended by the designers. The result may be that the receiving device may crash, execute a hacker's program, or behave in such a way as to impact other devices, such as becoming an unintended participant in a DoS attack.

Message Authentication Code (MAC)   A cryptographic method for assuring the integrity of data. A MAC is produced through the use of a hash algorithm in conjunction with randomly generated keys.

Multiplatform   Software-supporting, multiple operating systems and/or computer hardware (such as an IBM PC-compatible and a Macintosh). A multiplatform standard is one that can be implemented on multiple operating systems.

NAT   *See* IP address.

Network Application Framework   The collection of interoperable technologies that, when combined, allow the network and its applications to operate seamlessly as one distributed computing system.

Network Basic Input Output System (NetBIOS)   A Microsoft network naming scheme, network protocol, and application programming interface. Several vulnerabilities have been previously exposed in NetBIOS.

Network segment   A large private network is typically divided into small parts called network segments. These segments are logically separated from one another, often separated within a local hub or LAN switching device. At the IP network protocol level, this separation is achieved through the establishment of a separate IP subnetwork (subnet) for each segment. Security planners work to isolate specific types of traffic on only those network segments where they must be. They achieve this by filtering and disabling data packets before sending them from one subnet to another, or before allowing them to leave a computer.

Network Time Protocol (NTP)   One example of a network protocol used to distribute time within a network. There are secure versions of NTP, and there are also other time distribution protocols. Most protocols in use today lack sufficient security. They do not operate on the assumption that time synchronization is a security-sensitive operation. As discussed in this book, it is an important aspect of security.

Network-borne virus   Malicious software that makes use of the network in order to attack one or more systems. A network-borne virus may come to you in an email message or may be hidden within software you have installed (also sometimes called a Trojan). The virus may install itself on your machine and then attack your machine and others. Network-borne viruses are particularly dangerous when they are installed deep within corporate networks (behind the firewall) because they can then gain unauthorized access to high impact systems. For example, a network-borne virus may sniff all data packets on a sensitive corporate network. It may then email that information back to a hacker or otherwise tunnel the stolen information back to its source. Many security administrators mistakenly believe that, because their firewall filters so much, that even if a network-borne virus is present behind the firewall, this virus cannot reach the open Internet. This assumption is false. A virus could, for example, simulate a simple browsing session by a user and make this stolen information transmission appear to be nothing more than simple Web browsing.

Novell Directory Service (NDS)   A directory service software product developed by Novell.

NR   An acronym used in this book for the term nonrepudiation.

NT LAN Manager (NTLM)   The authentication mechanism used in Microsoft environments prior to the introduction of Kerberos with the release of Windows 2000.

Obfuscation   *See* code obfuscation.

Object signing   *See* code signing.

Open Source   An Open Source Initiative licensing standard stating that the source code for a computer program is made available free of charge to the general public. The standard sets forth specific criteria that must be met by the open source software product.

Patch   When software needs to be updated, such as when a change is required to fix a security vulnerability, the vendor issues a software patch. A patch is a collection of changes to a currently installed software program. Also, a software update.

Practical Extraction and Report Language (PERL)   A scripting language commonly used in conjunction with CGI on Web servers and for general system administration.

PHP Hypertext Preprocessor   A scripting language that can be embedded within Web pages, similar to JavaScript.

Plaintext   Before information is encrypted, it is referred to as plaintext.

Port number   Application protocols in an IP environment are typically written using either TCP or UDP. TCP and UDP applications such as FTP, Telnet, and http are differentiated from one another within the computer, and within network devices such as firewalls, by a port number. For example, the port number commonly used for http is TCP port 80 and that for https is TCP port 443.

Pretty Good Privacy (PGP)   A software package and format for the secure exchange of electronic mail messages.

Private key   One of two keys used in public key cryptography. *See* Public key cryptography.

Promiscuous mode   A computer's LAN interface (as in an Ethernet interface) can be configured by the hacker to operate in promiscuous mode. In this mode, all information sent along the LAN can be read by the hacker, not just information intended for the computer.

Protocol   A previously agreed-upon format and method for sending and/or receiving information between two devices. Protocols may be layered on top of one another. For example, FTP is an application-layer protocol that makes use of the TCP protocol for end-to-end guaranteed delivery and IP for basic transmission services.

Proxy server   A server that "stands in" on behalf of other servers behind it. The most common implementation of a proxy server is for purpose of managing the security and performance of Web browsing within an organization. With a Web proxy server, clients inside the organization (inside the firewall) attach to the proxy server whenever they wish to communicate over the Internet. The proxy server pretends to be the Web browser to the rest of the world (to the Internet), inserting its own IP address into packets instead of the internal client's IP address (the proxy server in this example, therefore, implements NAT). With this approach, the Web browser within the organization is never directly exposed to the Internet. Proxy servers can also enhance performance by storing (caching) frequently accessed Web pages, conserving Internet bandwidth by responding to Web browser requests with Web pages stored in its cache rather than repeatedly fetching that information from the Internet. Proxy servers can also be used to manage content (as in content and executable management) by blocking Web browser requests for content considered dangerous by the security planner. They can be used to disable and filter content, executables, and network traffic in general in conjunction with firewalls and routers. The example of a Web proxy server just provided is just one example of a proxy server. The concept of a proxy server is generic—one can proxy any application, not just Web applications. Doing so can be a powerful way to improve security by shielding internal network devices from direct access to more hostile external networks, as in the Internet. The proxy server can then become a more centralized focus of protection.

Public key   One of two keys used in public key cryptography. *See also* Public key cryptography.

Public key cryptography   A cryptographic mechanism relying on two keys, one *public* and the other *private*.With public key cryptography, you have two keys, one public and the other private. The private key is secret; you should not share it with anyone. The public is public, everyone can know it. For example, you may have your own public and private key. Public key cryptography allows for *asymmetric encryption*. An important property of asymmetric encryption is that, once information is encrypted with your public key, one must have the private key in order unencrypt it. If someone wishes to asymmetrically encrypt information so that only you can read it, then he or she will encrypt the information with your public key. In this way, only you can read information that has been encrypted with your public key, because only you have the private key. When you wish to *digitally sign* information, you apply your private key to the data. Because only you have that private key, then only you could have signed the document. Therefore, a digital signature on a document provides the characteristic of *nonrepudiation* . Because applying your private key to large amounts of data can be CPU-intensive and can, over time, weaken the security of the cryptographic key pair, applications digitally sign the hash of data, not all of it. The digitally signed hash is most commonly referred to as the *digital signature*. A popular implementation of public key cryptography is RSA. *See also* RSA.

Public key infrastructure (PKI)   The combination of public key cryptography technology, certificates, certificate authorities, directory servers used to manage certificates and authorization, methods for revoking certificates if an employee leaves a company for example, and applications supporting public key cryptography such as S/MIME and SSL.

Python   An interpreted programming language sometimes used by system administrators.

Remote AIMS Data Input User System (RADIUS)   Authentication protocol for dial-up connections such as when you dial-up to the Internet (or to an organization's private network) from home. A RADIUS server compares the username/password you entered into your computer to one stored in a secured database. If the RADIUS server is compromised or is forced to crash, then you cannot get access to the network.

Router   Provides communication between different IP subnetworks. Routers are used to connect to the Internet and to connect different subnets within your organization and between remote sites of your organization. They determine where traffic is routed next on its way to its destination. Routers should be configured to filter traffic as part of your security plan. Examples of routing protocols include the Routing Information Protocol (RIP), Open Shortest Path First (OSPF) protocol, and the Border Gateway Protocol (BGP).

RSA (Rivest, Shamir, and Adelman)   A public key cryptographpic algorithm developed by the people it is named after, Rivest, Shamir, and Adelman. At present, RSA is the most popular algorithm for use with PKI. RSA defines cryptographic algorithms for creating and making use of a public and private key pair to implement asymmetric encryption and digital signing.

Secure Multipurpose Internet Mail Extensions (S/MIME)   An electronic mail standard leveraging public key crytography for the exchange of authenticated, integrity-checked, and encrypted messages. S/MIME support is included in many popular email packages.

Scalability   The capability of a system to accommodate large increases in usage without experiencing substantial problems. For example, a customer database that performs well with 100 customers in it, but performs very poorly when there are 10,000 customers entered, offers poor scalability.

Schema   *See* directory service.

Scripts   A computer program, often written to provide additional Web server functions and for system administration.

Secure Sockets Layer (SSL)   A secure transport protocol most commonly implemented between a Web browser and a Web server for added security, such as when making an online purchase or performing a sensitive corporate transaction. The SSL protocol was first specified, implemented, and deployed by Netscape. Today it is a ubiquitous security protocol available in just about every Web browser and server available, to even include Web browsers in handheld computers. SSL is a secure transport protocol, a tunnel between two endpoints such as a client and a server. It can be directly integrated with another application so that all communication to/from the application is sent through the SSL tunnel. Examples of this include https and LDAPS. SSL is based on public key cryptography always makes use of a server certificate. That is, in order for a Web server to support SSL, it must obtain a digital certificate from a certificate authority (CA). In this way, SSL always supports server authentication because the server must present a digital certificate that has been digitally signed by a CA that is configured as trusted within your Web browser. SSL also supports client authentication wherein the Web browser can contain an individual's digital certificate, and that certificate can be presented as part of the SSL connection. This allows the server to authenticate the Web browser based on their digital certificate. Today, fewer organizations use SSL client authentication though this may change in the future. Instead, browser users are often asked to enter their username and password during the SSL session in order to authenticate themselves. The SSL protocol was submitted to the Internet Engineering Task Force (IETF) standards group and, at that time, was renamed the Transport Layer Security (TLS) protocol. TLS is heavily based on SSL, and Web browsers and Web servers today commonly support both SSL and TLS.

Security association (SA)   An IPSec SA is an agreement between two IPSec-capable devices on methods for secure communication. SAs can be defined for any combination of IPSec AH, ESP, and IKE relationships between devices. For example, a single IPSec authentication SA can exist between two endpoints, with intermediate firewalls establishing their own encryption and authentication SAs to apply corporate firewall policies. The encryption of a connection can be broken at the firewall with one SA, allowing the firewall to inspect the session's contents.

The contents can then be reencrypted for transmission to the destination using another SA. In this way, two endpoints can securely authenticate themselves, but intermediate firewalls can also inspect contents of the IPSec connection and perform their own authentication as required.

Shockwave   A technology developed by Macromedia, Inc. for adding multimedia capabilities to a Web page. Requires that a browser plug-in be installed.

Signature (attack signature)   Within the context of intrusion detection, a signature is a recognizable pattern of a hacker attack. For example, a particular sequence of packets or log entries may be a signature of a particular attack. IDSs look for signatures while looking out for hackers.

Single sign-on   The ability to log in just once, such as entering your username and password, to multiple applications rather than having to do so multiple times.

Smartcard   A smartcard contains an embedded chip that can be programmed to send and receive data and perform computations. The underlying electronics are small and can be shaped into a wide range of physical packages. Most smartcards are driver's-license- or credit-card-shaped. There are three categories of smart cards: (1) *Memory-only*, which is capable of storing and returning information but no more. Such devices have limited use in network security and are generally relegated to applications such as phone cards, gift cards, and the like. (2) *CPU-based*, which is capable of processing information. (3)*CPU- and crypto-coprocessor-based*, which is typically tied to a public key infrastructure (PKI) and sometimes called *PKI-enabled smartcards*. PKI is a combination of software, services, and encryption technologies that facilitate secure communications and transactions. The only way to get a card to perform private key operations is to provide a password or biometric information.

Sniffing (Sniffer)   *See* promiscous mode.

Simple Network Management Protocol (SNMP)   A network management protocol used for device configuration and statistics gathering.

Source code   The instructions for a computer program (software), written in programming languages such as Java, C, and C++.

Spoof   Pretending to be someone or something that you are not. For example, IP address spoofing is a technique used by a hackers to hide their identities (to prevent you from knowing where they are in the network) as well as to fool devices on the network into trusting their spoofed packets as if they came from trusted IP addresses.

Secure Shell (SSH)   A secure transport protocol commonly used by security-aware system administrators. Many excellent SSH-enabled tools are available for system administrators including SSH-enabled versions of FTP and Telnet.

Subnet(work)   *See* IP Address and network segment.

Switch   A network device capable of separating traffic coming from different parts of the network. IP switching is a technique whereby traffic from different network segments can be fast-switched with minimal intelligence and processing using simplified traffic forwarding rules rather than more complex routing protocols. In doing so, simplified filtering can be performed and routing protocol vulnerabilities can be more easily isolated to the fewer devices performing routing functions.

Symmetric encryption   Scrambling information in such a way that only one key can be used to de-scramble it. Both the sender and the recipient must have the same encryption key when symmetric encryption is used. In contrast, with asymmetric encryption, two different keys are used.

Synchronization   As relates to directory service; as relates to time.

Tcpwrapper   An open software program that, once installed, allows for greatly enhanced logging and address filtering control for computers communicating over an IP network.

Telnet   TCP/IP-based terminal emulation commonly used by system administrators to maintain network devices. To improve security, Telnet should be combined with SSH.

Time server   Distributes the time to devices within your network.

Timestamp   Time recorded for an event is referred to as a timestamp.

Token   Something you have; used during authentication. A smartcard is an example of a token. *See* smart card.

Trace   The act of recording the individual instructions executed by a software program to determine what has transpired while it is running. Also refers to the act of recording individual data packets sent over the network, from source to destination.

Transmission Control Protocol (TCP)   Protocol riding "on top" of IP providing guaranteed end-to-end delivery of packets through the network.

Transport Layer Security (TLS)   *See* SSL.

Trojan horse   *See* network-borne virus.

Tunnel   A contiguous network connection between two endpoints established through disparate intervening components.

User Datagram Protocol (UDP)   Like TCP, UDP also rides "on top" of IP; however, unlike TCP, UDP does not guarantee end-to-end delivery of packets. If the underlying network loses a packet, UDP will not request a retransmission of that lost packet.

Virtual IP address   When multiple devices on the same subnetwork must appear to the rest of the world as the same device, they can be configured with a virtual IP address. For example, if you install multiple redundant firewalls on the same LAN and want all of them to appear to other devices as one firewall (so that if there is a failure in one firewall, the other can take over and the changeover is transparent), then you can configure all firewalls with the same virtual IP address.

Virtual private network (VPN)   A secure "tunnel" established through an unsecured public network. A VPN is a "virtual" private network simply because data is still transmitted over a public network; however, it offers the benefits of a private network by providing security for transmitted information. IPSec is an example of a protocol that can be used for implementing a VPN.

Virus   A software program used by hackers to instruct your computer to perform actions dictated by the hacker.

Visual Basic   A programming language. There are versions of Visual Basic that can be used for scripting or for developing standalone compiled programs. Visual Basic scripts can be embedded in Web pages.

Vulnerability analysis (VA)   The act of probing a device for known vulnerabilities in the same manner that an experienced hacker would.

Wide area network (WAN)   A network providing connectivity between larger distances, such as between towns in a country or between countries. The Internet is a WAN.

Windows Internet Naming Service (WINS)   Used within Microsoft Windows environments to dynamically assign and manage the association between network addresses and network devices.

Worm   A virus that replicates itself from one computer to another within your network. Hackers use worms to spread their programs across multiple systems. Worms are often used as part of a DoS attack.

X.500   International Standards Organization (ISO) standard for directory services. X.500 is a comprehensive directory service standard. Because of its complexity, simpler standards such as LDAP gained in popularity.

X.509   International Standards Organization (ISO) standard. *See* certificate.

Index

A

Access Certificates for Electronic Services (ACES), 349

access control
  directory service authentication, 240
  directory services interface support, 237
  disablement responsibility, 313
  operating system privacy, 174
  physical attack prevention, 265
  secure software, 284
  security plan template element, 51–52
  Security Stack Worksheet, 92–97
  single points of failure, 253
  staff management element, 309
  surveillance systems, 208
  time services, 298

access control list (ACL), 51

access control matrix, 91–92

access control systems, 144

accounting service, PKI, 343

accounts, disabling after attempts, 109

ACES. *See* Access Certificates for Electronic Services

activities, incident response, 38–44

addresses, 191

addressing
  authentication effects, 196
  Business Worksheet, 201–204
  hacked systems, 42
  importance of, 189

Intrusion Detection and Vulnerability Analysis interaction, 266

Life-Cycle Management Worksheet, 197–199

security plan template element, 58–59

Security Stack Worksheet, 190–197

Selling Security Worksheet, 204–206

address spoofing, protection, 192–193

Administration and Management Worksheet, 321, 322

administration, security plan, 69–70

administrators, 113, 302

alarm events, intrusion detection, 192

alarms, 265, 273

algorithms, 128, 134–135, 143

anecdotes
  biometrics backlash, 54
  chmod command, 96
  credit-report theft, 10
  incident response, 40
  NMC hacker attack, 70
  password cracking, 111
  physical security (watching the door), 74

anti-virus software, signature reliance, 221

application guidelines. *See* Security Stack Worksheets; Selling Security Worksheets

application layer, 46, 254

application-level integrity, 145